What If the Babe
Had Kept His Red Sox?

What If the Babe Had Kept His Red Sox?

*And Other Fascinating Alternate Histories
from the World of Sports*

Bill Gutman

Skyhorse Publishing

Skyhorse Publishing books may be purchased in bulk at special discounts for sales promotion, corporate gifts, fund raising, or educational purposes. Special editions can also be created to specifications. For details, contact Special Sales Department, Skyhorse Publishing, 555 Eighth Avenue, Suite 903, New York, NY 10018 or info@skyhorsepublishing.com.

www.skyhorsepublishing.com

10 9 8 7 6 5 4 3 2 1

Library of Congress Cataloging-in-Publication Data
    Gutman, Bill.
    What if the Babe had kept his Red Sox? : and other fascinating alternate histories from the world of sports / Bill Gutman.
        p.   cm.
    Includes index.
    ISBN 978-1-60239-629-6 (alk. paper)
    1. Sports—United States—Miscellanea.   2. Sports—United States—History.   I. Title.
    GV583.G868   2008
    796.0973—dc22
    2008006689

Printed in Canada

To Arthur Friedman,
a good friend and great sports fan who has vivid memories
of many of the people depicted in this book.

Contents

Introduction

Sports arguments can be endless exercises in frustration because they normally produce no real answers. Despite an array of available statistics—batting or scoring average, wins and losses, yards gained, touchdown passes thrown, earned run average, blocked shots—people will still debate and usually disagree about who's the best hitter, pitcher, shortstop, centerfielder, running back, quarterback, pass receiver, point guard, center, tennis player, or golfer. Or they may argue about specific teams (Yankees vs. Red Sox, Lakers vs. Celtics) or maybe teams from different eras (Lombardi's Green Bay Packers vs. the recent version led by Brett Favre) or about players from different eras (Nicklaus or Woods, Laver or Federer, Koufax or the Big Unit). Let's face it, sports fans can argue about almost anything, including whether the odds on an upcoming game are fair or accurate. It really is endless.

There is, however, a more interesting arena in which to debate when it comes to sports, and that's the great **WHAT IF?** In other words, what if a certain player hadn't been traded, a coach had taken a different job, a league had not expanded or merged and thus certain franchises had never existed, or what if it was the "other" boxer who won the championship fight? This kind of speculation is far more fascinating because it delves deeper than who's-the-best? debates. The reason is simple. If just one part of history is changed, then the domino effect takes over and many other things will subsequently change as a result. In fact, there are some events that, if they had happened differently, might well have affected the entire career of a player, the history of a team, or the direction of a sport.

What If the Babe Had Kept His Red Sox? examines a number of high-profile situations that could have been very different if just one part of the equation had been altered. Just think about the consequences if Babe Ruth had remained with the Boston Red Sox his entire career instead of being sold to the New York Yankees in 1920. Look at how many things would have been affected—the early history of two great franchises, the career of the most widely known baseball player of all time, Yankee Stadium, Murderers' Row, the Curse of the Bambino, and the home run records considered sacred all these years. That's the What-If domino effect.

Not surprisingly, What-Ifs like this can be found everywhere. Did you know, for instance, that the legendary Vince Lombardi was offered his dream job to coach the New York Giants after the 1960 NFL season? What if he had accepted and left the Green Bay Packers? Or suppose Muhammad Ali, in the midst of dancing around the ring in his first fight against Sonny Liston, had been caught by a devastating punch and KO'd? How would the history of boxing and the personal history of the most recognizable sports figure in the world have changed? What if the Dodgers and Giants had not gone west in 1958, but had instead moved to new stadiums and remained in New York? The ramifications would be felt to this day.

Everyone knows that Jackie Robinson became the first African-American to play big league baseball in more than sixty years when he took the field for the Brooklyn Dodgers in 1947. But what if some enterprising owner had said "to hell with the gentlemen's agreement" and signed black superstars Satchel Paige and Josh Gibson in the mid-1930s? Would that have thrown baseball into complete turmoil? Or consider this. What if Arnold Palmer and Jack Nicklaus had just been mediocre professional golfers instead of the charismatic superstars they became in the 1950s and '60s? Without that dynamic duo leading the way would professional golf have grown so quickly into the mega-dollar sport it is today?

These are just a few of the topics covered in the following pages, which will take a close look at some of the most intriguing what-ifs in the annals of sport. Whether you agree with the conclusions or not, they will certainly give you grist for additional debate and speculation. And that, really, is why this intriguing question is posed so much in the first place. **What if . . .**

What If the Babe
Had Kept His Red Sox?

The Boston Babe

On December 26, 1919, the New York Yankees received a belated Christmas gift. They completed a deal that would bring Boston Red Sox pitcher/outfielder George Herman "Babe" Ruth to New York. The Yanks had purchased the young slugging sensation for the then unheard-of price of $125,000, more than double the highest price ever paid for a ballplayer. The deal between the New Yorkers and Boston owner Harry Frazee wasn't all that simple. There were more reasons for it than people think, but the bottom line was that it brought the Babe to New York, where he would proceed to turn the baseball and sporting world on its ear, and begin in earnest a record-setting career that also launched a Yankee dynasty which seemed to never die. It also left the floundering Red Sox with collateral damage that would come to be called "The Curse of the Bambino," and which wouldn't end until the Sox finally won the World Series in 2004. Babe Ruth is still mentioned with great reverence today and continues to be, in some ways, the face of the Yankees.

But what if the Babe had kept his Red Sox?

★   ★   ★   ★   ★

In a sense, Babe Ruth was an unlikely hero, an unlikely superstar, and most unlikely—at least at the beginning—to become arguably the greatest baseball player of all time. He came from proverbial humble beginnings, and by the time he was seven years old, his parents could no longer handle him. So they sent him to the St. Mary's Industrial School for Boys, which was, in essence, a reform school run by Catholic brothers in Baltimore. This happened back in 1902 when not only the Babe but baseball itself was in its early days. It would have taken one helluva soothsayer to predict that this out-of-control youngster would grow into a national hero and, in the eyes of some, the man who saved baseball.

By now the story is well known to real baseball fans. At St. Mary's, Babe came under the tutelage of Brother Matthias, the school's disciplinarian, who took a liking to the incorrigible kid and subsequently introduced him to baseball. Before long it was apparent that young George Ruth was a natural, and by 1914 Jack Dunn, who owned the minor league Baltimore Orioles, had signed the nineteen-year-old to a contract with plans to use him as a left-handed pitcher. Dunn also became the teen's legal guardian. Legend has it that on the first day of spring training, as Dunn took his rookie out to the mound, someone yelled: "Hey, look at Dunnie and his new babe."

And so a nickname for the ages was born, followed soon after by a very talented ballplayer. By early July, the young Babe had a 14-6 record, but the Orioles were losing money fast and on July 8, Dunn sold the Babe, along with pitcher Ernie Shore and catcher Ben Egan, to the Boston Red Sox for $8,500. Ruth signed a two-and-a-half year contract valued at $3,500 a season to pitch for

Boston. Three days later he beat Cleveland 4-3 for his first big league win. He would finish the year in the minors, but beginning in 1915 the Babe quickly established himself as the best young left-handed pitcher in the majors, compiling records of 18-8, 23-12, and 24-13 over the next three seasons. And in those latter two campaigns, 1916 and 1917, he finished with earned run averages of 1.75 and 2.01, respectively. That's how good he was.

But the big guy—and at 6'2", 190 pounds, he was big for a ballplayer in those days—could also do something else very well. He could hit better than any other pitcher in the league and better than many of his teammates. On May 6, 1915, the Babe blasted his first big league home run against the Yankees at the old Polo Grounds. He would hit four that season, which is nothing to brag about today, but in the dead-ball era, that was good enough to lead the Red Sox. And it didn't hurt that his team also won the pennant.

Led by a very strong pitching staff, Boston would take three pennants over four years, winning the World Series in both 1916 and 1918. The Babe was 3-0 in the pair of Fall Classics, setting a record along the way by throwing 29 straight scoreless innings, and having a combined 0.87 earned run average. By 1918, the Sox realized they had something special in the big guy, something other than his valuable left arm. His pitching record was just 13-7 because he was now spending more time in the outfield. The team wanted his potent bat in the lineup. He played enough to get 317 at bats and lead the American League with 11 home runs while hitting an even .300. Not counting his mound appearances, he played 59 games in the outfield and another 13 at first base. With the Sox dominating the American League and Ruth emerging as a huge star, the question in 1919 was how much he would pitch and how much he would play the outfield.

THE WORLD OF HARRY FRAZEE

Harry Frazee owned the Boston Red Sox from November 1916 to July 1923. That isn't a long time in baseball years, but fans in Beantown even today know his name and continue to rank him as the biggest villain in Red Sox history. Why? It's easy. He's the guy who sold Babe Ruth to the Yankees and brought upon the Red Sox the infamous Curse of the Bambino, which would haunt the Sox from 1920 to 2004. Many people think that Frazee sold the Babe to the Yanks to finance the Broadway show *No, No, Nanette*. But it wasn't quite as simple as that.

The Illinois-born Frazee always had a penchant for show business, and in those days that meant Broadway. By 1907 he had built his first theatre in Chicago and then, in 1913, he opened the Longacre Theatre on Broadway in New York. He also acquired a theatre in Boston and subsequently produced a string of hit shows. When his latest offering, *Nothing but the Truth,* was a success on Broadway in late 1916, Frazee decided to do something else with the profits. He bought the Red Sox on November 1, from Joseph Lannin, for the sum of $675,000. As it turns out, he didn't pay in full. He gave Lannin some of the cash and the rest in the form of notes. But he owned the team and one of the stars he inherited was a young left-handed pitcher, Babe Ruth.

"I have always enjoyed the game," Frazee said after the purchase. "Now I think I shall have a chance to show what I know about handling a baseball club. I think that by giving the public a first-class article, I am bound to hold their support. And this goes double for Boston, by all odds the greatest ball town on earth."

The Sox, of course, had just won the World Series when Frazee bought the team, and they duplicated that success two years later. So he had bought his way into one of baseball's best. But in 1918, the season had ended a month early because of the United States' participation in World War I. Frazee and the ballclub lost revenue, and it didn't help that his string of hits on Broadway and elsewhere suddenly became a string of flops.

There was a portent of things to come shortly after the championship season of 1918 ended. In December, Frazee sent two of his best pitchers, Ernie Shore and Dutch Leonard, along with outfielder Duffy Lewis to the New York Yankees in return for four lesser players and cash. One source says it was $50,000, another just $15,000. But one thing was certain: Frazee needed cash and one way to get it was to sell ballplayers. His team felt the loss of these players the following year, plummeting to sixth place with a 66-71 record. Not only did the Sox lose top hurlers in Shore and Leonard, but Babe Ruth only pitched enough to compile a 9-5 record. The rest of the time he was in the outfield, where he quickly emerged as the American League's premier slugger.

The Babe set a new major league home run record by blasting 29 round trippers, also leading the league with 114 RBIs while batting .322. And he did it in just 130 games. Even more amazingly, he got those hits off the old dead ball. The previous home run record had been 27, set by a National Leaguer named Ned Williamson way back in 1884, when the rules of the game were somewhat different. The next best total in 1919 was just 12 and several players hit 10. No wonder the Sox decided that Ruth should play in the outfield.

The Sox were now losing, and Harry Frazee was still in debt, so after the season he began talking again with the New York Yankees' co-owners, Colonel Jacob Ruppert and Colonel Tillinghast Huston, about their taking the big guy off his hands. The deal was completed in late December and announced on January 5, 1920. The Yankees had paid the huge sum of $125,000 for the Babe, more than twice what had been paid for any ballplayer to that time. In addition, the two co-owners agreed to loan Frazee anywhere from $300,000 to $350,000.

When Frazee told his manager, Ed Barrow, about the Yankees' offer, adding, "I can't turn it down," Barrow is said to have replied, "You think you're getting a lot of money for Ruth, but you're not."

THE REAL REASONS

Over the years, many Red Sox fans have lamented Frazee's interest in financing Broadway shows and the resulting loss of Babe Ruth to New York. In truth, there were a number of elements that led to Frazee approaching the Yankees and subsequently making the deal. For starters, the Red Sox owner had a long-running dispute with American League founder and president Ban Johnson. Their dispute came to a head in the summer of 1919 when pitcher Carl Mays bolted from the Sox. Johnson wanted him suspended, but Frazee turned around and sold him to the Yankees. Somehow, this dispute resulted in the American League being divided into two opposing factions—the Yanks, Red Sox, and White Sox versus the other five clubs, which became known as the "Loyal Five" due to their deference to Johnson. Thus when Frazee decided to move Ruth, the Loyal Five wouldn't deal with him. He could only turn to the Yanks or White Sox. There was one story that the White Sox offered Shoeless Joe Jackson and $60,000 for Ruth, but Frazee wanted strictly a cash deal. He needed the money more than another star player that he'd have to pay.

Then there was the Ruth factor. The Babe was simply not easy to handle. His upbringing at St. Mary's had been rough; once he found success in baseball, though, he was like a kid in a candy store. He wanted more of everything—food, drink, women, fun, and money. He was tough enough to contain during the 1919 season, but after it ended he began talking about forging a new career in the movies. In Oakland, for a series of post-season exhibition games, he began talking money, saying things like, "A player is worth just as much as he can get," and citing Detroit's Ty Cobb as a player who got all he could. Cobb responded by calling the Babe a "contract violator" and Ruth promptly challenged Cobb to a fight, adding, "I wouldn't say anything against Cobb if he held out for $100,000, so why should he say anything about me? He ought to be tickled to see any player get as much as he can . . ."

By that time, Frazee probably saw the Babe as a player he couldn't control and one who was going to bleed him for every last dollar he could get. And after Babe blasted those 29 home runs, he was obviously going to ask for plenty. At the same time, there was little doubt about his talents. During a spring training game in April of 1919 against John McGraw's Giants in Tampa, Florida, the Babe connected on a pitch from George Smith and sent the ball high and far over the right-centerfield wall, and into a hospital yard next door. After the game, Giants rightfielder Ross Youngs, who saw the ball land, went out and stood on the spot. Someone found a surveyor's tape and measured. The ball, it was said, traveled 579 feet. No wonder the Yanks were willing to pay so much.

So the Babe joined the Yankees, walloped 54 home runs in 1920, and then another 59 the following year. He quickly became the biggest attraction in baseball and, after the Black Sox scandal of 1919, when eight members of the Chicago White Sox were accused of taking bribes to throw the World Series and subsequently banned from baseball for life at the conclusion of the 1920 season, it was thought to be the Babe's prodigious home runs that brought many disillusioned fans back and, in effect, saved baseball. But . . .

WHAT IF FRAZEE DIDN'T NEED THE MONEY?

In 1919, America was on the brink of that unprecedented boom period known as the Roaring Twenties. It was a great time for both sports and entertainment, especially in the larger cities. There wasn't a better time—and wouldn't be again for more than a half century—for sports heroes to emerge. Boxing had Jack Dempsey, football had Red Grange, tennis had Bill Tilden, golf had Bobby Jones, even horse racing had a star in Man o' War, and, last and best, baseball had the Babe. It was also a time in which Broadway flourished, as new composers came on the scene and shows that are now classics started their runs on the Great White Way. Before the decade ended with the great stock market crash of 1929, the movies would even begin to talk.

It would seem, then, to be the perfect time for a Broadway entrepreneur like Harry Frazee to make his fortune. The problem was that it came a bit late. *No, No, Nanette* didn't hit Broadway until 1925 and would net Frazee about $2.5 million. By then, Frazee had not only sold Ruth, but also shipped Wally Schang, Everett Scott, "Bullet" Joe Bush, Joe Dugan, "Sad" Sam Jones, Herb Pennock, and Waite Hoyt to the Yankees, where a number of them joined the Babe to help create the first Bronx Bombers' dynasty and ultimately the team known as Murderers' Row. But what if Frazee had yet another string of hits in 1918 and 1919, and didn't need money? What if he had held on to Babe Ruth, told the big guy not to worry about money, that he would be paid in full for his talent?

If the Babe had not made the trip south from Boston to New York, the course of Major League Baseball may have been different, and the history of the game altered. There are a number of ways to look at this, from the standpoint of both the Yankees and the Red Sox, from the record book, and from the history of baseball itself. Put them all together and this is a fascinating supposition.

The evidence shows that Harry Frazee was never the kind of baseball owner a team would prefer. Despite his protestations to the contrary, he obviously cared more about his theatrical endeavors than about building a great baseball team. People may have been fooled by the fact that the Red Sox were a great baseball team when he bought it. But once he began unloading talent, the team sagged and would be a second-rate club throughout the 1920s, a bad baseball team that left the loyal fans of Boston with a continuing case of the what-might-have-beens.

But had Frazee taken the advice of baseball people, like manager Ed Barrow, he certainly would have kept the Babe in the fold. And perhaps he would have done it had his shows continued to prosper immediately after the war ended. Then he certainly would not have come out with the kind of statements that suggested he was justified in selling off his star player. Today we call it "spin."

"Twice within the past two seasons Babe has jumped the club and revolted," Frazee said. "He refused to obey the orders of the manager and he finally became so arrogant that discipline in his case was ruined. . . . He had no regard for the feelings of anyone but himself. He was a bad influence upon other and still younger players."

Had Frazee only known!

THE BABE IN BOSTON

Anyone with half a baseball brain could have seen the amazing talent in Babe Ruth right from the start. When he shattered the home run record with 29 in 1919 while still going 9-5 on the mound, it was more than apparent that he was special. And then, as now, Red Sox fans were rabid about their team. The club drew more than half a million fans in 1915 and nearly that many a year later. Recovering from the war, more than 417,000 fans came to Fenway in 1919. But once the Babe was gone and the team began losing, attendance dropped markedly. By 1921 only 279,273 fans pushed through the turnstiles and two years later paying customers were down to 229,688, an average of fewer than 3,000 a game. This is something that definitely would not have happened if Babe Ruth had remained in Boston.

Had the Babe remained, chances are that Frazee would have also kept the rest of the club intact, especially his fine pitching staff. With guys like "Bullet" Joe Bush, Herb Pennock, Carl Mays, and Waite Hoyt forming a Red Sox rotation, and the Babe hitting home runs, the Sox may well have had a chance to dominate the American League again in the 1920s. At the least, they would have revved up the heated Red Sox/Yankees rivalry a lot earlier. Once the Babe and those top pitchers were gone, the Sox had only one place to go. So that is the first trickle-down from Frazee dealing his players. He broke up a very good team and it didn't have to happen.

As for the Babe, there's little doubt that the Sox would have done the same thing the Yankees did and made him a full-time out-fielder. He was already moving down that road when he was dealt. The young Babe was the consummate five-tool player of his time. He could do it all—hit for average, hit for power, field, throw, and even run. Before he put additional weight on his large frame later in his career, the Babe was pretty quick on the basepaths and in the outfield. And with his keen sense of the game he knew how to steal a base when he had to. Had he remained in Boston, Ruth the batter would certainly have turned heads at Fenway during the 1920s. But would he have turned them as much as he did in New York?

First there was the Fenway Park factor. The venerable old sta-dium was opened in 1912 and, like so many of the old ballparks, it had rather gargantuan dimensions. For a southpaw swinger like the Babe, it was only 314 feet to the seats down the right field line. But from there the wall jutted out sharply and it took nearly a 400-foot poke to get the ball into the seats in right center. Dead center was some 488 feet from home plate. Remember, these early parks were built during the dead-ball era when home runs weren't a big part of the game. Having a huge outfield made the gap hitters more effec-tive and it seemed in the early days that there were as many inside-the-park home runs as four-baggers that cleared the fences.

But Ruth was different. He was big and strong, swung a very heavy bat, and didn't choke up. He had small hands for a man his size and thus the handles of his bats were thinner than most, which probably helped his bat speed, a term not used back in his day. In addition, he had a big swing with a slight uppercut. Most of the top hitters of the day took level swings with the object being to make solid contact and hit the ball hard and to a place where the fielders wouldn't get it—the old Willie Keeler "hit 'em where they ain't" theory. The consummate hit was a hard line drive. But the Babe, as teammate Joe Dugan once observed, "swung from Port Arthur, Texas, on every pitch." And many of his homers were high, deep, majestic drives that not only cleared the outfield wall, but sailed far over it.

But if the Babe had played his entire career in Fenway Park he would still have been a great hitter and most likely the premier slugger and home run hitter of his day. But he may not have been quite the Sultan of Swat that he became with the Yankees. Remember, once he went to the Yankees he played three seasons at the Polo Grounds. Both the Yankees and Giants were using the old bathtub-shaped ballpark then and the right field fence was just 256 feet down the line. While centerfield was a country mile away, right field was a much more inviting target than the corresponding dimension at Fenway.

Then there was Yankee Stadium. The legendary House That Ruth Built opened in 1923 after the Giants asked the Yanks to leave the Polo Grounds. They were actually bent out of shape because the "other" New York team was outdrawing them at the gate. So the Yankees built their own ballpark. And since the Babe was already attracting all kinds of attention with his home runs (54 in 1920 and 59 in 1921), the team is said to have wanted a ballpark to suit his prodigious talents. Thus right field at Yankee Stadium was just 295 feet away. And while left center and center at the original Stadium were 460 and 490 feet deep, right field and what would become known as the "short porch" was an inviting target for left-handed sluggers, and none was better than the Babe.

Suppose Fenway Park and its deeper right field dimension cost the Babe five homers a year. If so, Babe still would have retired as the all-time home run leader, but would not have had his magical 714 career total. The most he might have hit in a season would have probably been in the 55 home run range. The 60 he slammed in 1927 was such a gold standard for so long, even after Roger Maris hit 61, that it really helped make the Babe a legend. But if the most he hit had been 55, then Jimmie Foxx would have become the single-season record holder with his 58 in 1932 and would have been tied by Hank Greenberg in 1938. Before the Great Depression was over, the Babe would have been in third place.

As for his career total, without the Polo Grounds and Yankee Stadium, the Bambino might have lost about 75 home runs from his career total. That would have left him around the 639 mark for his career. He would have still retired as the all-time leader, but Henry Aaron (who finished with 755) would have passed him first, followed shortly afterward by Willie Mays, who finished with 660. The Babe would have continued as a superb hitter, a great slugger, and one of the all-time greats, but with his home run figures diminished even slightly, some of the mystique would clearly have been gone.

WHAT ABOUT YANKEE STADIUM AND MURDERERS' ROW?

The Babe remaining with the Red Sox begs yet another question. What about Yankee Stadium, arguably the most famous ballpark in baseball history and by far the most modern and innovative stadium when it was first opened in 1923? Without the Babe, the Yankees certainly would still have wanted their own home. So it's not a matter of if, but when, and would it have been any different?

Jealousy over the Yanks drawing bigger crowds is often given as the reason that the Giants were no longer willing to share the

Polo Grounds, but without the Babe and his record-breaking home runs, it's doubtful that Yankees attendance would have outstripped that of the Giants. As it was, the Yanks drew 1,289,422 paying customers in 1920, while the Giants brought just 929,069 through the gates. There were similar disparities over the next two seasons. Remember, Babe had set a new home run record with 29 his final year with Boston in 1919. Not only did he break it the next year, he obliterated it, with 54, standing the baseball world on its collective ear. And a year later, he had what is still considered one of the great seasons in baseball history. He hit a robust .378, walloped another record 59 homers, drove home 171 runs, and scored 177 times. No wonder fans wanted to come out and see him.

Without the Babe, the Yankees would have generated considerably less excitement, the crowds wouldn't have been the same, and the Giants may well have allowed their tenants to stay. Without a huge gate attraction and a pennant-worthy team, Yankee owners Ruppert and Huston would probably not have wanted to spend the $2.5 million it would take to build the new park they envisioned. More likely they would have waited until perhaps the late 1920s, after Lou Gehrig joined the team, and then built the first Yankee Stadium. The same tract of land in the Bronx, across the Harlem River from the Polo Grounds, may still have been available since it was the home of a lumberyard. So the location may well have been the same and the team would still have built baseball's most modern stadium. But the dimensions may have been altered slightly. Without the need to showcase the Babe and his home runs, Yankee Stadium may well have been deep in both right and right centerfields. There wouldn't have been that short rightfield porch, and it would certainly not have become the House That Ruth Built. On the contrary, it might have become the House That Gehrig Built.

As for the Yankees themselves, without Babe Ruth, the face of the team certainly would not have been the same. With the Babe, the Yanks won their first ever American League pennant in 1921. That was the year he belted his 59 homers. It didn't hurt that a couple of former Boston hurlers, Carl Mays and Waite Hoyt, won 46 games between them. Outfielder Bob Meusel supported Ruth at the plate with a .318 average, 24 homers, and 135 RBIs. The only problem was that the team lost in the World Series to the rival Giants, 5-3, in a best of nine series. They won a second pennant the next year with former Red Sox pitchers Hoyt, Mays, and Joe Bush winning an aggregate 58 games. So Frazee's fire sale was benefiting the Yanks in more ways than one. Though the Giants again won the Series there was little doubt that the Yanks were coming.

A year later they won it all. The Babe hit an amazing .393 that year, with 41 homers and 131 ribbies. Ruth, of course, was great. But you could make a real case that the castoff Boston pitchers won it for them. Bush, Herb Pennock, Hoyt, and Sam Jones accounted for 76 of the Yanks' 98 victories. Thank you once more, Harry Frazee. Though the Washington Senators took the next two pennants, the Yankees bounced back the following three years, unveiling a powerhouse team still known today as Murderers' Row. The 1927 team won 110 games and lost just 44, then swept the National League Pittsburgh Pirates in the World Series.

That was the year Babe Ruth hit his epic 60 home runs. But he had plenty of help. Lou Gehrig was starting his third year with the Yankees, and the big first baseman really came into his own. He batted .373, followed the Babe with 47 homers, and drove home a league best 175 runs. Centerfielder Earle Combs hit .356, Meusel came in at .337 with 103 RBIs, while young second sacker Tony Lazzeri hit .309 with 18 homers and 102 runs batted in. This was a Murderers' Row attack. Hoyt and Pennock won 41 games between them, but it was the Babe and his fellow bashers who set the tone for this team. They won it again a year later with the same formula, their sixth and final pennant of the decade.

What would have happened to this ball club if it didn't have the Babe to set the tone? Chances are if the Babe had remained in Boston, those outstanding pitchers would have remained there, as well. So the Yankees would not only have been deprived of the game's greatest slugger, they also would not have had pitchers Mays, Bush, Pennock, Hoyt, and Jones. That's a complete rotation, though all five didn't pitch at the same time during the decade. There's no doubt that Harry Frazee gave the Yankees a lot more than Babe Ruth.

Without the Red Sox to supply arms, the Yankees would have had to develop their own or look elsewhere for trades. With the Babe removed from the equation, there's a very good chance the New Yorkers would not have won any of those first three pennants between 1921 and 1923. In fact, they may well have been a second-rate team as the Red Sox continued to thrive. So the roles of the two teams would have been reversed in the early 1920s.

In 1925, the Yankees made Lou Gehrig their regular first baseman. Gehrig had been signed out of Columbia University two years earlier and would emerge as a major star, an all-time great who normally batted cleanup for the Yanks, right behind the Babe. Together, they became arguably the greatest 1-2 batting punch in baseball history. Gehrig, however, lacked the Babe's flamboyance. He was self-effacing, quiet, and modest, but a rock in the lineup who wouldn't miss a game for more than thirteen years until he contracted the illness that now bears his name. Though he would hit 493 home runs in his career, Gehrig was more of a line-drive hitter than the Babe, and didn't hit the same kind of long, majestic homers. But he was an RBI machine and a .340 lifetime hitter.

Had Ruth remained in Boston, Gehrig would have become the face of the Yankees, albeit a more subdued face, and the leader of a team that may well have fallen well short of greatness during the

1920s. There were some other fine hitters, such as Lazzeri, Meusel, and Combs, but without the Babe's bat and those pitchers delivered to the Yanks by Harry Frazee, the Yankees may well have gone through the entire decade of the 1920s without a single pennant. In fact, the Yankees as we know them today might not have really existed until 1936, when a rookie named Joe DiMaggio teamed with Lou Gehrig to give the team the same kind of 1-2 punch that Ruth and Gehrig had given it in the '20s. These Yanks would win four straight pennants and World Series through 1939 and would go on from there.

Had Babe Ruth stayed with the Red Sox for his entire career there's a good chance the Yankees would not have become baseball's best team until 1936. Lou Gehrig would have been the first Yankee legend with the addition of DiMaggio helping Gehrig to his first World Series. The history of the New York Yankees from 1936 on would probably closely resemble what it is today. But without the Babe the team definitely would not have found its early success, and Yankee Stadium might not have been quite the same ballpark.

THE BABE RUTH LEGEND

Even today, there is no icon in sports who can match Babe Ruth for his larger-than-life status. During World War II, Japanese soldiers, answered American taunts of "The hell with the Emperor!" with "The hell with Babe Ruth!" In fact, there were already those who loved him in Japan since he had barnstormed there before the war. The Babe simply *was* baseball. Who didn't love the Babe? As Harry Hooper, an early teammate of Ruth's in Boston, said in later years, "I still can't believe what I saw. A nineteen-year-old kid, crude and poorly educated, only lightly brushed by the social veneer we call civilization, gradually transformed into the idol of American youth, and the symbol of baseball the world over. [He was] a man loved by more people and with an intensity of feeling that perhaps has never been equaled before or since."

But would this same thing have happened if the Babe had remained a Red Sox? Not in the same way and not with the same intensity, and for a lot of diverse reasons. For one thing, Boston wasn't New York. Sure, it's a large, cosmopolitan city, but New York was special, maybe even more so back in the 1920s with sports, Broadway, speakeasies, music, restaurants, movie theatres, and even the stock market. And the Babe was made for New York. He loved the nightlife and he showed up everywhere. Being a record-setting home run king during what was called the Golden Age of Sports and a New York Yankee made the Babe special. It was really the catalyst that spawned the legend.

And remember, in Boston the Babe would not have been quite the home run hitter he was in New York. He'd have still been great, a surefire Hall of Famer with ease, but the mystique wouldn't have been as striking. Babe Ruth and New York were made for each other. The Boston Babe just doesn't have the same ring. And while the Red Sox would have remained a much better team had they retained Ruth and some of those pitchers, they wouldn't have had the amazing success of the Yankees, especially the teams from 1926–1928, when everyone knew about Murderers' Row. And let's not forget that incredible 1927 Yankees team that won 110 games as the Babe blasted his 60 and Gehrig followed with 47. That never could have happened in Boston, because the entire Yankee team, including Lou Gehrig, couldn't have been duplicated.

Then there was the Babe's flair for the dramatic, like the aforementioned 60th home run on the final day of the 1927 season. He never would have hit 60 playing in Boston. And there were plenty of other epic moments, as well. When Yankee Stadium opened in 1923, it was the Babe who provided the margin of victory with a three-run homer before 74,000 fans. At Fenway he would be lucky to play before half that number. In the first All-Star Game ever, played in 1933 at Comiskey Park in Chicago, it was the Babe's third inning, two-run homer that insured the American League of a 4-2 victory. That certainly could have happened if he was in a Red Sox uniform, but the meaning would not have been quite the same because the Babe never would have hit his 60 homers and Jimmy Foxx's 58 the year before may well have been the record.

And finally there was the 1932 World Series. The Yankees were playing the Chicago Cubs and there was a lot of animosity between the two teams. Game 3 was being played at Wrigley Field in Chicago, and the game was tied at 4-4 when the Babe came up against pitcher Charlie Root in the fifth inning. The Babe had already hit a three-run shot in the first inning. This time, Root's first two pitches were right down the middle and each time the Babe held up a finger to show everyone he knew the count. The next two pitches were balls, running the count to 2-2. That's when the Babe held out his bat with his right hand. Some felt he was just indicating that he had yet another strike left. More have insisted that he was pointing to the centerfield bleachers. He's also said to have remarked to catcher Gabby Hartnett, "It only takes one to hit it."

At any rate, when Root threw again the Babe took his huge swing and sent the ball soaring deep into the centerfield seats, one of the longest home runs ever hit at Wrigley Field, before or since. As he circled the bases, the big guy taunted the Cubs' bench. The Yanks eventually won the Series in four straight and the legend grew immediately that the Babe, by pointing with his bat, had called his shot. Babe would never confirm or deny this, but admitted later that it was one of the most gratifying home runs of his career.

"As I hit the ball, every muscle in my system, every sense I had, told me that I had never hit a better one," he said. "As long as I lived nothing would ever feel as good as this one."

Yet the legend that the Babe called his shot persists to this day, part of baseball lore and something never to be forgotten. It wouldn't have been remembered if the Babe had stayed in Boston because it simply wouldn't have happened.

Another part of the Ruthian legend was the huge salary he commanded. By 1930 the Yankees were paying him $80,000 a year, a sum that was incredible for that time and dwarfed the paychecks of all other ballplayers. That made the Babe one of New York's big spenders and tippers, something else that has contributed to his legend. The Red Sox could never have afforded a salary anywhere near that, and the world at the time would have been deprived of watching the legendary star drop $100 bills as tips and spend lavishly wherever he went. So high was the Babe's salary that year that someone pointed out that he was earning $5,000 more than Herbert Hoover, the president of the United States. To that, the Babe supposedly replied, "So what? I had a better year than he did."

DID THE BABE REALLY SAVE BASEBALL AND COULD HE HAVE DONE IT IN BOSTON?

For years it has been said that Babe Ruth almost single-handedly saved baseball after the Black Sox scandal of 1919. Eight members of the pennant-winning Chicago White Sox had conspired with gamblers to throw the World Series, which was won by the underdog Cincinnati Reds. While the drama played out, the conspirators played one more season and then were banned from baseball for life by new commissioner Kenesaw Mountain Landis. Once that happened many people were said to have perceived baseball as being "crooked." There had been fixed games earlier in the century, but this one involved the World Series. The lords of the game were worried. Would the fans stay away in droves?

The prosperous 1920s were just beginning and there is usually a post-war spike in sporting events, but big league attendance did indeed drop the next season, from 9,120,875 in 1920 to 8,607,042 the following year. That was also the year the Babe hit a whopping 59 home runs for the Yankees. Yet despite this, attendance budged very little over the next two years, as the Babe became the biggest star in the game. Then the people began returning. Total attendance went from 8,672,409 in 1923 to 9,596,083 in 1924. That was the year the Washington Senators won the American League pennant. It would crest at 9,922,868 in 1927, when the Babe hit his 60, but by looking at those numbers it's difficult to make a case for the Babe saving baseball. Rather, it was probably a matter of more people becoming interesting in sports and having the money to attend while the Black Sox scandal slowly receded into the background.

The Babe did have an effect on attendance once he began playing in the huge Yankee Stadium. People definitely came out to see him take his mighty swings with the hope he would connect. Would it have been the same in Boston? Again, it would have but to a lesser extent, which seems to be the catchphrase for almost everything the Babe would have accomplished if he had stayed with the Red Sox. He still would have been one of the greatest ever, a Hall of Fame pitcher who then became the greatest slugger of his generation and maybe of all time. When the Babe died in 1948 he was the possessor of fifty-six major league batting records. Some have since been eclipsed, but not the mythical proportions of the man. He remains a megastar, and his larger-than-life presence is associated instantly with the New York Yankees, his team from 1920 to 1934.

Had the Babe remained in Boston he would undoubtedly be revered there, as he is now in New York. But his mystique wouldn't have been nearly as great. And, as many of his records have now been eclipsed, his memory might have begun to fade. There would have been no plaque in Monument Park at Yankee Stadium and none of the other priceless amenities that the Yankees can bring to

the table, including his place in New York history, and the continued merchandising of products, as well as his name and like-
ness. Being sold to the Yankees by Harry Frazee was not only the
best thing that happened to the Yankees, it was the best thing for
the Babe and for baseball, as well.

But one other thing is certain. Had the Babe remained in
Boston, there definitely wouldn't have been that catchphrase that
fans of the Red Sox have hung their hats on for so long. There
would have been no "Curse of the Bambino"!

Clay Gets Crushed

On February 25, 1964, twenty-two-year-old Cassius Clay stepped into the ring at Convention Hall in Miami, Florida, to challenge Charles "Sonny" Liston for boxing's heavyweight championship, one of the most prestigious prizes in all of sports. Liston, a ferocious ex-con with a menacing glare and a punch like a sledgehammer, was a prohibitive 7-1 favorite, with many wondering if the cat-quick Clay would get out of the ring alive. By now, everyone knows what happened. The impetuous Clay used his speed to befuddle and then batter the overconfident and out of shape Liston, who quit on his stool as the bell rang for the start of the seventh round. Cassius Clay was the new heavyweight champion. Days later, he officially changed his name to Muhammad Ali and a legend was born.

But what if Liston had KO'd Clay to retain the heavyweight championship?

★　★　★　★　★

It wasn't exactly a match made in heaven, but it was very intriguing. Boxing was very different back in the early 1960s. There were fewer divisions without the in-betweens, and only a single champion in each. And of those, it was the heavyweights who always caught the fancy of the fans. From John L. Sullivan to Jack Johnson, from Jack Dempsey to Joe Louis, and from Rocky Marciano to Floyd Patterson, the heavyweight champ was the guy to watch. When the Liston-Clay match-up was announced in November 1963, the interest level was immediately high. In the minds of many, this was going to be a battle between good and evil. In fact, many fans felt that evil, embodied in the champion, Sonny Liston, shouldn't have had a chance to fight for the heavyweight title in the first place.

Sonny Liston wasn't certain when or where he was born. He guessed it was 1932 or '33, but some felt it might have been as far back as 1927 or '28. He knew he was born in a small Arkansas farming town, but wasn't sure which one. His father, Tobe Liston, worked in the fields, moving from job to job. He was said to have fathered eleven children with Sonny's mother, Helen, and before that at least twelve more with another woman.

Sonny himself would later admit, "We grew up like heathens. We hardly had enough food to keep from starving, no shoes, and only a few clothes. And nobody to help us escape from the horrible life we lived."

Despite this, Sonny Liston grew to be big and strong. By the time he was sixteen he was nudging past six feet in height and weighed about 210 pounds. For all intents and purposes, he was already a heavyweight. But he wasn't a fighter. Rather, he was an uneducated kid who would soon begin having trouble with the law. His mother left his father and moved to St. Louis in 1946. Soon after, Sonny ran away from home and joined her there. Four years later he received a five-year prison sentence for the armed robbery of two gas stations and a diner. Behind bars in the Missouri State

Penitentiary, Sonny Liston was introduced to boxing. He was 6'1½" and weighed a rock-solid 215 pounds, and could punch with either hand. And it didn't hurt that he also had massive, fourteen-inch fists.

He was released on parole by October 1952 and became a professional boxer the following September. His first fight lasted all of thirty-three seconds, and when it ended it wasn't Sonny Liston who was stretched out on the canvas. It was a journeyman named Don Smith who tasted just one of Liston's punches. That's all it took. The boxing career of Sonny Liston had officially begun and soon the word was out—heavyweights beware.

During the next several years Liston alternated between winning fights and getting in various scrapes with the law. A confrontation with a St. Louis police officer in May 1956 earned him yet another nine months of incarceration. Soon after his release he left St. Louis and moved to Philadelphia, where his contract was purchased by a group that included Frankie Carbo and Frank "Blinky" Palermo. Both men had ties to organized crime and also to the boxing world. Back then, the two were often linked and Liston, with his checkered past, seemed the perfect fit for their machinations.

By 1958 he had KO'd such highly-regarded fighters as Cleveland Williams and Zora Folley, but his continued problems out of the ring finally led to a suspension by the Pennsylvania Athletic Commission in July 1961, a suspension honored by all other states. Yet three months later his license was reinstated and that December he knocked out fourth-ranked Albert Westpahl. Suddenly, Charles "Sonny" Liston, the poor sharecropper's kid and ex-con, was in line to fight for the heavyweight championship of the world.

PATTERSON, THE POPULAR CHAMPION
The reigning heavyweight king in 1962 was Floyd Patterson, a smallish 190-pounder and a guy many thought of as a natural light-

heavyweight. But when Floyd knocked out ageless Archie Moore, the longtime light-heavyweight champ, in November 1956, he ascended to the top of the sports world. He was the natural successor to Rocky Marciano, who had held the crown from 1952 to 1956 before becoming the only heavyweight king to retire undefeated. Marciano had followed the great Joe Louis, who had owned the title for twelve years, between 1937 and 1949. So there was a lineage and the public responded to it.

Patterson, however, wasn't the big bomber that Louis and Marciano had been; he fought with his gloves high by his head in what was called the "peekaboo" style. Floyd had quick hands and a sharp left hook, often leaving his feet when he threw it, but he was also vulnerable to a good puncher and that was part of the reason fans rooted for him. He lost the title to Sweden's Ingemar Johansson in a stunning knockout in 1959, and then became the first ever to regain it when he KO'd the Swede the following year, knocking him out with one of those leaping left hooks. Now, on September 25, 1962, Patterson would have to defend once more, this time against the big bear, Sonny Liston.

As a reflection of the times there were protests against Liston getting a title shot. Many pointed to his prison record and felt that he lacked the character to be the heavyweight champ. Even the NAACP didn't want to see the fight happen because they felt that the big man's reputation as a thug-like felon would hurt the growing civil rights movement. But Liston had earned his shot where it counted—in the ring—and the boxing world couldn't deny him.

The fight was almost a sham. If Liston's menacing glare hadn't unnerved Patterson, his physical presence backed up by his fists did. It was like a bully picking on a little kid as Sonny dispatched Floyd at 2:06 of the very first round to become the new heavyweight champ. The two fought a rematch the following July in Las Vegas and the result was eerily similar. It took Liston just four seconds more this time, at 2:10 of the first round, to once again knock Patterson out. Now Liston stood alone; his destruction of Patterson was so complete that many people felt he was virtually unbeatable. In fact, one of his trainers, Johnny Tocco, put it this way: "In the ring, Sonny was a killing machine."

ALONG COMES CLAY

Because of Liston's background, suspected mob ties, and surly demeanor, he was never a popular champion, and almost immediately fight fans looked for someone who could defeat the new champ, someone worth rooting for. Within a short time they found him in an up-and-coming, handsome youngster with the intriguing name of Cassius Marcellus Clay. He was born in Louisville, Kentucky, on January 17, 1942, began training as a fighter at the age of twelve and soon began winning titles. By the time he was eighteen, his resume included six Kentucky Golden Gloves titles, a pair of national Golden Gloves championships, and an Amateur Athletic Union national title. All told, he would have more than a hundred amateur bouts and lose just five times.

Then, in 1960, young Cassius Clay became a member of the United States Olympic team. Tall and well built, he would compete at 175 pounds in the light heavyweight division. He already had a special grace and tremendous foot speed in the ring, though he wasn't known as a particularly big puncher. At the Olympic Village in Rome, he wandered about, introducing himself to athletes from all over the world and, when asked, predicting he would win a gold medal.

His first bout was against Yan Becaus of Belgium and Cassius won easily, knocking out his opponent in the second round. He did it with flash and verve, firing lightning-quick combinations, then holding his hands low and almost daring his opponent to try to hit him. He followed up his opening win with lopsided decisions over

Gennady Schatkov of the Soviet Union, Tony Madigan of Australia, and then Zbigniew Pietrzykowski of Poland, easily winning the gold medal.

Not long after the Olympics ended Cassius Clay announced he was turning pro and would campaign as a heavyweight. Many wondered if the still-growing teenager could compete in boxing's premier division, where he could encounter bigger, stronger fighters. And could he punch hard enough to pose a real threat? After he won his first fight, a six-round decision against Tunney Hunsaker in October 1960, people realized the kid could more than hold his own.

Fighting often and learning his craft as he went, young Clay began beating everyone and knocking out most of his opponents. Unlike Liston, he wasn't a one-punch knockout guy, but with his speed and ability to throw blazing combinations, he simply wore his opponents down. He was also extremely entertaining, talking constantly, exhibiting slick footwork never before seen in a heavyweight fighter, and often doing a quick, dance-like maneuver that would later be called the Ali shuffle. He went into the ring eight times in 1961 and another six times the following year, when his last fight, in November 1962, ended with a fourth-round knockout of the wily former light-heavyweight champ Archie Moore.

All along, the brash Clay seemed to be gaining in confidence. He was soon telling anyone who would listen that he couldn't be beaten, that he was the greatest, and he backed it up by often predicting the round in which his opponent would be stopped—and getting it right more often than not. In 1963, Clay knocked out a fighter named Charlie Powell in January, and went on to beat a couple of tough, ranked fighters, decisioning Doug Jones in March and knocking out England's Henry Cooper in June. There was no denying that the kid was ready. He was unbeaten and getting better. In November, the fight was made: Cassius Clay would challenge Sonny Liston for the heavyweight championship of the world.

CLAY'S PRE-FIGHT ANTICS PUZZLE EVERYONE

It quickly became apparent that Cassius Clay was going to do a lot more than just train for the fight. To everyone's surprise, he began dogging the menacing Liston, showing up at his training site and heckling him, calling him names. Clay referred to Liston in the press as "the big ugly bear." As for Liston, he couldn't understand why this kid was showing absolutely no respect for him as the champion. He even began questioning the youngster's mental state. But, unbeknownst to Liston, there was a method to Clay's feigned madness.

"The big thing for me was to observe how Liston acted outside the ring," Clay would say later. "I read everything I could where he had been interviewed and talked to people who had been around him or had talked with him. I would think about them and try to get a picture of how his mind worked."

But could a guy like Liston be unnerved? After all Clay's antics, it would ultimately come down to those minutes in the ring, the two of them trying to knock each other senseless. In fact, the ring seemed to be the one place where the champ could be himself and just let his furious fists do the talking. Still, Clay persisted. He drove his bus to Liston's house one night and had an associate actually ring the doorbell before they left. When the two met at the Miami airport shortly before the fight, his continued needling resulted in Liston throwing a punch . . . that missed.

Then came the pre-fight weigh-in. When the challenger, Clay, saw the champ come in, he seemed to go berserk, screaming, "You chump, you ugly bear, I'm gonna whip you!" Doctors measured Clay's heart rate at 110 beats a minute, more than double its usual 54. The lead doctor on the scene, Alexander Robbins, said that

Cassius was "emotionally unbalanced, scared to death, and liable to crack up before he enters the ring." But once the weigh-in ended, Clay's vitals quickly calmed down and returned to normal. It had all been a calculated act.

There was yet another element in play as the fight approached. Word came out that Cassius Clay was about to join the Nation of Islam, the Black Muslims, considered by many to be a militant civil rights organization that would stoop to violence if necessary. The Black Muslims frightened a lot of people, and now this popular and charismatic young man who would be fighting for the heavyweight championship of the world was about to join them. Yet, personalities aside, the fight was still considered a mismatch, with Liston a staggering 7-1 favorite. Because so many people assumed that big, bad Sonny would knock the seemingly unstable Clay senseless, the Convention Center in Miami was only about half full, with some 8,297 people in attendance. But, at last, the battle was at hand.

THE FIGHT . . . AND WHAT IF?

Liston, of course, feared no man, but just before fight time Cassius Clay was nervous. He would say, years later, "I was scared. Sonny Liston was one of the greatest fighters of all time. He hit hard and he was fixing to kill me . . . But I didn't have no choice but to go out and fight."

It was Clay's veteran trainer, Angelo Dundee, who really thought his young fighter could win. "I felt he'd win because he had the speed to offset Liston's jab and Liston's jab was the key to everything. Liston had a jab that was like a battering ram. If he got you at the end of that jab, you were gone, but Cassius was able to surround the jab, side to side, with quickness and agility."

That's just how the fight started; in the first round, Liston rushed out of his corner as if to make quick work of his latest nemesis, just as he had against Patterson, whom he handled like a rag doll. To Sonny's surprise, when he threw his first few shots at his opponent, Clay wasn't there. His superior footwork was keeping him out of harm's way. So were his head movements as he leaned away from the end of Liston's strong punches. Sonny threw a big right hook that also missed, and at the end of the round Clay suddenly exploded on Liston with a flurry of quick punches. He returned to his corner with renewed confidence.

In the second round, Liston continued to mainly miss while Clay began connecting with his own quick jab. By the end of the round, there was a small welt rising under Liston's left eye. Sonny connected with a left to the jaw toward the end of the round that shook Clay, but he didn't follow up and Clay recovered. In the third, the young challenger opened a cut on Liston's face with a quick, sharp left-right combination. He continued to pepper Liston for the rest of the third round and for most of the fourth. It became all too obvious that the champ wasn't in good shape. He hadn't trained for a long fight, figuring he could take his opponent out easily, and now he appeared to be tiring badly. But toward the end of round four, Clay found himself in trouble. His eyes began stinging and tearing, and he was struggling to see.

Back in the corner, he told Angelo Dundee what was happening, and the veteran trainer suspected that a coagulant that Liston's cornermen were using to stop the bleeding had gotten onto his gloves and subsequently into his fighter's eyes. Clay was on the verge of panicking and told Dundee he didn't want to continue. No way, Dundee thought. He quickly washed his fighter's eyes out with a wet sponge and hollered, "Cut the bullshit. We're not quitting now. You gotta go out there and run." He felt that if Clay could avoid Liston's bombs for a couple of minutes, his eyes would clear up.

But here's what could have happened. Clay went out for round five, began backpeddling immediately while still dabbing at his eyes with his gloves. Liston, finally sensing a weakness in his opponent, saw his opportunity and took it. He gauged Clay's movements and finally succeeded in cutting off the ring, trapping the young fighter in the corner. Then he connected with that long, hammer-like jab, snapping Clay's head back and stunning him. Before Cassius could react, Sonny threw his massive right and Clay tumbled to the canvas. The ref began his count. Even then, the youngster could take a punch. He got to a knee at the count of six and was up at nine. But the punch had temporarily short-circuited his greatest asset, his legs.

With his movement still hampered, he couldn't get away. Liston summoned his remaining stamina to attack the youngster and suddenly it looked like the Patterson fight all over again. As Clay covered up, Liston landed two huge shots to his side and then got the big right in once more. As the challenger sagged to the canvas, the ref rushed in waving his arms. The fight was over. Sonny Liston had retained his championship with a dramatic, fifth-round knockout.

THE POSSIBLE AFTERMATH

It's not easy to think about what might have happened if Clay had been knocked out by Liston back in 1964. One reason is that Cassius Clay, who officially became Muhammad Ali just days after winning this fight, has become a worldwide icon, perhaps the most popular and certainly most well-known athlete of the second half of the twentieth century. By the same token, had he been KO'd by Liston's big punches on that hot night in Miami some things would have surely changed, not only for Muhammad Ali, but for Sonny Liston as well.

With Liston, it's much easier to speculate. Having retained his title, Sonny might well have realized that there's no sure thing and that he had better not come into a fight so overconfident and under-conditioned again. He would have realized that he was tiring badly and if he had not caught his young opponent with such a telling punch, he might have run out of steam and suffered the ultimate embarrassment in the only place where he was the best— in the ring. That could have led him to train with renewed vigor and vow to hold his title as long as he possibly could.

Judging from the fighters Muhammad Ali would defeat in the ensuing three years—Floyd Patterson, George Chuvalo, Henry Cooper, Brian London, Karl Mildenberger, Cleveland Williams, Ernie Terrell, and Zora Folley—it's hard to see any of them standing up to Liston's powerful fists. In fact, he had already beaten several of them and they might not have wanted to get back in the ring with him a second time. Liston, of course, was already on the far side of thirty when he fought the young Clay—how far, no one knew—so the chances were good that he was about to begin fading. To hold the title and earn enough money to hopefully keep him solvent, he would have had to train diligently.

To achieve the complete acceptance of the boxing and sporting public, and to be recognized as a great heavyweight champion, Sonny Liston would also have had to straighten out his personal life and his boxing associations. Had he retained the title he might have shied away from any further confrontations with the law. That, of course, isn't always easy for certain individuals, as another great champion, Mike Tyson, would learn in later years. But with a forgiving public and maybe some smart advisors on board, Liston certainly would have had the chance to clean up his image.

Whether he could have extricated himself from the likes of Frankie Carbo and Blinky Palmero is another story. Sonny's original contract with them, by all accounts, pretty much left him on the short end of the financial stick. But this was also a time when organized crime's fairly widespread influence over boxing was starting to wane and, again, with the right people in his corner, he might have been able to find a better management group that would have had his best interests at heart. And who knows, if these things had occurred sports fans might well have seen a headline in 1968 that read, "Frazier KO's Liston to Win Heavyweight Title."

Had it all come together for Sonny, he might have lived a better life. As it was, some ten months after losing to Cassius Clay, the two had a rematch in a tiny arena in Lewiston, Maine. In that one, Muhammad Ali KO'd Sonny in the first round with a right hand many at ringside didn't even see. The so-called "Phantom Punch" put the big guy on the canvas for a controversial ten-count. When Liston went down, Ali stood over him, screaming for him to get up. The referee, former heavyweight champ Jersey Joe Walcott, in trying to get Ali to go to the corner, lost track of the count and some estimate Liston was down for at least 17 seconds. When he finally got up, Walcott motioned for the fight to continue. It wasn't until a journalist at ringside shouted to Jersey Joe that the time-keeper had counted Liston out that the fight was stopped. Fans at ringside couldn't believe that Liston could be KO'd by such a quick punch and thought the fight was fixed. Some even speculated that Sonny had thrown the fight for fear that the Black Muslims would murder him. The truth may never be known.

After that, Liston disappeared from the ring for a whole year, but then came back to win four straight fights in Sweden. Returning to the United States, he then won ten more and had begun talking about another title fight when Leotis Martin knocked him out in late 1969. Depending on his hazy birth date, he could have been pushing, or perhaps over, forty by then. The final chapter came on January 5, 1971, when Charles "Sonny" Liston's body was found at his Las Vegas home by his wife, Geraldine, on her return from visiting family. Officially, the cause of death was listed as heart failure and lung congestion, but needle marks were found on his arm leading to speculation that he might have died of a heroin overdose. There were also some who thought he was murdered by mobsters. Either way, the mostly sad and violent life of Sonny Liston had ended. Had he won the fight that night in Miami, the ending could have been very different.

WHAT ABOUT MUHAMMAD ALI?

This one is much harder to gauge because it leads to a much more complex scenario. Had Cassius Clay been knocked out by Sonny Liston in his first try for the heavyweight title, one of the greatest careers in boxing history might have been very different. Not only that, but a loss for Clay that night might have changed the course of a story that began playing out during the turbulent 1960s and has continued ever since.

For starters, there's the political question of the Black Muslim movement. There's no question that Cassius Clay was committed to joining them, and as part of this he changed his name to Muhammad Ali. Like so many young black men at that time, he was tired of the incessant racism that still permeated much of the land. After returning from the Rome Olympics with a gold medal in 1960, young Cassius was refused service at a Louisville restaurant. He was so upset that he told people at the time that he threw his Olympic medal into a nearby river. Later, he would say it just came up missing, but there's no doubt he was severely troubled by the racial attitudes in the country at the time. So there's no doubt that if he saw the Nation of Islam as the best way to invoke change, he would willingly become part of them. And as he has shown over the years, his conversion to Islam was no whim. He has remained true to his adopted religion ever since. But an overriding question remains.

Had he lost to Sonny Liston, would the Black Muslims have been so anxious to embrace him? After all, having the heavyweight champion of the world in their fold was certainly a huge plus, a way to attract more attention to their movement. But a beaten fighter who had just been knocked out and whose ring future was suddenly uncertain? It's doubtful the Nation of Islam would have rejected him completely, but he certainly may not have played as prominent a role in the movement as he ultimately did. As it was, there were many who refused to recognize his name change and continued to call him Cassius Clay for years. Had he been on the losing end of Liston's fists, even more people would likely have scoffed at or simply rejected the name change. Or, had he been defeated, he might have postponed the change until a later time, or perhaps have taken on a different name. As one story recapping the fight put it, had Angelo Dundee not pushed his fighter back out for the fifth round after his eyes began burning, "there might have been no Muhammad Ali."

At the same time that this was playing out, the Vietnam War was polarizing the country. President John Kennedy had been assassinated in 1963. In 1968, both Robert Kennedy and Martin Luther King, Jr., were shot and killed. After the Reverend King's death there were riots in the streets as many young African-Americans began to feel that peaceful change would never come, or would come much too slowly. And in the middle of all this stood Muhammad Ali, brash and bold, the greatest fighter in the world and the heavyweight champ. On April 28, 1967, Muhammad Ali would publicly refuse induction into the United States Army after he was drafted. He felt that since African-Americans were not given equality in the United States, it was wrong for them to fight in a foreign war. At first he was classified as a conscientious objector, but after saying he was not opposed to all wars and would likely fight in an Islamic holy war he lost his conscientious objector status and was ultimately sentenced to five years in prison. What's more, he was stripped of his heavyweight title.

But had he lost to Sonny Liston, that momentous event, too, might well have been altered. If Muhammad Ali were not the heavyweight champ, thus not a noteworthy celebrity, he probably would not have become the face of the Black Muslims and would not have attracted the kind of media coverage that always surrounded him. Had he then refused induction to the service under the same circumstances, he most likely would have served his prison time. As it was, he never went to jail and had his conviction overturned four years later by the United States Supreme Court on procedural grounds. Muhammad Ali had taken a stand and, as a result, lost four prime years of his boxing career. If Ali had lost to Liston, he still might have taken the same stand, but without the resultant publicity and celebrity status. There would have been little press and a good chance of jail time.

WHERE WOULD ALI'S BOXING CAREER HAVE GONE?

Perhaps the biggest question left to answer in the face of a Liston victory is that of Muhammad Ali's continuing boxing career. Ali admitted that he was scared before the fight, and if he had been KO'd by Liston's enormous power punches, chances are, at his young age, he wouldn't have relished a second chance against the big man right away. And Liston, seeing Ali's speed in the early rounds, might well have realized that he was lucky to catch his youthful opponent and certainly wouldn't want to give him another opportunity. So it's pretty safe to say there wouldn't have been a rematch, at least not in the foreseeable future.

What then, for Ali? Though he fought at 175 pounds in the 1960 Olympics, the 6'3" Ali weighed close to 215 when he took on Sonny Liston. If he had lost, he would have been left with three choices. One would be to leave boxing, but it's very doubtful Ali would have taken that path, for two reasons—he was very good at it and he had nothing to fall back on. If he chose to continue, he would have had to decide whether to remain a heavyweight or perhaps drop back down to the light-heavyweight division. Despite his extra weight, it wouldn't have been too difficult for him to drop down to 175. He was still very young, with a supple body, so the weight wasn't firmly established. And fighters often make weight the day before a fight, then rehydrate and come into the ring the next day sometimes ten or even close to twenty pounds heavier than at the weigh-in. So Ali conceivably could have made the 175 pound weight limit for several years and climbed into the ring at perhaps 185 to 190.

If Ali had decided to remain a heavyweight, his goal obviously would still have been the title and the renewed Liston would be standing in his way. But had he dropped down to fight in the light-heavyweight division, Muhammad Ali might have, indeed, dominated for years. The light-heavy champ from 1963–65 was Willie Pastrano, a solid boxer who really didn't have much of a knockout punch. If Ali had quickly become a contender he most certainly could have easily defeated Pastrano. Following Pastrano to the title were Jose Torres (1965–66) and Dick Tiger (1966–67), two very good fighters but both smaller men. Each had grown up from the middleweight division and it's difficult seeing either posing much of a threat for the tall, quick, and more powerful Ali. So Muhammad could have conceivably dominated the light-heavyweight division up until the time he refused to be inducted into the army.

It's an interesting scenario, but something still would have been different. The light-heavyweight division has never attracted nearly the exposure or coverage of the heavyweights, and has never generated the same kind of excitement. In fact, back in the 1960s and '70s there was often more interest in big fights at the welterweight and middleweight levels than in the light-heavies. It was always something of an in-between weight class, and even today it's all but eclipsed by even the lighter weight classes. So even if

Muhammad Ali had dominated as a light-heavy, it's doubtful he would have created the same kind of buzz. He had too much natural charisma to have been totally anonymous, but the knockout loss to Liston would have hovered over his head like a dense fog.

Assuming Muhammad moved down to the lower weight class and won the title, his career still would have been derailed by his refusal to join the Army in 1967. Regardless of whether he spent time in prison or remained free pending an appeal, he would have been faced with a big decision when he returned to the ring in 1970. He would have been twenty-eight years old and, after the three-year layoff, would undoubtedly have had trouble getting back to the 175-pound limit. So this time, it seems logical that he would have tried his skills in the heavyweight division once again. By then, the unbeaten Joe Frazier would be firmly ensconced as the heavyweight champ. Frazier, a pleasant though reticent man, was nonstop in the ring. He was continually coming forward, bobbing and weaving, along with throwing the most lethal left hook in the business. Ali, with his great speed, would still probably felt he could beat Frazier, but before he could do that he would have to totally reestablish himself as a legitimate heavyweight contender.

NO SUPERFIGHT IN '71

With this scenario in place, one thing is certain: one of the greatest sporting events of the twentieth century would never have taken place. On March 8, 1971, the unbeaten Muhammad Ali, in his third fight since regaining his license, met the current heavyweight champ, Joe Frazier, who was also undefeated. The two fought a fifteen-round title bout at Madison Square Garden in New York that became a cultural event, a fashion show, and a place where the rich and famous gathered, as well as those who managed to get tickets and wanted to be seen in all their finery. Movie actor Burt Lancaster helped with the commentary while singer/actor/icon Frank Sinatra took photographs at ringside for *Life* magazine. It was the first ever boxing match that literally transcended the sporting world and it has since been called "The Fight of the Century." Frazier won a close, fifteen-round decision capped by a knockdown in the final round when he caught Ali with one of his patented left hooks.

Just that short description alone will give those unfamiliar with it an accurate picture of the ambience surrounding this fight. It really marked the return to center stage for Ali, a place he would occupy for the remainder of his career and beyond. It was also the defining moment of Smokin' Joe Frazier's career. There's a very good chance, though, that if Sonny Liston had beaten Muhammad Ali back in 1964 this fight, and the circumstances that surrounded it at this particular place and time, would never have happened.

If Muhammad Ali had followed the scenario where he dropped down to light heavyweight and held that title until being stripped of his title for refusing Army induction, he would have returned to the ring with a lot to prove before he had a chance at the heavyweight title. He may well have done it, but not before Big George Foreman defeated Frazier for the title on January 22, 1973, in Kingston, Jamaica. And there's no guarantee that he would have been the same wily fighter he had become, being able to adapt to losing some of his speed and dazzle during his forced layoff.

Chances are, even with this scenario, there would have been no "Rumble in the Jungle," the fight between Ali and Foreman in Kinshasa, Zaire (now the Democratic Republic of the Congo), on October 30, 1974. It was in that fight that Muhammad Ali regained the heavyweight title and surprised everyone by just laying on the ropes for several rounds while the powerful Foreman wore himself out throwing punch after punch that Ali mostly blocked with his arms. Ali called it the "Rope a Dope," another one of his clever catchphrases, and he finally came off the ropes to KO the tiring Foreman in the eighth round.

Had Ali lost to Liston in 1964, he might have fought Foreman differently when the two met. Knowing that Foreman punched just as hard as Sonny Liston, Ali may well have decided not to use the Rope a Dope, which allowed Foreman to pummel his arms and sides. He would have remembered Liston's crushing right catching him in the face. He might well have tried to fight Foreman in the center of the ring, using his superior speed. But with Big George's outstanding punching ability, there's no certainty that Ali, already in his early thirties, could have avoided the younger man's fists. Remember, the Rope a Dope caught everyone by surprise, including Ali's trainer, Angelo Dundee, and it perplexed Foreman. Had Ali fought a more conventional fight, the result might have been very different.

Another fight that would not have happened was the "Thrilla in Manila," which took place in the Philippines on October 1, 1975. Ali met Frazier for the third and final time in the rubber match of their trilogy of battles. It was a brutal fight in which Frazier didn't answer the bell for the fifteenth and final round. Ali himself admitted this battle was extremely brutal, and called it "the closest thing to death" that he had ever experienced. They say that all great fighters need a great opponent to cement their legacy. Muhammad Ali had Joe Frazier, and vice versa. Their battles, especially the first and third, will never be forgotten.

If, however, the first fight between the two had never taken place, there would have been no trilogy. Perhaps the two would have fought once after Ali turned heavyweight and Frazier had lost the title, but they never would have forged the great rivalry now etched in history by those three colossal battles. Boxing would have lost one of its most legendary rivalries and two of the greatest fights of the generation.

LATE CAREER AND BEYOND

There's no doubt in anyone's mind that Muhammad Ali fought for too long. Boxing is one sport in which many fighters have a hard time walking away, even the most successful ones. Maybe nothing beats that rush of walking into the ring to loud cheers, squaring off against an opponent in the ultimate one-on-one showdown, and being able to throw one's arms up in victory. Certainly more than a few fighters have announced their retirement only to re-emerge for a "comeback" a short time later.

Muhammad Ali was never quite the same after his forced exile. As a youngster, he had foot speed second to none, and he moved deftly around the ring with grace and guile. While he never had the punch of a Foreman or a Liston, he threw deadly combinations off an outstanding jab, and his hands were the fastest in the division. Once he returned from exile, though, he could no longer sustain his speed and movement, and he began developing other strategies, such as the Rope a Dope. Though he still won most of his fights, he now absorbed more punishment in the ring as he traded blows with some of the hardest punchers of his time. So while he was rarely cut, he did have some brutal, give-and-take fights, all later in his career. Though it probably hurt him in the long run, Ali also showed the boxing world that he could take a punch with the best of them.

Some of the battles he was in after returning to the ring included the three fights with Frazier, three with hard-punching Ken Norton (who won the first when he broke Ali's jaw), a battle with big punching Earnie Shavers, a pair with Leon Spinks (he lost the first, but won the second to regain the title for the third time), and one with champion Larry Holmes in 1980. For that one, Ali returned after a brief retirement, lost a lot of weight too quickly, took a brutal beating from Holmes (who idolized him and almost begged the ref to stop it), and was KO'd in the eleventh round. He fought once more the following year, losing a decision to Trevor Berbick, before calling it quits.

Within a decade of retiring, Ali began showing symptoms of the Parkinson's disease that would eventually limit his mobility and his ability to speak. Many feel the accumulation of punches taken late in his career may have contributed to his debilitating illness. Again, going back to the first title fight with Sonny Liston, a loss might have also changed the final course of his career. Once more, there are several possible scenarios. Had Muhammad remained a light heavyweight he undoubtedly would have retired as one of the division's greats, maybe the greatest. But he would not have had the accolades he received as the heavyweight champion and might have retired sooner.

But every fork in the road leads to a change. Had his career not taken the path that it did, Muhammad's post-boxing life also might have been different. It's hard to say, because he was still a charismatic figure who remained steadfast in his beliefs. He would go on to become one of the most well-known and well-respected figures in the entire world, and become involved with many humanitarian endeavors. He certainly could have taken a similar path had he lost to Sonny Liston. But he might not have had the same influence, and his work probably would not have been done on center stage. And center stage is where Muhammad Ali began and remained always. The only thing that might have derailed it are those two little words . . . What if?

New York or Bust

Once upon a time, New York was the only city with three major league baseball teams, and they all had long and interesting histories. The New York Yankees, from Babe Ruth to Joe DiMaggio to Mickey Mantle, had dominated baseball since the 1920s. The New York Giants were one of baseball's great early teams with a history going back to Christy Mathewson and John McGraw. In the 1950s they had Willie Mays and Leo Durocher. As for the Brooklyn Dodgers, well, they had an entire borough that worshipped them like gods. And from the 1940s through the 1950s they were also one of the best teams in baseball, not to mention the franchise that broke baseball's color line when Jackie Robinson joined them in 1947. Then in 1957 it all changed. Both the Dodgers and Giants announced they were packing up and moving their franchises to California. It marked the beginning of baseball's expansion era, broke the hearts of New York fans, and helped change the game forever.

But what if the Dodgers and Giants had decided to stay in New York?

★   ★   ★   ★   ★

If you told a baseball fan back in the 1920s, 1930s, or even the 1940s that someday the city of New York would be without the Giants and the Dodgers, they would immediately say you were crazy. The New York Giants and Brooklyn Dodgers were major league institutions, venerable old National League franchises that had grown up in Manhattan and Brooklyn. They were simply there to stay. And why not? Baseball was stable—eight teams in each league and none of them ever moved. They stayed where they were. If anything in the world was status quo, it was baseball. Unfortunately, that status quo couldn't last forever.

Just after the 1952 season, another old franchise, the National League's Boston Braves, received permission to move to Milwaukee. The Braves were playing in a small, old ballpark and simply couldn't compete with the more popular Boston Red Sox. It was the first franchise shift in a half century but it gave others serious food for thought. A year later it was the St. Louis Browns who followed suit. The American League team always played second fiddle to the Cardinals in St. Louis, so they decided to move to Baltimore, where they became the Orioles. And the year after that, the Philadelphia Athletics pulled up stakes and relocated to Kansas City. That would turn out to be merely a stopover. Soon enough, they would move again, eventually becoming the Oakland A's.

So by the mid-1950s, baseball was on the move and some teams began looking for more lucrative homes where they could find new and enthusiastic fans, and better ballparks. But the Giants and Dodgers? That simply couldn't happen. For one thing, the two teams had the most heated rivalry in sports. It had developed over the years, though prior to the late 1940s the Giants had been by far the more successful franchise. Then the rivalry took another turn when, in the middle of the 1948 season, the Dodgers fiery and successful manager, Leo Durocher, was suddenly dismissed by GM Branch Rickey and immediately hired by owner Horace Stoneham to manage the Giants. Durocher would never forgive Rickey and immediately took the rivalry to another level. Beating the Dodgers would always be special, and when the highly combative and abrasive Durocher wanted to win that badly, animosity usually followed.

In fact, Leo was a Hall of Fame manager who never took prisoners or hid his feelings. When he first walked into the New York clubhouse and saw the players staring at him as if he was still an enemy, Durocher ran his hand across his chest where the team's name was emblazoned on the uniform and said just one word: "Giants!"

He also didn't like the team he was given, a slugging outfit of slow-footed players who in 1947 had set a major league home run record with 221 and still finished fourth. The new manager immediately went to owner Horace Stoneham and voiced his dissatisfaction. When Stoneham asked what had to be done, Durocher answered, "Back up the truck!"

He then went about unloading sluggers like Johnny Mize, Walker Cooper, Willard Marshall, and Sid Gordon. He made a trade that brought him the keystone combination of shortstop Alvin Dark and second baseman Eddie Stanky—scratchers and divers, he called them—and slowly changed the face of the team. By 1950, Durocher's Giants were in contention. Following the lead of the Dodgers (Durocher was suspended as Dodgers manager when Jackie Robinson broke the color line in 1947, but he was all for allowing African-Americans to play), he quickly integrated his team, bringing in outfielder Monte Irvin and third baseman Hank Thompson. He also added the likes of Whitey Lockman, Don Mueller, and catcher Wes Westrum. On the mound he had a big three with Mexican League import Sal Maglie, Larry Jansen, and Jim Hearn. The Giants were 86-68 in 1950, three games behind the Dodgers and just five behind the pennant-winning Philadelphia

Phillies Whiz Kids. That set the stage for 1951, one of the most memorable seasons in New York baseball history.

LET'S VISIT THE DODGERS

In the early years of the game, the Brooklyn Dodgers were a laughing stock, a team that always seemed to dwell closer to the basement than to the penthouse. Yet playing in cozy Ebbets Field, they were beloved by their fans, who somehow took these lovable losers to heart. After all, this was the only baseball team ever named after a borough rather than a city, and those who lived in Brooklyn always claimed the team as their own.

In 1938, with former pitcher Burleigh Grimes in the manager's chair, the Dodgers finished near the basement once again, this time seventh with a 69-80 record. A year later, Leo Durocher took over the managerial reins and suddenly "Dem Bums" were no longer a joke. Leo the Lip had the Brooks in third place with an 84-69 record. And he was still occasionally playing shortstop for them as well. The team was second the following year, and in 1941 they won 100 games and a pennant.

Suddenly, there were ballplayers in Brooklyn: Dolph Camilli, Billy Herman, Dixie Walker, "Pistol" Pete Reiser, Joe "Ducky" Medwick, and a young shortstop named Harold "Pee Wee" Reese. Though they lost the World Series to that "other" team from New York, the Yankees, the Brooklyn Dodgers were here to stay. In 1942 they won 104 games—and were second, as the Cardinals won 106, in one of the greatest pennant races in National League history.

The war years created an uneven playing field for many teams, but by 1946 the Dodgers were again in the thick of things, finishing second to the Cards. Then Durocher was suspended in 1947 by Commissioner Happy Chandler for reasons that were never crystal clear. With veteran Burt Shotton managing the team, the

Dodgers won the pennant once more, this time with Jackie Robinson, who was the talk of baseball that year, as well as National League Rookie of the Year. The next year Durocher made his famous switch to the Giants, but by 1949 the Dodgers were pennant winners again.

Now the team was made up of many of the players who would become known as "The Boys of Summer," and they would remain one of the sport's elite squads for the next decade. There were Robinson and Reese at second and short, Gil Hodges at first, Billy Cox at third, and Roy Campanella behind the plate. Duke Snider and Carl Furillo were the outfield stars, and the pitching staff featured Don Newcombe, Preacher Roe, and Ralph Branca. That Dodger team lost to the Yanks once more in the World Series, as they had in '41 and '47. But there was no denying their talent.

NEW YORK TEAMS DOMINATE

The 1951 season was a classic. That was the year the Giants trailed the Dodgers by 13½ games in mid-August and made their mad dash to tie it all up on the final day of the season. It was also the year a twenty-year-old centerfielder named Willie Mays joined the Giants and began establishing his own great legacy. The two teams had to play a best of three-series for the pennant and it came down to the final inning of the final game. With the Giants trailing, 4-2, third baseman Bobby Thomson hit a two-out, three-run homer off reliever Ralph Branca to win it in one of the most dramatic moments in baseball history. It forever cemented the Giants-Dodgers rivalry and is still talked about to this day. It almost didn't matter that the Yanks again took the World Series, beating the Giants in six games. New York baseball was at its apex.

In 1952 and '53 it was the Dodgers and Yanks in the Series again, the Bronx Bombers winning each time. Then in 1954, Durocher's Giants, sparked by Willie Mays, who was returning after two years in the army, won the pennant and then swept the highly-favored Cleveland Indians (a team that won 111 games) in the World Series. A year later, the Dodgers finally broke through, winning their only World Series in Brooklyn when they beat the Yanks in seven games. The year after that the Yanks got revenge, topping the Dodgers in seven. In 1957, the Milwaukee Braves were National League champs and upset the Yanks in seven games to become champs. A year later, the Yanks got even, topping the Braves in seven.

It was an amazing run. In the twelve years from 1947 to 1958, at least one New York team was in the World Series eleven times. The Dodgers were there six times, the Giants twice, while the always-powerful Yanks visited the Fall Classic on ten occasions. Those years are considered a golden age for New York baseball. Each team had multiple stars, and fans in the five boroughs and sur-rounding suburbs argued incessantly over which team had the best centerfielder. Was it Willie, Mickey (Mantle), or the Duke? It was hard to see anything changing in this huge city that had always sup-ported its three teams. But things often aren't what they seem.

THE WINDS OF CHANGE WERE ALREADY BLOWING

Though most fans didn't know it at the time, neither the Giants nor the Dodgers were completely happy in their ballparks with the problem coming to the fore—especially with the Dodgers—after World War II, when there was a spike in attendance and the fan de-mographic changed. Ebbets Field, which opened in 1913, had a cozy setup that kept the Dodger fans close to the playing field and to the players; they loved the place. But there were just 32,000 seats and, worse yet, parking facilities for only 700 cars.

As early as 1946 Walter O'Malley, then the Dodgers vice-president and general counsel, wrote the city about the need to either expand Ebbets Field or build a new facility. Four years later,

O'Malley bought the controlling interest in the ballclub and became its president. Always considered more of a businessman than a baseball man, he soon began thinking in earnest about a new stadium for a ball club that was becoming one of baseball's best. At first, he looked to stay in Brooklyn rather than leave town.

O'Malley did not ask for New York City to put up money. He wanted to build and operate his own stadium, and picked out a tract of land at the intersection of Atlantic and Flatbush Avenues in downtown Brooklyn. But to do that, he needed the approval of Robert Moses, the New York City parks commissioner, a man considered the most powerful nonelected official in the city. O'Malley, thinking business all the time, also realized the borough of Brooklyn was changing as people moved to the suburbs. Along with the new stadium, he wanted the adjacent Long Island Railroad station renovated to make the trip to and from the park easier. There was also access to every subway line in New York. O'Malley planned to improve and redevelop the area. In June of 1953, he wrote Moses and the City Council, saying in part, "It is my belief that a new ballpark should be built, financed, and owned by the ball club. It should occupy land on the tax roll. The only assistance I am looking for is in the assembling of a suitable plot . . ."

Robert Moses had other plans. He had visions of building a 50,000 seat municipal stadium in the borough of Queens, at the site of the 1939–40 World's Fair at Flushing Meadows. He offered to house the Dodgers there as a tenant, but O'Malley felt that if he moved his team to Queens, they would no longer be the *Brooklyn* Dodgers. That was number one. Number two was that O'Malley wanted to own the ballpark, not be a tenant. He and Robert Moses would clash over this for several years.

During this time, O'Malley's eyes began to wander. He watched the Braves move to Milwaukee in 1953 and suddenly draw 2 million fans to County Stadium, and he started thinking that moving the Dodgers to a new location might not be such a bad idea. If he could find a place to build his own stadium, a huge fan base, and a great television contract he could possibly make more money than the team would ever make in Brooklyn. He made a last-ditch attempt in 1955, offering to put up $6 million to build and operate a domed stadium in downtown Brooklyn, still at the intersection of Atlantic and Flatbush. Moses rejected the offer, and that was probably the last straw for O'Malley.

It wasn't quite the same with the Giants. The Polo Grounds had capacity for some 55,000 fans, but the seats were rarely filled. The ballpark, however, had a long history and its odd shape made it unique. So did the clubhouse, which was some 480 feet away in dead centerfield. When a pitcher was removed from the game he wouldn't go to the dugout. Instead, he'd make that long walk to the centerfield clubhouse. There had been some talk of a new stadium, but it wasn't the same kind of issue it was with the Dodgers. What riled Horace Stoneham was the city's announcement that it was going to take a good portion of the Polo Grounds parking area to build a new school. The timing of the announcement was also bad. The announcement was made just after the Giants had swept the Indians to win the 1954 World Series.

Stoneham wasn't stupid. The Giants' owner knew that many of the team's fans were moving out of the city, to the northern suburbs and to Long Island. More people would be driving their cars to the game and he knew that convenient parking was important. He tried to persuade the city to change the location of the school. They refused. And that's when Stoneham and the Giants began looking for greener pastures.

CALIFORNIA, HERE THEY COME

Horace Stoneham's first choice for the Giants' new home was Minneapolis, where their top farm club played. But Walter O'Malley had a more grandiose plan. He knew that the city of Los Angeles had talked about getting a major league team since 1954. California had long been a hub of minor league baseball. Back in the 1930s, some players could make more money playing for the San Francisco Seals of the Pacific Coast League than they could in the majors. Then in 1956, when Los Angeles County supervisor Kenneth Hahn was in New York for the World Series and a meeting with Washington Senators owner Calvin Griffith, O'Malley had a note delivered to Hahn that simply said, "Don't sign anything."

Not long after that, O'Malley visited Los Angeles, and as soon as he saw a 350-acre tract of land that was available in Chavez Ravine, he was sold. He set the wheels in motion to build a stadium there and move the Dodgers across the country. He also persuaded Stoneham to forget about Minneapolis and bring the Giants to San Francisco, where the longtime rivalry could resume immediately without missing a beat. Even though fans, especially those in Brooklyn, continued to doubt the move would actually happen, it finally came to pass. Giants attendance had fallen dramatically in 1957. Durocher left after the 1955 season and the team was losing. As Stoneham put it, "I feel sorry for the kids, but I haven't seen many of their fathers at the ballpark lately."

The Giants announced their move on August 19, 1957. Though the Dodgers delayed a formal announcement until after the season, all the players and many of the fans knew they were going. But it didn't really sink in until the beginning of the 1958 season. The *Los Angeles* Dodgers opened up in the mammoth Los Angeles Coliseum, a stadium not configured for baseball, but a temporary home until their new stadium was ready, while the *San Francisco* Giants opened at their temporary home, Seals Stadium, until Candlestick Park was completed. New York had suddenly lost two of its baseball teams. Only the Yankees remained.

But what if . . .

THE DODGERS AND GIANTS GOT NEW BALLPARKS?

Some historians maintain to this day that the only man who really wanted to leave Brooklyn was Walter O'Malley. Though O'Malley tried for a number of years to build a new stadium in Brooklyn, he reached a point where he probably saw mountains of money in the bright sunshine of Los Angeles. As longtime Dodger executive Buzzie Bavasi said, years later, "[O'Malley] did it for a reason: money. All those acres in downtown Los Angeles. He could have taken the Dodgers a few miles to where Shea Stadium is, but he took them 3,000 miles. We had a vote among the eight top people in the front office, and the vote was 8 to 1 not to go to California, but the one vote was Walter's."

Several things could have happened to change this. It's doubtful O'Malley would have ever taken the Dodgers to Queens, to the site of the present day Shea Stadium. He was right—there was no way you could call the team the Brooklyn Dodgers if they played in Queens. But if Robert Moses and New York City had allowed O'Malley to build his stadium in Brooklyn, domed or not, there's a good chance it would have been accomplished before O'Malley was seduced by the riches of Los Angeles. Because the Dodgers were such an institution in Brooklyn and one of just a handful of teams turning a profit in the 1950s, it's hard to imagine them not being eminently successful in a spanking new ballpark with a larger capacity. If the railroad station had also been upgraded and the entire neighborhood developed, the new ballpark could have changed the face of the entire borough. In that sense, it's a shame it didn't happen that way.

By remaining in Brooklyn, the great Dodgers tradition could have continued unabated. It's possible that no group of fans was ever as close to their team and its players as the people who went to Ebbets Field. It was a unique situation, and since the team was in a separate borough from the Giants (Manhattan) and the Yankees (the Bronx), the Dodgers became a major part of Brooklyn's identity. That not only would have continued, but would have grown as the nation's media outlets grew and expanded. The players themselves helped foster this identity. Many of them lived in Brooklyn, and they would walk the streets, go to movies with their families or each other, talk to and mingle with the fans. Leaving hurt many of the Dodgers deeply and some never adjusted to the move west.

"It was a very emotional situation for some players," Buzzie Bavasi remembered. "Gil Hodges' family never came to Los Angeles, and he was a real family man. Carl Furillo wasn't happy [in Los Angeles]. Brooklyn was still on their minds."

A number of the veteran Dodgers moved with the team to Los Angeles. Hodges, Furillo, Duke Snider, and Jim Gilliam, as well as pitchers Don Drysdale, Clem Labine, Johnny Podres, and young Sandy Koufax all moved to L.A. The great Pee Wee Reese played sparingly in 1958. At the age of forty he was about done. Don Newcombe, who had been so great for the Brooklyn pennant-winning teams, was traded to Cincinnati midway through the season after the move. Newk was one of those players who hated to fly and despised the cross-country trips. There were also a number of other young players who started in Brooklyn, but didn't have the same longstanding identification with the borough. The Boys of Summer, however, were all Brooklyn guys and some of them might have had longer careers if the team had remained there.

It's also interesting to think about the fates of several players had the Dodgers remained in Brooklyn. Left-hander Sandy Koufax got his first "cup of coffee" with the Dodgers in 1955, appearing in 12 games as a hard-throwing nineteen-year-old. It would take Koufax six years before he really pulled it all together. By the time he was 18-13 in 1961, the Dodgers were firmly entrenched in Los Angeles. From there, Koufax put together five more of the greatest seasons any pitcher ever had before an arthritic left elbow forced his premature retirement at the age of thirty-one. How good was he? Not only did he throw four no hitters and set a strikeout mark of 382 hitters in a season, but in his final year he was 27-9, completing 27 of 41 starts and striking out 317 hitters. His earned run average was a paltry 1.73.

Sandy Koufax wasn't really a Hollywood guy. He was born in Brooklyn, and if the Dodgers had remained there, Koufax would have been one of the biggest sports stars in New York City history. Though he wasn't the kind of guy who reveled in the spotlight, he still would have become a New York icon, worshipped throughout the city to this day.

Then there were two of the greatest Dodgers ever—Roy Campanella and Jackie Robinson. Campy, a three-time National League Most Valuable Player, had all intentions of going to Los Angeles with the Dodgers even though he was thirty-six years old. That winter, he was in a one-car auto accident on an icy road and suffered a broken neck. He would spend the rest of his life in a wheelchair, though he often went to spring training with the Dodgers and worked with the catchers. Since every little thing that happens in life can alter others, it's still possible to wonder if Campy would have been in the same place at the same time if the Dodgers remained in Brooklyn. Maybe there would have been a team function that night, or he would have been out with some of his teammates. It may seem far-fetched, but had the Dodgers remained, Roy Campanella might not have had his accident.

As for Robinson, as the first African-American in the big leagues, he may well have been baseball's preeminent pioneer. Robinson went through a torturous time in breaking the color line, especially during his rookie season in 1947, when he was already twenty-eight years old. His short career ended after the 1956 season, when the Dodgers tried to trade him to the Giants. Instead of joining the hated rivals, Jackie retired. Once the Dodgers moved west, Robinson continued to live in Connecticut and went into the working world. He was elected to the Hall of Fame in 1962, but by the time of his premature death, ten years later, he was somewhat forgotten as the great pioneer and exciting player he was. It wasn't until many years later that baseball began honoring Jackie Robinson everywhere, finally permanently retiring his number 42. If the Dodgers had remained in Brooklyn, Robinson might well have been a much more visible presence around New York baseball, especially at Dodgers reunions and at games. He would have remained a hero in Brooklyn and the baseball world would have been much more aware of him from his retirement until his death, and then beyond.

WHAT ABOUT THE GIANTS?

In a way, the Giants were the forgotten team in the equation. Owner Horace Stoneham wasn't actively seeking a new ballpark, but he was beginning to look for greener pastures. When just 629,000 fans attended Giants games in 1956, the smallest attendance in the league, Stoneham was duly concerned. Though he felt the city should help his team, he looked first to Minneapolis, and then finally to San Francisco as a place the Giants might settle. The strange part is that while Robert Moses offered to build a ballpark in Queens for the Dodgers, he never made a similar offer to the Giants. And if you think about it, Queens may have been the perfect fit for the team, especially if the Dodgers remained in Brooklyn.

The Polo Grounds was located right across the Harlem River from Yankee Stadium. If you took the subway, the two ballparks were a stop apart. So, in essence, they were sharing the same fan base, and Yankee Stadium was a much superior venue at which to watch a game. As soon as the Giants' championship team of 1954 fell apart, the fans stopped coming.

But had the city shown the initiative and foresight to put the Giants in Queens (where they still could accurately be called the New York Giants), it could have opened up a whole new demographic and fan base, and the city's three teams would have been geographically separated from one another in just the right way. Brooklyn was Brooklyn, a great place for the Dodgers. The Yankees still had the Bronx and Manhattan, as well as fans in the suburbs to the north and in New Jersey. The Giants, operating out of Queens, would have had that borough as well as all of Long Island, and fans in the northern suburbs could easily get there by car. It's a scenario that could have worked and could have kept all three teams in New York forever.

The Giants also had the most charismatic and dynamic player in the game at the time. Willie Mays was a superstar, a supremely talented, five-tool player whose enthusiasm for the game matched his ability. When the Giants played at the Polo Grounds, Mays used to go into the streets of Harlem and play stickball with the local kids. On the diamond, he was magic. He hit for both power and average, ran the bases with abandon, and was by far the best centerfielder in baseball. He could catch everything, had a great throwing arm, and did it all with a flair. Most flies he caught at his waist, a basket catch that no one would dare teach a young player, and yet he never dropped one. When he ran, his hat invariably flew off his head. Willie Mays had it all and he was made for New York.

Once the Giants moved to San Francisco, it wasn't the same. Mays continued to be a great player, but the city by the bay never took him to heart the way New Yorkers did. San Francisco fans tended to root more for young slugger Orlando Cepeda and, while Mays could never go unnoticed, he was never the same kind of icon, not to mention playing in a wind-driven ballpark made it tougher for a right-handed batter to hit home runs.

Had the Giants and Dodgers remained in New York, Willie Mays would have been a king. He would have ultimately surpassed the exploits of the other two great centerfielders playing in New York—Mickey Mantle and Duke Snider—and might have had an even greater career, especially if the team's new ballpark in Queens was hitter friendly. Mays could easily have topped 700 home runs for his career (he finished with 660) and maybe even challenged the record 714 held by Babe Ruth. Though it was Henry Aaron who ultimately broke it, imagine how it would have been if Mays was approaching that mark in New York City—one great New York ballplayer trying to top the record of another.

WHAT WOULD HAVE HAPPENED TO EXPANSION?

It was inevitable that baseball would expand and become a coast to coast endeavor. In fact, the other major sports (basketball, football, hockey) all had similar expansions during approximately the same era. Had the Dodgers and Giants remained in New York, only the demographics would have changed, and perhaps a bit of the timing. California was already big baseball country. It had great weather and some outstanding minor league teams, notably the San Francisco Seals, Hollywood Stars, and Los Angeles Angels. The city of Los Angeles began actively seeking a big league team as early as 1954, so even if the Dodgers hadn't gone west, Los Angeles would have eventually found a big league team to call its own.

Two early teams that looked to L.A. were the St. Louis Browns and Cleveland Indians, but not as a duo. The American League rejected both efforts. The prevailing thinking was that having just one team on the west coast would not be a smart move financially. In fact, when the Dodgers and Giants finally went, the stipulation was that both had to go for the move to be approved.

In 1957, perhaps the only other team that might have had a reason to move would have been the lowly Washington Senators.

Remember, the Boston Braves were in Milwaukee, the old St. Louis Browns had already relocated to Baltimore, and the Philadelphia A's had just gone to Kansas City. The rest of the league was pretty stable then. So had the Giants and Dodgers stayed in New York, chances are that California would have had to wait for a big league team until 1961, when the Los Angeles Angels joined the American League.

The problem with that scenario is that without the Dodgers and Giants, California needed a second team. The same year that the Washington Senators moved to Minnesota and became the Twins, 1961, a new expansion Washington Senators team took over in D.C. Perhaps that second expansion team would have been placed in California, either in San Francisco or San Diego, cities that have National League teams today. The Padres joined the National League in 1969 and the A's moved to Oakland in 1970, the same year the Seattle Pilots joined the league. West Coast expansion was in full swing. Baseball also went south and north: to Atlanta (with the Braves in 1966), to Texas (the Colt .45s, later the Astros, came to Houston in 1962, and the Senators moved to Arlington as the Rangers in 1972), and to Canada (in Montreal in 1969 and Toronto in 1977).

So there would have been no stopping expansion. But had the Dodgers and Giants stayed in New York, the West Coast move would have been delayed several years and the league placements might have been different. But one expansion team has been left out of the equation, and that's because this one directly involves the Dodgers and Giants, and if they had stayed the whole history of New York baseball would have been altered in yet another way.

THE METS
When the Dodgers and Giants headed west, the question of another team immediately arose in New York, as the city was simply too

big to house just one baseball team. Plans for a new National League team began almost immediately, and in 1962 the New York Metropolitans were born. The Mets, as they were called, played their first two seasons in the ancient Polo Grounds, then in 1964 moved to brand new Shea Stadium in Queens. Does that site for a stadium sound familiar? Now, more than forty years later, the Mets have a history of their own and are firmly entrenched as New York's "other" team. They even battled the Yankees in the 2000 World Series, a revival of the old "subway" series from Yankees-Dodgers and Yankees-Giants days. And they were World Champs in both 1969 and 1986, giving their many fans the ultimate baseball thrill.

In 2009, the Mets will have a brand new stadium, Citi Field, built alongside the old Shea Stadium in Queens. Shea will then be demolished. The new ballpark will have the retro look of Ebbets Field on the outside and will be state-of-the-art inside. How ironic that Queens was one place Walter O'Malley refused to take his Dodgers and now the new Mets ballpark is being designed to remind fans of Brooklyn's Ebbets Field. But if the Dodgers and Giants had stayed, there would have been no New York Mets. The franchise might have indeed been located elsewhere as baseball expanded, and then its history would have been very different.

Here are a few things New Yorkers would have missed had there been no New York Mets: For starters, the city of New York would not have had a last act from Casey Stengel. Ol' Case was the Yankees' skipper from 1949 to 1960 and led the Bronx Bombers to ten pennants and seven World Series triumphs. The Yanks let him go after the 1960 season, implying that at seventy he was too old to manage the team. Two years later he was back, at the helm of the hapless Mets, a team destined to lose 120 games. "Can't anyone here play this game?" Casey asked of his struggling team. He would entertain New Yorkers for three and a half years as the Mets struggled for respectability, and was the team's top attraction. He was a lovable character and a wise baseball man. Without the Mets, Stengel would not have had his encore.

Had the Dodgers and Giants stayed, there would have been no Miracle Mets of 1969. Before '69, the team had never finished higher than seventh place, but during the first year of divisional play, they won the N.L. East, defeated the Atlanta Braves for the pennant, and then upset a superior Baltimore Orioles team in five games to win the World Series. They were one of the great sports stories of the decade and their exploits in '69 thrilled all New Yorkers and baseball fans everywhere.

What made the story of the '69 Mets even greater was the fact that the team was managed by Gil Hodges, the former Dodger first sacker during their glory years of the 1950s. Hodges was not only a New Yorker through and through, but proved a brilliant manager after coming over from skippering the Washington Senators. All the players credited Hodges with making the Miracle possible. He continued to manage the Mets until his tragic death from a heart attack just prior to the 1972 season.

The Mets' ace pitcher in 1969 was Tom Seaver, who would go on to enjoy a Hall of Fame career, winning more than 300 games. If the Dodgers and Giants had stayed, New York fans would have likely seen Seaver only when he pitched as a member of a visiting team. The same holds true for Nolan Ryan, who also pitched on the '69 team. Ryan spend most of his Hall of Fame career with other clubs, but Mets fans saw him at the beginning and saw the early stages of a career that would result in more than 5,700 strikeouts.

Fans would also not have had the pleasure of seeing the outstanding Mets teams of the mid-1980s that featured the likes of Dwight Gooden, Darryl Strawberry, Gary Carter, Keith Hernandez, Tug McGraw, and others. That group provided fans at Shea with many memorable moments, including a great, come-from-behind victory in the 1986 World Series.

It's difficult now not to think of the Mets as a New York team, through and through. By the year 2012 they will have been in existence for half a century. And by that time, the numbers of fans who remember the Dodgers and Giants when they were in New York will be dwindling. Yet had they never left, their own histories in New York would have another half century added to them, and the Mets, well, they simply wouldn't have existed for New York baseball fans.

THE RIVALRIES

When the Dodgers and Giants went west, baseball lost a trio of its greatest rivalries. Dodgers-Giants, Dodgers-Yankees, Giants-Yankees. It was only natural that rivalries like these would be intense, especially in a city like New York, which was the only city with two teams in the same league. The Dodgers and Giants battled for years, but the rivalry was never as intense as in the '40s and '50s, when both teams were outstanding and led by combative personalities like Leo Durocher and Jackie Robinson. The 1951 pennant race and playoff, with its dramatic ending, would have stayed a focal point for many, many years had the teams remained in New York—a thorn in the side of the Dodgers and a feather in the caps of the Giants.

With the Dodgers playing in a new, downtown Brooklyn Stadium and the Giants playing at a new stadium in Queens, these two National League rivals would have battled it out for years and the ballparks would have been filled nearly every time they met. Sure, they went west together, but the distance between Los Angeles and San Francisco made the rivalry somewhat less fierce. They were still in the same state, but not the same city, and that's a huge difference. In New York, fans of both teams rubbed elbows everywhere—at the ballparks, at work, in the bars and clubs, at parties and family gatherings, almost everywhere. Dodger-Giant talk could come up at any time. In California, the fans were separated by many miles. And they simply didn't have the same kind of passion for the game that always fueled the intensity in New York.

The 1962 season is the perfect example of how things changed, and it happened just five years after the two teams left New York. It was a race for the pennant all the way by the two best teams in the National League. When the regular season ended, the Giants and Dodgers were tied with identical 101-61 records. Once again, as they had in 1951, the two teams met in a best-of-three playoff, and once again the Giants won it late in the third game. Despite the repeat ending, it lacked the excitement of 1951, as well as the extra intensity the New York rivalry between the teams fostered. It simply wasn't the same and it isn't remembered in nearly the same way as the Game Three Thomson home run in '51.

Finally, there are the Yankees. Baseball's most dominant team since the 1920s, it is the Yankees–Boston Red Sox rivalry today that is the most intense in the sport. But what if the Dodgers and Giants had stayed? Sure, they were both National League teams, but that really didn't matter in New York and it especially wouldn't today, with the advent of interleague play. The Yankees-Giants rivalry was spawned in the 1920s when the two teams shared the Polo Grounds (until 1923) and met each other in several World Series. It cooled somewhat after that but was renewed in the 1950s. When the teams met in the 1962 World Series, the Giants were rooted in San Francisco and the sense of rivalry was gone. But if they had still been in New York, there would have been that special something that only comes about in a subway series. The baseball attendance boom of the 1990s and into the twenty-first century certainly would have exacerbated the rivalry, and interleague games at Yankee Stadium and at the Giants' ballpark would be packed with fans.

The Dodgers and Yankees had the more intense rivalry since they kept meeting in the World Series during the 1940s and 1950s. The Yanks whipped the Dodgers six of seven times, losing only in 1955. The teams met again in the Fall Classic in 1963, 1977, 1978, and in 1981. The '63 Series featured some great pitching by Sandy Koufax as L.A. won. Both '77 and '78 were exciting, with Reggie Jackson having a record-setting performance in the former and the New Yorkers winning twice. The teams met once more in '81, with the Dodgers coming out on top. Still, none of these encounters matched the excitement of all those subway series of the '40s and '50s. If the Dodgers were still in Brooklyn, each would have been a classic. And who knows if the results would have been the same?

In a nutshell, the city of New York has had two distinct and separate baseball traditions. The first one ended in 1957 when the Dodgers and Giants went west. The second began in 1962 when the New York Mets were born. Each is special in its own right. But if the Dodgers and Giants had remained in New York and continued to play in the Big Apple today, the tradition would be, by far, the richest in the sport and the rivalries as intense as any. With interleague play, the Dodgers and Giants might have even developed an intense rivalry with the Red Sox, and that would have been yet another great baseball treat.

4

Lombardi Comes Home

When Vince Lombardi became the head coach of the Green Bay Packers in 1959, he gathered his team around him and held a ball high above his head. "Gentleman," he said. "This is a football, and before we're through, we're gonna run it down everyone's throats." Lombardi proceeded to produce teams that did exactly that. His Packers would win five National Football League titles and the first two Super Bowls, and he became a coaching legend along the way. Thanks to Lombardi, the city of Green Bay was known as Titletown, USA, and even today the winning team in the Super Bowl is presented with the Vince Lombardi Trophy. More than three decades after his death, Lombardi continues to be a benchmark against which other coaches are judged. But there was one job Vince Lombardi never had. His dream job was to coach the New York Giants. When he was finally offered the job in 1960, he was already committed to Green Bay, so he turned it down.

But what if Vince Lombardi had left Green Bay to become head coach of the New York Giants?

* * * * *

Vince Lombardi always did things the old-fashioned way. Dedication, perseverance, hard work, sacrifice—these were all Lombardi trademarks and he transformed them, along with his talent for leading men, into one of the great coaching careers in football history. Lombardi took over a Green Bay Packer team in 1959 that was coming off a horrendous 1-10-1 season and hadn't produced a winning record since 1947. As one of the NFL's oldest and most celebrated franchises, one that had taken six NFL titles under legendary coach Curly Lambeau, the Packers had spend a decade going nowhere and both club officials and fans were restless. They wanted a head coach who could win, and win quickly.

But where to look? After taking stock of various candidates, Packers President Dominic Olejniczak began to focus seriously on an assistant coach with the New York Giants, Vince Lombardi, despite the fact that Lombardi had never held a head coaching position outside of a small high school. At that time, he was simply a lifelong assistant couched in the kind of anonymity that made one member of the Packers executive committee remark, "Who the hell is Vince Lombardi?"

The world would soon find out. Vincent Thomas Lombardi was a New York guy, through and through. Born in Brooklyn on June 11, 1913, he had never strayed very far from his roots. After starring as a fullback for his high school team, St. Francis Prep, he went to Fordham University in New York City, where he became a top guard on the Rams' fabled "Seven Blocks of Granite" offensive line. He graduated cum laude in 1937, but before beginning his coaching career, he worked at a finance company while taking night classes at Fordham's law school. He also played semipro football in Delaware. Then in 1939 he took a teaching and coaching job at St. Cecilia High School in Englewood, New Jersey. In addition to coaching football, Lombardi took charge of the basketball and baseball teams. For all that and teaching four different subjects, Lombardi was paid the grand sum of $1,700 a year.

He left St. Cecilia in 1947 to coach Fordham's freshman football team and the next year became an assistant with the varsity. Then in 1949, Army's renowned coach, Red Blaik, brought Vince to West Point to coach the Cadets' defensive line. Under Blaik's tutelage, Lombardi learned to stick with basic plays and to execute those plays to perfection, lessons that stuck with him for the rest of his coaching career.

Slowly, this little-known coach was moving up the ladder. In 1954 Jim Lee Howell, the head coach of the NFL New York Giants, hired his former Fordham classmate to work with the team's offense. The Giants were coming off a 3-9 season and Howell was under pressure to turn his team around. One of the first things Lombardi did with the Giants was move USC alum Frank Gifford from defense to offense. Gifford would become an All-Pro, all-purpose halfback, and within two years the Giants were a championship team, beating the Bears 47-7 in the NFL title game. Much of the credit went to Lombardi, on the offense, and another assistant, Tom Landry, on the defense.

With his coaching roots firmly established, Lombardi was getting restless. He felt he was ready to lead a team. But which one? Back in 1958 there were far fewer teams and far fewer coaching positions. Finally, in February of 1959, he was called to Green Bay for an interview. Never a shrinking violet, as he stood facing the executive committee, Lombardi made his intentions crystal clear.

"I want it understood that I am in complete command here," he said. Maybe it was the way he presented himself, his confidence and desire to run the show in an obvious no-nonsense way, that convinced them to hire him. He was not only made the head coach, but the committee gave him the vacant general manager's job as well. So in 1959, the lifelong New Yorker took his wife and son, and moved to the tiny city of Green Bay, Wisconsin, ready for his first challenge as a head coach.

QUICK SUCCESS

During training camp, Lombardi put his principles into action quickly. Any players who didn't give 100 percent, had sloppy practice habits, or seemed to be shirking at all didn't last long under the new coach. He weeded out the deadwood immediately and then made a promise to the players who remained, telling them that if they obeyed his rules and followed his methods, he would shape them into a championship unit. In many cases, such platitudes become meaningless words and empty promises. Anyone hearing him talk about a championship probably would have thought the new coach was just spouting gas; after all, the Packers had been a laughing stock for years, especially after coming off a 1-10-1 season.

A look at the roster prior to the 1959 season makes one wonder just how the Packers could have been that bad. Already on the team were guards Fuzzy Thurston and Jerry Kramer; running backs Paul Hornung and Jim Taylor; quarterback Bart Starr; receivers Max McGee, Boyd Dowler, and Ron Kramer; tackles Forrest Gregg and Henry Jordan; and middle linebacker Ray Nitschke. Many of these players would form the foundation of the Packer dynasty that would follow shortly.

The Packers shocked everyone by going 7-5 in Lombardi's first season—winning their first three, dropping the next five, and closing with wins in their last four games. A year later, the Pack won the NFL's Western Division title with an 8-4 record. In the title game against the Philadelphia Eagles, Green Bay held a 13-10 fourth-quarter lead, only to have the Eagles score with 5:21 left to take a 17-13 advantage. The Packers drove again and the game ended with the Eagles' Chuck Bednarik tackling fullback Jim Taylor at the eight-yard line—eight yards away from victory—as time ran out. From that point forward, none of Lombardi's teams would ever lose a championship contest again.

By 1961 the Packers had arrived. They were 11-3 in the regular season and defeated Lombardi's old team, the New York Giants, by a 37-0 score to win the championship. Then they repeated the next season, again topping the Giants, this time 16-7 in the title game. Despite an 11-2-1 record, the Packers finished second to the Bears in 1963, but came back to win it all in 1965. Lombardi's charges also won NFL titles in 1966 and 1967, and, as an added victory, they also won the first two Super Bowls. In fact, with the pressure of defending the honor of the NFL against a team from the upstart AFL, the Packers won with ease. With five NFL titles and no more worlds to conquer, Lombardi stepped down as the team's head coach, but kept the title of general manager.

In his nine seasons as head coach, Vince Lombardi's Packers won six divisional titles, five NFL crowns, including two Super Bowls. His ballclubs went a combined 98-30-4, a remarkable achievement during a time when there were a number of outstanding teams and when a rival league (the American Football League) was rising to prominence and forcing an eventual merger.

However, Lombardi would only stay out of coaching for a year. Getting the old itch again, he accepted the job as the Washington Redskins' head coach in 1969 and seemed on the way to repeating a familiar pattern as he took over a losing team and brought them home with a 7-5-2 record his first year. Unfortunately, he never got the chance for more. Diagnosed with intestinal cancer after the season, Vince Lombardi died on September 3, 1970, at the age of fifty-seven, leaving a great legacy behind.

Despite all his success and the creation of a coaching legend which continues to this day, Vince Lombardi never had what many people knew was his dream job, which was to coach his beloved hometown Giants. Instead, he ended up beating them twice for the

NFL championship. If Lombardi wasn't a man of extreme character, though, he could have had the job.

Just weeks after his Packers had lost the 1960 title game to the Eagles, the Giants were in the process of making a coaching change. Jim Lee Howell was retiring and owner Wellington Mara looked to his former assistant Vince Lombardi to take over the team. Mara was clearly impressed by how quickly Lombardi had turned the Packers around, and he offered him the job. There it was, right in front of him, his dream job sitting on the table. But Vince Lombardi turned it down. He had signed a five-year contract with the Packers and to him that was a commitment you didn't break. It wasn't like the game of musical coaches played today, when contracts aren't worth the paper on which they're written. Nope. Lombardi would stay with Green Bay and coach his way into history.

But what if . . .

What if he had forsaken the Packers to take over a very good New York Giants team in 1961? How would things have changed?

THE PACKERS WITHOUT LOMBARDI

It's hard to imagine the Green Bay Packers of the 1960s without Vince Lombardi, but it easily could have happened. If Lombardi had been simply unable to pass up a chance to coach the New York Giants, he would have resigned from the Packers following the 1960 season, leaving a team that had just played for the NFL championship, but lost. While this was a team that already had a core group of individual stars, many of whom would eventually go to the Pro Football Hall of Fame, it's very easy to make a case that they would not have continued to develop the same way without the leadership and prodding of the taskmaster Lombardi. With another coach, it's possible that this group of Packers could have won an NFL title, maybe two. But it's very doubtful that they would have become the five-time championship dynasty that would represent the NFL in the highly-charged, pressure-filled atmosphere of the first two Super Bowls. Let's look at some of the possible reasons why.

For starters, Lombardi was a coach who stuck to the basics—running, passing, blocking, and tackling. He took stock of the players he had and knew immediately what he had to do—develop a rock-ribbed, unyielding defense and add to that an offense that would do as he promised, run the football down everyone's throats. To that end, he developed the famous "Packer Sweep." It was a simple play: at the snap, guards Jerry Kramer and Fuzzy Thurston would pull off the line and together lead the running back to the right or left. They would prove a devastating combination. And carrying the ball was either the tough fullback Jim Taylor or the patient halfback Paul Hornung. The Packers didn't perfect it overnight, but once they did, they were almost invincible. Other teams knew it was coming, but as Lombardi learned from his mentor, Red Blaik, if you execute to perfection, you can't be stopped.

Paul Hornung was a special project. A Heisman Trophy-winning quarterback out of Notre Dame, it soon became obvious that he wasn't cut out to be an NFL signal caller. Still, Lombardi saw something in the player who would become known as the Golden Boy. Hornung wasn't fast, but he was tough and smart, and knew how to follow blockers. He was the perfect guy to compliment the powerhouse Taylor in the backfield. Thanks to Lombardi, Hornung became a star.

Former Oakland Raiders coach and current broadcaster John Madden saw firsthand how complex a simple play could be. While coaching at a junior college, Madden attended a clinic in Reno that featured Lombardi as a guest speaker. John Madden remembers it this way: "I thought then I knew everything about coaching. But that day Lombardi spoke for eight hours . . . about one play, the Green Bay sweep. . . . I learned about real depth that day, about how much knowledge goes into what can seem the simplest of things. . . . He was truly an incredible coach."

Just the fact that Lombardi could speak for an entire day about one play indicates how much time he must have spent with his team preparing to execute it and then practicing it over and over again. As one of his guards, Fuzzy Thurston, said, "He prepared us so well, and he motivated us so well, I felt he was part of me on the field."

The sweep was the cornerstone of the Packers' attack. Had Lombardi left the team after the 1960 season, the sweep simply might have faded away as part of the team's offense. Whoever replaced Lombardi might not have wanted to run it that much, or might not have had the ability to perfect it. Without the sweep, the Packers offense would not have been the same, and there might have been more pressure on quarterback Bart Starr and his receivers, since the sweep was the great equalizer that made the passing game work.

Starr was another player who blossomed under Lombardi. A thin and undersized quarterback out of Alabama, many thought he didn't have a strong enough throwing arm to make it in the NFL. But in the Lombardi scheme, he didn't need a cannon for an arm. The coach saw that his quarterback was an extremely accurate passer, a clutch performer, and a leader. He tapped into all of those qualities and utilized Starr's talents in the best way. Years later, Starr gave his coach full credit for making him into a Hall of Famer.

"Coach Lombardi showed me that by working hard and using my mind, I could overcome my weakness to the point where I could be one of the best," he said.

Again, had Lombardi left for the Giants in 1961, Bart Starr might not have developed into the quarterback he became, a cornerstone of the dynasty right through the first two Super Bowl triumphs. If you just take away the perfection of the Packer sweep and cut into the effectiveness of Bart Starr, the Green Bay offense takes two steps backward, and the Packers don't have a dynasty. That's how instrumental Lombardi was in all aspects of his team's play.

The Green Bay defense was also full of stars and more continued to come in during the Packers' winning streak, all drafted or traded for by General Manager Vince Lombardi. Without Lombardi, there's a good chance the personnel would have been altered. Take two, three, or four of Green Bay's players away and the defense changes. Take away the master motivator and the defense changes. As the great defensive end, Willie Davis, once said, "He made you a believer. He told you what the other team was going to do, and he told you what you had to do to beat them, and invariably he was right."

Probably the most accurate statement describing the influence Vince Lombardi had on the Green Bay Packers comes from one of his star guards, Jerry Kramer. Kramer said simply:

"He made us all better than we thought we could be."

WHAT ABOUT THOSE FIRST TWO SUPER BOWLS?

The American Football League began play in 1960 with eight teams, and at first those in the NFL simply ignored them. People had tried to form new leagues before to compete with them and they'd always failed. In 1950, the NFL broke precedent by taking in three teams from the dying All-America Football Conference, all located in cities that the older league wanted to inhabit anyway. So the Baltimore Colts, Cleveland Browns, and San Francisco 49ers joined the National Football League. As always, the NFL said their brand of football was superior to that of the AAFC, but the Cleveland Browns proved them wrong, winning the NFL championship its first year in the league and having a near dynasty throughout the 1950s. The Baltimore Colts—though a second incarnation of the franchise—turned out to be pretty good, as well, winning titles in 1958 and '59.

Now there was another new league. At first it didn't look as if the AFL would succeed, but with a television contract and some wealthy owners, the new league began corralling players, going after strong-armed quarterbacks, and even raiding players from some NFL teams. It sent salaries skyrocketing during a time when most players earned very little. When the New York Jets, one of the flagship AFL franchises, signed strong-armed and flamboyant quarterback Joe Namath out of Alabama in 1965 and paid him the then-unheard-of sum of $427,000 for his talents, it's said the new league came of age—at least on the publicity front. Down on the field they played a more wide-open passing game that excited the fans, but the NFL continued to scoff. They didn't play the same kind of hard-nosed, basic football, the pundits said, so they couldn't compete on the same gridiron.

Namath's signing started a bidding war for talent with the top college players being drafted by teams from both leagues, giving them the luxury to negotiate, pick, and choose. By mid-1966 both leagues were tired of battling for players and the rising cost, and they soon announced a merger in which the entire AFL would become part of the NFL to form a huge, 24-team league that would expand to 28 by 1970. The AFL would retain a separate identity until the 1970 season, but a common draft would begin immediately, thus ending the ever-escalating bidding war, and there would also be a championship game between the winners in each league beginning in January 1967, after the 1966 season. This was the game that would ultimately become known as the Super Bowl and, as soon as it was announced, the men who ran the older league realized it was the NFL who had the most to lose. If an AFL team were to win the first-ever Super Bowl, what would happen to the myth of NFL superiority?

Enter Vince Lombardi. His aging Packers were once more moving toward another NFL title and, admit it or not, most NFL supporters wouldn't have wanted anyone else standing on the sideline to meet the Kansas City Chiefs, the AFL representative. When the Pack defeated a rapidly improving Dallas Cowboys team (coached by Lombardi's old Giants cohort, Tom Landry), 34-27, they had the NFL title and a trip to the first-ever Super Bowl.

The bottom line is easy. The Packers won the game 35-10, giving the bragging rights to the NFL, and a sense of validation about the superiority of their league. What many people tend to forget is that the Chiefs had an outstanding football team on both offense and defense. They had huge offensive and defensive lines, bigger than those of the Packers, an intimidating corps of linebackers, and two all-AFL defensive backs. On offense, quarterback Len Dawson was a lot like Bart Starr. Running back Mike Garrett was all-league, and wide receiver Otis Taylor was big, fast, and strong. This was a team that played the Packers tough in the first half, trailing by just four points at 14-10. But as was so often the case, Vince Lombardi had seen what the Chiefs could do and he made the necessary halftime adjustments.

Sure enough, basic mistake-free football won again. Defensive back Willie Wood intercepted a Dawson pass early in the second half and the rout was on. From that point forward, it was all Packers and they cruised to an easy victory. A year later, the Pack was back in the Super Bowl, this time facing the Oakland Raiders. Despite the fact that the Packers were aging and some of their old stars were gone or second string, they still had Vince Lombardi. Though the Raiders had obvious talent, the Packers again imposed their will and that of their coach, winning the game, 33-14. No doubt now, the NFLers said. Our league is still better.

But was it? After Super Bowl II, Vince Lombardi retired and the aging Packers began descending toward mediocrity. If the NFL was in fact the superior league, they should continue to dominate in the Super Bowl, at least for the next few years. In Super Bowl III, the Baltimore Colts, a team that had lost just one game during the regular season, were made 17-point favorites to beat Joe Namath and the New York Jets. Before the game, though, it was Namath who made the headlines by "guaranteeing" a victory. Sure enough, the Jets shocked the football world and prevailed, 16-7. And the year after that, the Kansas City Chiefs returned to win Super Bowl IV, easily defeating the favored Minnesota Vikings, 23-7. So in the four Super Bowls before the complete merger between the leagues, Lombardi's Packers had won two and the American Football League had won two.

Take away the Lombardi factor and all bets are off. Had Lombardi gone to the Giants back in 1960, there's certainly no guarantee he would have had his Giants teams in those first two Super Bowls. The AFL's top teams were already on a par with the NFL—we can admit that now—and without Lombardi it's entirely possible that the Chiefs and Raiders would have won those first two games, or at least one of them, something that would have totally embarrassed the older league. So the NFL should count itself fortunate that Lombardi had the integrity to honor his contract and not make the jump to the Giants.

GREEN BAY AND THE LOMBARDI PHILOSOPHY

There's no denying that Vince Lombardi was old school. He preached basic football and broke the game down into individual confrontations. "You never win a game unless you beat the guy in front of you," he said. "The score on the board doesn't mean a thing. That's for the fans. You've got to win the war with the man in front of you. You've got to get your man."

He also knew what it meant to lead and put up with no nonsense. When his starting center, Jim Ringo, brought in an agent to negotiate a new contract at a time when agents were rarely used, Lombardi excused himself and left the room. He returned five minutes later and informed Ringo that he had just been traded to the Philadelphia Eagles. Was he a dictator? Perhaps. He certainly didn't want anyone to question his decisions or to be distracted by any outside influences.

"It is essential to understand that battles are primarily won in the hearts of men," he said. "Men respond to leadership in a most remarkable way and once you have won his heart, he will follow you anywhere."

So his Packers responded. And that's why he felt basic football— blocking and tackling—would win games if everything was executed to perfection. His style of football wasn't flashy. It wasn't quite the "three yards and a cloud of dust" that Woody Hayes used to preach at Ohio State, but the Packer sweep was always the focal point of the offense and set up Bart Starr's pinpoint passing. When the AFL was formed in 1960, the league certainly looked to the NFL in order to figure out their basic philosophy. Perhaps the question they began asking was, How can we counter Lombardi and the Packers? The league wasn't doing much business the first few years as the Packer dynasty grew.

Then around 1964, the AFL really began opening it up, going after big time quarterbacks (Namath, John Hadl, Len Dawson, Daryle Lamonica) who could throw downfield and fill the air with passes. It's very possible that the new league went to the wide-open game to give fans a choice, to present a different kind of football from that of the Packers and the NFL. So you might say that if Lombardi switched over to the Giants, while his philosophy wouldn't have changed, he would have been less a symbol of NFL success and there's a chance the AFL might well have approached their game differently, perhaps a bit more conservatively, more traditionally. Would that have affected the eventual merger? Probably not. At best, it might have altered the timing a bit. And remember, once Lombardi was gone, pro football as a whole began gravitating to a more wide-open passing game almost immediately. And that still continues today.

THE GIANTS AND LOMBARDI

The other intriguing part of the equation is what might have happened to the Giants had Lombardi decided to take their offer. With a pretty clear picture of the kind of man and kind of coach Vince Lombardi was this poses some very interesting questions. It was no secret that coaching the Giants had always been the native New Yorker's dream job and suddenly, at the end of the 1960 season, it was there for the taking.

With the Packers, Lombardi was brought on board to rescue a struggling 1-10-1 team. But the Giants of that same era were another story. Under Jim Lee Howell (assisted by Lombardi), they were 8-3-1 in 1956 and then won the NFL championship. The next three years the team finished at 7-5, 9-3, and 10-2. The latter two years they won divisional titles only to lose to John Unitas and the Baltimore Colts in a pair of NFL Championship games.

The classic 1958 game went into sudden death overtime before the Colts prevailed, 23-17, a contest so hard-fought and dramatic that it is still often referred to as "The Greatest Game Ever Played." A year later the Colts won again, this time by a 31-16 count. But there was no denying that this was a very good Giants team even after the assistant coach departed for Green Bay. Then in 1960, as Lombardi's Packers won the Western Division title, the Giants stumbled a bit. They finished at 6-4-2 and were third in their division. That's when longtime coach Jim Lee Howell decided to call it quits and owner Wellington Mara decided he wanted to reel in the one that got away.

Had the coach said yes, a number of interesting possibilities could have resulted. For one thing, Lombardi probably would have been vilified in Green Bay for breaking his five-year contract after just two years. Fans in Wisconsin would never have forgiven him for leaving right after taking their team to the NFL title game. Then the newly-vilified coach would have come home, taking over a Giants team that had been built around defense. Because he had been an assistant under Howell through 1958, Lombardi would have been very familiar with many of the team's personnel, giving him an instant advantage.

One reason this is such an interesting dynamic is that the Giants and Packers were the teams that met for the NFL title in both 1961 and 1962. As mentioned earlier, take Lombardi off the Green Bay sidelines, add a change in coaching philosophy, and the Pack might not have continued to develop as rapidly. There's a 50-50 chance that they would have reached those title games in either or both years. But what about the Giants?

In Jim Lee Howell's final season, the Giants were far from an offensive powerhouse. The club was still built around its very good defensive line (Andy Robustelli, Rosey Grier, Dick Modzelewski, and Jim Katcavage), a charismatic middle linebacker in Sam Huff, and a very solid secondary that featured Jim Patton, Dick Lynch, and Erich Barnes. In a move to spice up the offense, the team acquired thirty-five-year-old Y. A. Tittle from the San Francisco 49ers to take over the quarterbacking duties in 1961. The team's best running back was fullback Alex Webster, with Del Shofner and Kyle Rote as top receivers. Shofner was the deep threat and Rote was the route-runner.

However, this was not exactly a Green Bay Packer-type offense. Tittle liked to throw deep to Shofner and he would become the hub of the attack for the next three years, with the running game playing a secondary role. This was not Lombardi's football philosophy, and chances are that the new coach would have altered the Giants' game plan. He might have looked to make some player moves in order to implement his favorite running play—the sweep—and pulled back a bit on the passing. At any rate, the 1961 season would have been one of adjustment, and there's a good chance that the 10-3-1 Giants of that year might have become something like the 8-5-1 Giants as the team adapted to the new style of play.

The Giants of 1962 and '63 were obviously one of the best teams in the league. Their combined record in those two division-winning years was 23-5, led by Tittle's super passing attack, with the running game reduced to a very secondary role. Alex Webster had been the team's leading rusher with 928 yards in 1961. A year later, Webster again led the ground attack, but this time with 743 yards. And in 1963 it was journeyman Phil King who led with just 613 yards. At Green Bay, Lombardi had an annual 1000-yard rusher in Jim Taylor, tough and tenacious. He always liked to have a runner he could count on, a guy willing to run through a brick wall to get a couple of extra yards.

Had Lombardi been unwilling to change his own philosophy and play the kind of game those Giants teams played best—with Y. A. Tittle throwing the football—then the Giants indeed might have fallen back again in 1962 and '63 and maybe finished short of a divisional crown. Of course, there is always an X factor or two. One is that Lombardi—who was above all a football coach—might have seen that the only way he could win with this kind of team was to let Tittle throw. Despite his age, Tittle passed for more than 30 touchdowns and 3,000 yards in both 1962 and 1963. It's possible that Lombardi could have tweaked the offense just enough to incorporate a better running game with the air attack.

The other possibility is that after his first year, the coach would have made huge personnel changes. He probably would have left the defense intact because they were very solid. But he probably would have looked to bring in another runner or two, and maybe made some changes on the offensive line in order to begin running the sweep more effectively. If Lombardi had done this, there is no telling whether the Giants could have won titles in '62 and '63. If Lombardi decided to play for the future he might well have sacrificed a couple of games. If, however, he saw the only way to win was to play the hand he was dealt, then the changes might have come more slowly and he certainly could have gone all the way with those two Giants teams. There's absolutely no doubt that winning was what Vince Lombardi was all about.

So the chances are probably greater that he would have tried to shape the Giants to his own thinking rather than shape his thinking to the Giants, and there's a very good chance the Giants would not have been as good a team from 1961 to 1963 as they were with Allie Sherman as head coach. That's not saying that Sherman was a better coach than Lombardi. Ask some people today and they'll still say there's never been a coach better than Vince Lombardi. But he was also a coach who wanted to shape a team to fit his own football philosophy. And had Lombardi coached the Giants there would have been yet another problem.

AN AGING TEAM

When Vince Lombardi took over the Green Bay Packers, he inherited a team with a core group of young players. He built on that core, adding just the right touches every year to tweak the team and keep it in peak playing condition, and that's one reason why they won five titles in seven years. Some of his stars were with him right from the beginning and the players he added blended in perfectly, with a number of them becoming stars in their own right. Coaching the Giants, though, Lombardi eventually would have run into a problem that didn't exist in Green Bay.

The Giants were an aging team. Some of the stars on the 1961–63 teams had also been on the 1956 title team. Y. A. Tittle was already thirty-seven years old when he led the team into the 1963 championship game. Frank Gifford, the versatile halfback, sat out the 1961 season with a head injury, and while he was a serviceable player the next two years, he was far from the triple-threat superstar he once was. Even the reliable Alex Webster was visibly on the downside. The defensive unit was aging as well. Remember, a lot of these guys had been through the two title games against the Colts in '58 and '59. There were a lot of tough football wars already under their belts.

Proof of the Giants' decline came in 1964, when the team absolutely crashed. As hard as it is to believe, essentially the same team that went 11-3 and played for the title in 1963 finished the 1964 season with an abysmal 2-10-2 record. They rebounded to 7-7 the following year, then bottomed out at 1-12-1 in 1966, the worst season in the team's long history. Their once-vaunted defense allowed more than 500 points, and these dismal seasons would eventually cost Allie Sherman his job.

But what about Lombardi? How would he have dealt with a team loaded with thirty-year-old-plus veterans? There's no doubt he would have seen the potential problem almost immediately. Even though the team continued to perform at a high level, Lombardi probably would have been more aggressive about bringing in younger players to bridge the gap and give the team more balance. Again, this scenario could have played out in two ways.

The first way is that Lombardi could have begun making changes immediately. If he put too many new pieces into the 1961–63 teams, he might have lost some of the chemistry and thus a few more games while continuing what would have been an internal rebuilding program, potentially costing them those three straight division titles. However, had he gone for the second option and kept that team intact in an effort to win immediately, then he would have had to really scramble to keep the 1964 team from crashing the way it did. And there just doesn't seem to be any conceivable way a Vince Lombardi–coached team would have bottomed at 1-12-1 the way the '66 Giants team did. Remember, when Vince Lombardi took over the Packers one of the first things he said was, "I have never been on a losing team, gentlemen, and I do not intend to start now."

He wasn't, ever. And there's no reason to think that Vince Lombardi wouldn't have kept the Giants on the winning side of the ledger, even if those teams didn't win championships. He was that good.

But the bottom line is this: Had Vince Lombardi left the Green Bay Packers to take over the New York Giants in 1961, the course of pro football would have changed. The Packers probably would not have been a dynasty in the 1960s and the Giants, too, might not have had quite the same early success at the outset of the 1960s, though they would have had greater success than they did in the latter part of the decade. And the outcome of the first two Super Bowls might indeed have been different.

One thing, however, is certain. No matter which direction he took, Vincent Thomas Lombardi would still be in the Pro Football Hall of Fame and a legendary coach.

Satch and Josh in '36

On April 15, 1947, Jackie Robinson trotted out of the Brooklyn Dodgers' dugout and took his position at first base. The eyes of all 26,623 fans at Ebbets Field were on number 42 as he began tossing warm-up grounders to his infield teammates. There's no doubt that it was an occasion of monumental importance. Jackie Robinson was about to become the first African-American to play major league baseball in the twentieth century. The so-called "gentlemen's agreement," or color line, was about to be broken. During his first two seasons, Jackie Robinson went through hell. The old ways would die hard, and many players, especially those from the South, didn't want to play with or against a black man. Robinson persevered, and the Dodgers' Branch Rickey, who had chosen him to be the first, was vindicated. The Great Experiment was a success and other black players would follow. There wouldn't be a stampede, but the majors would finally be integrated. What's amazing is that it took so long, and that great African-American players like Satchel Paige and Josh Gibson were denied the chance to show their talents before big league fans.

But what if Satchel Paige and Josh Gibson had signed big league contracts in 1936?

★   ★   ★   ★   ★

Believe it or not, the first mention of a "color line" in the sport of baseball goes back to 1868, just three years after the end of the Civil War. The league in question was called the National Association of Baseball Players, and on December 11, the NABB's governing body voted unanimously to bar "any club which may be composed of one or more colored persons." The country had just been at war and one of the results was freedom for all black people formerly held as slaves, and it would understandably take people some time to adjust to this sweeping change in the social structure of the nation.

Flash forward to 1884. Baseball was growing rapidly. The National League, the same one that exists today, had been formed in 1876, and now there was a second big league, the American Association. The Toledo team had joined the Association that year and brought with them an African-American catcher named Moses Fleetwood "Fleet" Walker. Walker was the son of a doctor and had played baseball for both Oberlin College and the University of Michigan before becoming a pro, but his tenure with Toledo wasn't easy. It was a time when racism, if not rampant, was very much overt. One time Walker was forced to sit out a game in Louisville when a white player on the home team refused to play on the same field with him. He also sat out a game in Richmond, Virginia, when the Toledo manager received a letter that threatened an attack on the team if Walker played.

Chicago White Sox standout Adrian "Cap" Anson also gave the Toledo team some problems. Cap was one of the biggest stars of the day, a future Hall of Famer who would finish his career with a .329 lifetime batting average and 2,995 hits. He was also outspoken when it came to race, and when he saw Fleet Walker, he immediately threatened to pull his team off the field if the Toledo catcher played. But when told if he forfeited the game, he would also lose his share of the gate receipts, Anson decided he'd rather fatten his wallet and allowed his team to play, even with Walker in the Toledo lineup.

The Toledo team folded after the 1884 season and Walker subsequently joined Cleveland in the Western League. At that time there was no official or unofficial ban and it's estimated that there may have been up to fifty or so black players throughout the minor leagues during this period. By 1887, Walker was playing with the Newark Little Giants of the International League, where he often caught pitcher George Stovey, a black Canadian. The two formed baseball's first black battery. Newark had a July exhibition game against the White Sox and this time Cap Anson was ready. Because the game was played in Chicago, Anson felt he had the upper hand. He allegedly flew into a rage, looked at Stovey, and said, "Get that nigger off the field!" This time Anson didn't back down, so Stovey faked an injury in order to allow his team to play the game. Walker was already hurt and the two watched the game from the bench. To some baseball historians, this is the game that drew the "line in the sand."

That same day, owners of the International League formally voted not to sign any black players and, before long, the National League and American Association did the same thing. By 1897, blacks were totally excluded from all minor and major league rosters. Though nothing was ever put in writing, the infamous color line had been drawn. But because he appeared with the Toledo Mud Hens in 1884, Moses "Fleet" Walker is considered the first African-American to appear in the big leagues—and also the last until Jackie Robinson in 1947. But to point out more accurately the tenor of the time, on July 11, 1887, three days *before* the game between Newark and Chicago, the following editorial appeared in *The Sporting News* and stated, in part, that "a new trouble has just arisen in the affairs of certain baseball associations [which] has done more damage to the International League than to any other we know of. We refer to the importation of colored players into the ranks of that body."

Not the kind of sports writing you see today, but its ominous message is crystal clear. An awful lot of people back then simply did not want black players participating at any level of professional baseball. Amazingly, the unwritten edict would remain in effect for more than a half century.

As for Moses Fleetwood Walker, he played two more seasons with Syracuse, then returned to Ohio where he ran both a newspaper and an opera house. He also became an advocate of black emigration to Africa, a feeling spurred no doubt by his own experience in baseball and the racism in America that he had felt first hand.

THE NEGRO LEAGUES

Despite the imposition of the so-called color line, black Americans were not about to stop playing baseball. Since they couldn't play in the major or minor leagues, the formation of all-black teams and leagues was inevitable. The Cuban Giants, organized in 1885, are generally considered to be the first all-black team. Other teams began springing up and they all played independently until the first league was formed in 1920, when Rube Foster, often called the Father of Black Baseball, founded the Negro National League. Three years later, Ed Bolden formed the Eastern Colored League and both operated successfully for several years before financial problems caused their demise.

A new Negro National League was organized in 1933 and four years later the Negro American League began play. These two leagues would continue until Jackie Robinson took the field for the Dodgers in 1947. During the time they existed, the various Negro Leagues played eleven World Series (1924–1927, 1942–1948) and created their own All-Star Game, which was played from 1933 to 1948. In fact, the All-Star Game eventually became the biggest black sports attraction in the country. But once Robinson broke the color line, young black players (as well as older ones) started looking to the majors. The Negro National League folded after the 1948 season and the all-black teams that kept playing for several years after that were no longer big league caliber.

Negro Leagues generally consisted of just six teams. Baltimore, Chicago, Kansas City, New York, and Philadelphia were almost always represented. Other cities with franchise teams included Atlantic City, Birmingham, Cleveland, Detroit, Indianapolis, Memphis, Newark, Pittsburgh, St. Louis, and Washington. Schedules were usually very flexible so that teams could also play against other competition, often semipro white teams. Many of these black teams, even the top clubs, played more non-league than league games. The leagues, on average, played between 50 and 80 games a year.

But none of that diminishes the skills of the black ballplayer. Many were on a par with the best the major leagues had to offer and would have been big league stars had they been allowed to play. Finally, after too many years, the stars of the Negro Leagues have taken their rightful place alongside their white counterparts in the Baseball Hall of Fame at Cooperstown, New York. Visitors can now read about the likes of Satchel Paige, Josh Gibson, Cool Papa Bell, Oscar Charleston, Ray Dandridge, Martin Dihigo, Rube Foster, Judy Johnson, Buck Leonard, Turkey Stearnes, Smokey Joe Williams, and others. In fact, in 2006 there were seventeen additional inductees elected by a special committee, some having played even before the Negro Leagues were formed.

These are players who should not be forgotten. As Satchel Paige, long considered one of the greatest pitchers of all time, once said in referring to the players in the Negro Leagues, "There were many Satchels, many Joshes."

WHY NOT SOONER?

Looking back, it's really difficult to believe that it took until 1947 for the color line to finally fall. While there was still strict segregation in many parts of the country and a great deal of obvious racial hatred, most of the major league baseball teams were situated in the Northeast and Midwest, with Washington being the southernmost city and St. Louis the city furthest west. There were a number of efforts made to integrate the majors before it finally happened in 1947, and although many of the people involved in those efforts are now forgotten, they did lay the groundwork for the eventual desegregation of baseball.

Surprisingly, other nonwhite players were allowed to play in the early part of the twentieth century, including light-skinned Hispanics and Native Americans, a rationale that was part of the illogical nature of racial bigotry. In 1901, before he earned his reputation as one of the greatest skippers in baseball with the New York Giants, the legendary John McGraw became the manager of the Baltimore Orioles. No matter where he managed, McGraw was always extremely competitive and combative, and always looking for the edge, which is why he tried to get Charlie Grant onto his team. Grant was an African-American second baseman with obvious talent and McGraw, ever the schemer, tried to sign him by passing him off as a Cherokee Indian named Tokohama. Needless to say, the ruse didn't work and Grant never got to a play a game. Even back then, an astute baseball man like John McGraw knew that there were talented black players who could help his team, and he probably would have signed several if the color line had not been so recently drawn.

After that initial effort, it took until the 1930s before people were willing to challenge the color line again. In 1935 a man named Ferdinand Morton became president of the then struggling Negro National League. An Ivy League–educated attorney, and son of former slaves, Morton thought about the inequities facing black players after he took over the Negro National League, and in 1936 he approached National League President Ford C. Frick. Morton presented a proposal to Frick that not only would have integrated organized baseball, but would have provided the groundwork for African-American management and ownership.

Morton's proposal would allow the Negro League teams to become part of minor league baseball. Teams would remain segregated at first with full integration occurring sometime in the future. Morton may have figured that the Negro League teams would be far superior to the minor league teams they played and that, at some point, owners would want to level the playing field and would do it by integrating. Frick, however, rejected the proposal outright.

Then there was the case of Lester Rodney and the *Daily Worker*. Rodney became sports editor of the United States Communist Party's daily newspaper in 1936, long before the communist witch hunts of the 1950s, but even then the paper wasn't very popular among those who didn't agree with the communist philosophy. Rodney not only wanted to establish a real sports section within his paper, but he also saw the racial inequities in baseball and intended to make some noise about it.

"Other papers just said, 'The Kansas City Monarchs will play the Baltimore Giants at such and such a time tomorrow,' with no mention that any of them could have played big league baseball or even minor league baseball and were banned from both," Rodney explained, years later. "It was amazing. You go back and read the great newspapers in the thirties; you'll find no editorials saying,

'What's going on here? This is America, land of the free and people with the wrong pigmentation of skin can't play baseball? [There was] nothing like that. No challenges to the league, to the commissioner, to the league president, no interviewing the managers, no talking about Satchel Paige and Josh Gibson, who were obviously of superstar caliber."

Rodney felt that most people didn't even think about it, that they just accepted that not allowing blacks to play was part of baseball culture. Rodney wasn't about to ignore the color line, and he soon began crusading in his paper's pages for blacks to be allowed to play on major league teams. The *Daily Worker* also developed a relationship with the black press, and they began to print each other's articles about the Negro League players and the color line, which opened up new audiences for each of them.

Rodney began speaking to more big league players about racial inequalities in baseball and printed everything he could in his paper. For example, in 1937 he was in the dressing room at Yankee Stadium when someone asked the young centerfielder, Joe DiMaggio, Who was the best pitcher he ever faced? Without hesitating, DiMaggio said, "Satchel Paige." He had apparently played against Paige in an exhibition game. But Rodney also reported that DiMaggio did not add that Paige should be in the major leagues. Another time, he asked Cincinnati pitchers Johnny Vander Meer and Bucky Walters if blacks should be allowed in the majors and one of them answered, "I don't see why they shouldn't play." Despite this, owners continued to say that white players wouldn't stand for it.

Another reason often given was that Negro League teams rented out big league stadiums for their games. The owners felt that if blacks were allowed in the majors the Negro Leagues would quickly fold and they would lose their rental money.

Two prominent black reporters who also led the crusade for the integration of the major leagues were Sam Lacy and Wendell

Smith. Lacy wrote for the Baltimore *Afro-American* and Smith for the *Pittsburgh Courier*. In 1937, Lacy arranged an interview with Clark Griffith, the owner of the Washington Senators, who told him that the "time was not far off" when black players would be in the major leagues. But Griffith was just blowing smoke. After Jackie Robinson debuted with the Dodgers, it took Griffith another seven years before he signed a black player for his ballclub.

As early as 1933, White Sox president J. Louis Comiskey said this about integrating baseball: "The question has never crossed my mind. Had some good player come along and my manager refused to sign him because he was a Negro, I am sure I would have taken action or attempted to do so, although it is not up to me to change what might be the rule."

Well, there was no rule, per se. Even baseball commissioner Kenesaw Mountain Landis admitted that, but he did little or nothing to improve the situation. He said that in order to integrate, owners of Negro League teams would have to be heavily compensated because of the loss of revenue that would occur if their best players went to the majors. He mentioned that the minor leagues would also have to be integrated and there were a significant number of minor league teams throughout the Deep South, and integrating those teams could prove more difficult than integrating the largely northern teams of the major leagues.

There were always stories and rumors throughout the 1930s. In early 1937, a sportswriter quoted Brooklyn Dodgers president Steven McKeever stating he would like to sign black players but the decision would be his manager's. Burleigh Grimes, the former pitching star who was managing the Dodgers then, quickly deflected the question to N.L. President Frick. It was a constant game of pass the buck. Grimes did admit in an interview with Lester Rodney that he had been impressed with a number of black players during barnstorming exhibition tours, but when asked about putting a Dodger uniform on Satchel Paige or Josh Gibson, Grimes said, "You're wasting your time. That'll never happen as long as there are segregated trains and restaurants." So the buck was passed some more.

Then, in 1939, Pittsburgh Pirates president William Benswanger mentioned to someone that he was thinking about purchasing Josh Gibson's contract. Apparently, Benswanger had seen quite a bit of Negro League baseball since the Homestead Grays played their games at Pittsburgh's Forbes Field. He supposedly asked the Grays' owner, Cumberland Posey, if he would sell Gibson. But nothing came of it. Even as late as 1942, Benswanger wanted to hold a tryout for several black players, but was pressured by others not to do it. He simply didn't have the strength that Branch Rickey exhibited when he signed Jackie Robinson and stayed with it, despite the criticism and predictions of failure.

There was a rumor in the early 1940s, during the war years, when baseball was scraping the bottom of the barrel for talent, that Bill Veeck—who would later be the maverick owner of the Cleveland Indians, St. Louis Browns, and Chicago White Sox at different periods—was planning to buy the Philadelphia Phillies and stock the team with black players. Veeck knew how talented many of the Negro League stars were, but the purchase never happened and some feel it was never a legitimate possibility. Veeck eventually brought an aging Satchel Paige to the Indians in 1948. Because he always loved to go against the establishment, had Veeck owned a team in the 1930s, he might well have been the one to break the color line.

Come to think of it, what if . . .

THE PHILLIES HAD MADE A HISTORIC SIGNING?

The team that was perhaps in the most disarray in the mid-1930s was the Philadelphia Phillies. They were near the bottom of the league every season and in 1935 they finished seventh with a 64-89 record. The Phillies were also a team that had virtually no big stars on the roster at the time, because owner Gary Nugent, who bought the team in 1933, was in constant financial crisis. As a result, he sold off or traded his best players, like slugger Chuck Klein, as well as promising youngsters, often receiving cash in return.

The National League would take the club away from Nugent in 1943, but things could have gone differently if the aggressive and innovative Bill Veeck had purchased the team prior to the 1936 season. Veeck could have decided that the quickest way to turn his club around and bring the Phillies back to respectability was to sign a pair of real superstars—Satchel Paige and Josh Gibson.

SATCH AND JOSH

The premise is simple. Satchel Paige and Josh Gibson were such immense talents that they would have been naturals for any big league club to sign. There are still some who call the lanky right-handed Paige the greatest pitcher of all-time, bar none, and the right-handed slugging Gibson the greatest hitter of all-time, bar none. Of course, you have to add the word *arguably* to make it all plausible. However, even to speak their names alongside the already-acknowledged greats of the game gives them an instant credibility, and to those who saw them play, the stories of their exploits are endless.

Let's face it, if any big league club had the guts to sign Paige and Gibson during the mid-1930s, their presence would have improved that club immeasurably. That's simply a fact that cannot be denied.

Leroy Robert Paige was born in Mobile, Alabama, on July 7, 1906, though some claim he was actually born in 1903 and others say it was 1908. He got his nickname, Satchel, because he carried bags at the Mobile railroad station when he was just seven years old. Though he was in trouble numerous times during his youth, he could always throw a baseball. In his late teens he signed on with a local black semipro team, the Mobile Tigers, and in 1924 is alleged to have won 30 games and lost just one. The Paige odyssey would continue for another three decades. He'd play for many teams, often pitching exhibitions and pitching against major league teams, usually beating them all. Though record-keeping was erratic or even nonexistent then, some estimate that Satch was winning in the neighborhood of 60 games a year and striking out between 10 and 18 hitters a game. At 6'3" and 180 pounds, he was tall and lanky with long arms, taller than most pitchers of the day, which gave him an advantage pitching off the high mound.

In 1931 Satch went north and joined Gus Greenlee's Pittsburgh Crawfords, one of the best black teams in the business. As the star pitcher, his salary was $200 a month. Satch's battery mate with the Crawfords was Josh Gibson, and the two stars were a devastating combination. With Josh providing his long home runs, Satchel was said to have won about 105 games over three years while losing only 37. Paige threw every kind of pitch there was, and gave them all special nicknames. His moving changeup was a "two-hump blooper," his medium fastball was "Little Tom," while his hard fastball was "Long Tom." He also threw a hesitation pitch, where he would stop his delivery halfway through just momentarily, then continue.

Satch pitched enough against the top big leaguers of the day to be considered the real thing. His barnstorming opponents included Babe Ruth, Bob Feller, and Rogers Hornsby, and legend has it that he once fanned Hornsby five times in a single game. After the 1934 season, he toured against the team anchored by Dizzy Dean, who had won 30 games that year, and Satch won four of the six games in which they pitched against each other. In fact, he beat Diz 1-0 in one of the games. The following year he defeated an all-star team lead by big leaguer Dick Bartell and featuring young Joe DiMaggio in center. That's when the future Yankee Clipper came to believe that Satch was "the best I've ever faced and the fastest." There's little doubt that, in his prime years, Satchel Paige would have been dynamite in the big leagues.

As for Josh Gibson, he's a guy who hit an estimated 800 or more home runs during his career, including 75 to 84 in one season! That can't be verified because of the shoddy record-keeping and the number of teams for which he played, but enough of those who saw him say he could hit as well as anyone. One of the nicknames he had was "The Black Babe Ruth." There's a story that says Gibson hit the only fair ball ever to leave Yankee Stadium, something not fully verified, but there are people who say it happened. He's also credited with having a .384 lifetime batting average in the Negro Leagues.

Joshua Gibson, Jr., was born in Buena Vista, Georgia, on December 21, 1911. He began playing ball as a youngster, graduated to the semipro level and was eventually signed by the Homestead Grays in 1930, when he was just eighteen years old. It didn't take long for his legend to grow. Roy Campanella, who saw Gibson play when he was in the Negro Leagues, had nothing but praise for his fellow catcher. Remember, Campy became a three-time National League Most Valuable Player with the Brooklyn Dodgers.

"When I broke in with the Baltimore Elite Giants in 1937, there were already a hundred legends about him," said Campy. "Once you saw him play, you knew they were all true. I couldn't carry his bat or glove. The stories of his 500-foot home runs are all true, because I saw them. And he was one of those sluggers that seldom struck out. You couldn't fool him; he was too quick with the bat. And he could do it behind the plate, including throw."

Gibson was 6'1", 215 pounds, with a short, compact swing. He often hit line drives that seemed to carry forever. Those who saw him remember a player with huge forearms and tremendous upper body strength long before anyone even thought about performance enhancers.

Like Paige, Josh Gibson often played in exhibition games against white stars. The great pitcher Walter Johnson, managing the Washington Senators in the 1930s, once saw him in an exhibition game against his team and said immediately, "There is a catcher that any big league club would like to buy for $200,000. His name is Gibson. He can do everything. He hits the ball a mile. And he catches so easy, he might as well be in a rocking chair. Throws like a rifle. Bill Dickey isn't as good a catcher. Too bad he's a colored fellow."

Monte Irvin, who began his career in the Negro Leagues and ended it as a successful major leaguer, had this to say about Gibson: "I played with Willie Mays and against Hank Aaron," the Hall of Famer explained. "They were tremendous players, but they were no Josh Gibson. Josh was better than those two."

There's little doubt about Josh Gibson's talent. When Branch Rickey finally decided to choose a player to break the color line Gibson was one of the players he considered. "For sheer talent alone, Gibson would have been the obvious choice," Rickey said, some years later. "You know what I feel about [Roy] Campanella, but whatever Roy can do, Josh could do better." Unfortunately, Gibson was thirty-four years old by the time Rickey began looking to choose the one, and he was also in declining health. He would die from a brain tumor on January 20, 1947, three months before Jackie Robinson would take the field for the Dodgers for the first time.

Both Satch and Josh most likely would have jumped at the opportunity to play in the majors. When Branch Rickey signed Jackie Robinson to be the first black player in the majors, Satchel Paige lamented, "I'd always figured it would be me. Maybe it had happened too late, and everybody figured I was too old. Maybe that's why it was Jackie and not me."

WHAT COULD HAVE HAPPENED?

In 1936, Satch wasn't too old. If you take 1906 as his birth year, he would have been just thirty and at his peak. Josh Gibson would have been twenty-five and ready to explode as a big-time power hitter. The new owner of the Phillies would have stated unequivocally that there was no written rule about signing blacks and, as far as he was concerned, it was an agreement not made by gentlemen, and it was about time someone stood up. The signings would have triggered a huge press response and, especially in the North, chances are that a good number of the newspapers would have examined their collective conscience and agreed that blacks should be allowed to play. But that doesn't mean it would have been easy. Here are some scenarios that could well have occurred.

The 1930s weren't the best time for race relations in the United States. The Great Depression characterized the decade leading up to World War II, a tough period for many and the competition for too few jobs naturally made people more aggressive in their desire to protect hearth and home. That damaged race relations, even in the North. But it was still markedly worse in the South, where segregation still reigned.

One only has to look at some of the black musicians—Duke Ellington, Count Basie, Jimmie Lunceford, Chick Webb—who traveled down South during the Swing Era, when their music was in demand. The bands and band members always had a difficult time in the South and they never could be sure when a racial incident would arise. It wasn't any better for white bands that had integrated and had one or two black musicians. The blacks were always singled out and treated badly. And when the whites stood up for them, they were treated poorly, too.

It wouldn't have been any different for the baseball teams of the day. Negro League teams knew where they were wanted and where they could go. Even when they barnstormed in the South, they played essentially in front of black crowds. But there still could be problems. The ordeal that Jackie Robinson had to endure in the minors in 1946 and with the Dodgers a year later is well documented. He was being threatened, baited, ridiculed, and challenged on an almost daily basis.

But if Paige and Gibson had been signed by the Phillies in 1936, there would also have been some big plusses. Jackie Robinson was a fine ballplayer, a catalyst with outstanding skills. He joined one of the best teams in the majors and made them better with both his presence and his talent. Paige and Gibson, by all accounts, were on another level completely. They were among the elite, and had they joined the Phillies together, they certainly would have brought excitement back to a dead team. If there's one thing fans everywhere want, it's a winner, and these two were superstars. If Paige had come in, for example, and won between 25 and 30 games while Gibson led the league with 45 homers (Mel Ott of the Giants led with 33 that year) and 145 RBIs (Joe Medwick was tops with 138), it's hard to see the fans in Philadelphia not cheering. In fact, outside of New York, Philly may have been the best place for them to have played in 1936. That doesn't mean all their teammates would have accepted them. But a strong manager and owner would have made it crystal clear what was expected and malcontents would be free to go. Those Phils didn't have a lot of premium players to lose. In addition, there would also have been a bottom line that might have quieted even their southern teammates. The presence of Paige and Gibson would have eventually put money in everyone's pockets.

Undoubtedly, it would have been different on the road. It was away from Ebbets Field where Jackie Robinson got the brunt of the abuse. But if Paige and Gibson had thick enough skin to weather the initial onslaught, the sheer magnitude of their talent might have turned things around pretty quickly.

THE OWENS AND LOUIS FACTOR

There were two other very significant events about this same time that certainly could have had some effect on an early effort to integrate baseball. The first was the 1936 Olympic Games, which would have taken place during Satch and Josh's first season with the Phillies. The Games that year were held in Berlin, Germany, where Adolf Hitler was determined to showcase his athletes and make a statement for the superiority of the Aryan race. Then in stepped Jesse Owens, the great African-American track star. Owens dominated the Games, winning an unprecedented four gold medals in the 100 and 200 meter dashes, the long jump, and the 4 x 400 relay, setting two Olympic records and a world record along the way. Adolf Hitler was so shaken that a black man had beaten his Aryan athletes that he wouldn't even appear on the victory stand to present Owens with his medals.

There was a sense of nationalistic pride among all Americans after Owens and his teammates excelled. The winds of war were already blowing through Europe and that made Owens's victory even more special. "I am proud that I am an American," he said upon returning in an interview with the *Pittsburgh Courier*. "I see the sun breaking through the clouds when I realize that millions of Americans will recognize that what I and the boys of my race are trying to do is attempted for the glory of our country and our countrymen. Maybe more people will now realize that the Negro is trying to do his part as an American citizen."

There was, of course, an immediate reaction and a long term reaction. The overriding sense of pride in Owens's accomplishments could have served as a foundation for the integration of the big leagues and more cheers for Paige and Gibson. Of course, the little day-to-day things don't change overnight; upon returning to the U.S., Owens and his wife were refused service in several New York hotels. One finally gave them rooms, but only on the condition that they use the service entrance. Promises that Owens would receive big money endorsements never materialized. Still, most people felt that Owens's Olympic success helped pave the way for Robinson's debut eleven years later, and it probably would have helped Paige and Gibson just as much, had they been playing in the big leagues in 1936.

Then there was Joe Louis, who was an up-and-coming heavyweight fighter when he was unexpectedly knocked out by Germany's Max Schmeling in 1936. Because of the political climate in Europe and fears that Schmeling might be a Nazi (he was apparently never an official member of the Nazi party), it was the defeated Louis who got the first crack at the heavyweight title. "The Brown Bomber" defeated James J. Braddock for the title in 1937 to become the first black heavyweight champ since Jack Johnson. Louis's first order of business as champ was to avenge his only defeat, and that meant fighting Max Schmeling once more. The big fight was set for Yankee Stadium on June 22, 1938. By that time, the war machine of the Third Reich in Germany was becoming more threatening, and the bout was looked upon as not only a heavyweight title fight, but a battle of fascism versus democracy.

With much of the world watching and 70,000 fans of all colors at Yankee Stadium cheering for Louis, the champ came out and destroyed Schmeling in the first round, knocking him out in just 124 seconds. Joe Louis became an instant American hero embraced not only by the black population, but by large segments of the white population as well. President Franklin Delano Roosevelt invited the champ to the White House, felt his biceps, and commented, "Joe, we need muscles like yours to beat Germany."

Years later his son, Joe Louis, Jr., said this about his father: "What my father did was enable white America to think of him as an American, not as a black. By winning, he became white America's first black hero."

And sportswriter Jimmy Cannon, when he heard the oft-used phrase that Louis was a credit to his race, quickly wrote, "Yes, Louis is a credit to his race—the human race."

Assuming that Satchel Paige and Josh Gibson had survived their first years, they would have already been playing in the big leagues for three seasons when Louis defeated Schmeling. Many white fans by that time would have realized that these two players were special and if they continued to put up the superstar-caliber numbers of which they were both capable, there's no reason to believe that they wouldn't have been widely admired as ballplayers by then. Add Louis's victory over Schmeling to the mix and more fans than ever would have realized that heroes don't have to be white to be admired. So Joe Louis's triumph could have made it even easier for Satch and Josh, because the powers that be in baseball might well have realized that integrating the big leagues was the right thing to do. By that time there even might have been a few more blacks coming into the league, but if not, the Louis-Schmeling bout could have served as a catalyst for other owners to begin ignoring a color line that was ridiculous in the first place.

THE WAR YEARS

When Pearl Harbor was attacked by the Japanese on December 7, 1941, plunging the United States into war, no one foresaw immediately what an impact it would have on baseball. It was huge. Before World War II ended in 1945, some 500 major leaguers and another 5,000 men from the minor leagues would serve in the military in one capacity or another. Many of the game's biggest stars, such as Hank Greenberg, Bob Feller, Ted Williams, and Joe DiMaggio lost several years of their careers to Uncle Sam. In fact, it was thought for a while that baseball might have to shut down, but President Roosevelt issued an edict saying that major league baseball should continue because it was a morale booster for the people at home. However, with virtually all the rosters depleted, what could baseball do? There was a logical choice, only it wasn't made at the time.

The war years presented baseball with the perfect opportunity to integrate its teams. The army was integrating to some degree as black and white soldiers for the first time fought beside each other. But instead of integrating, baseball began scraping the bottom of the talent barrel. More and more front-line players left for the military, and their replacements were somewhat questionable.

Here are just a few examples: In 1944 the Dodgers signed a seventeen-year-old shortstop named Tommy Brown who managed to hit only .164 that year. Cincinnati did them one better, signing fifteen-year-old Joe Nuxhall in 1944. Nuxhall pitched in one game, left after two-thirds of an inning with a 67.50 earned run average and didn't pitch in the majors again until 1952. On the other side of the coin, the Reds signed forty-seven-year-old Hod Lisenbee in 1945. Lisenbee had pitched in the majors in 1932, again in 1936, and then not until 1945. He was 1-3 in 31 games that year. Detroit needed a catcher in 1942 so they dipped into the minors to grab thirty-five-year-old Paul Richards, who was then a catcher-manager for the Atlanta minor league team. Richards hadn't played in the bigs since 1935.

Perhaps most emblematic of the lengths big league teams went to in order to fill rosters during the war was the signing of Pete Gray by the St. Louis Browns in 1945. Gray was an outfielder who would play in 77 games and hit .218 that year. What was so unusual? Pete Gray had just one arm.

With war raging in Europe and Asia, and the president specifically asking baseball to continue to operate, it was the perfect opportunity to integrate the majors. It could have been done in a number of ways. The Negro Leagues were also continuing and the talent pool was obviously there. All it would have taken was a group of owners who wanted to keep winning to begin signing black players. Baseball was entertainment and they could have increased attendance dramatically since they also would have had black fans coming out. African-Americans came in large numbers to see Jackie Robinson in 1947. There's no reason to believe they wouldn't have come from 1942 to '45.

Had Paige and Gibson broken the color line in 1936, there would have been a good chance that other black players would have already been in the majors by the time Pearl Harbor was attacked. If that had happened, there's no reason to believe that World War II would not have provided the perfect opportunity for a more complete integration of major league baseball. Remember, the war ended in 1945, just a year before Branch Rickey signed Robinson. So the climate was changing. It didn't happen overnight. There wasn't a flood of black players flowing into the majors after 1947. It was more like a trickle, in the National League first, then the American. The Yankees, for example, didn't have a black player until Elston Howard in 1955, and the Boston Red Sox were the last team to integrate, not signing an African-American until Pumpsie Green in 1959.

But if the flow had begun in 1942 the entire process could have been accelerated, and if a couple of players the caliber of Satch and Josh had arrived as early as 1936 it could well have happened. In fact, if the first two had weathered the storm and survived into the war years, they could have easily paved the way for others to follow.

ECONOMICS AND THE JIM CROW FACTOR

It would have taken a very strong owner, a strong manager, support from the president of the league and commissioner of baseball, but everything points to eventual success if Paige and Gibson had joined the Phillies in 1936. Jackie Robinson had all of that support he needed when he joined the Dodgers. It would have taken some real perseverance on the part of Paige and Gibson.

Playing in the Negro Leagues or with barnstorming black teams, the two stars always had a support group around them, especially when racial incidents arose. Robinson, of course, was alone when he joined the Dodgers that first year. Had Paige and Gibson signed with the same team, they would have had each other's support and a mission to show how good they were. There would have undoubtedly been problems with teammates, with players on other teams, with hotels and restaurants, and it wouldn't have been surprising if the two players and their families received threats of bodily harm or worse, so the pair would have needed dogged determination to deal with all of that.

Robinson was chosen by Branch Rickey because he had the character and tenacity to turn the other cheek. Rickey knew he'd be challenged on the field and didn't want him getting into fights that first year. Paige, being a pitcher, could undoubtedly protect himself. Anyone giving Satch a difficult time also knew they would have to get in the batter's box sooner or later and face his very live fastball. With his pinpoint control, Paige undoubtedly could have put the ball exactly where he wanted. In days when pitchers regularly brushed hitters back, that was a powerful weapon to have. He also could have protected Gibson. If an opposition player bowled Josh over at the plate, or if pitchers began throwing at him, Satch would get his chance at those same players when they came up to hit. Once more, that would have been a powerful equalizer.

Gibson, by all accounts, was the more mercurial of the two and might have had a more difficult time coping with the animosity he would face. Having Paige on the team definitely would have helped. And Gibson's bat would have been his other equalizer. While Jackie Robinson was a good hitter with a .311 lifetime average, he wasn't a real slugger. Josh Gibson was considered a devastating hitter, one of the best, and if he brought that same kind of big bat to the majors, he would have been a feared figure in the batter's box. The talent level of both players was so great that they probably would have won over their teammates and the fans rather quickly. And once that happened, they'd be halfway home.

The only downside would have been the economics of the day. Even back then, those opposed to integrating the majors would use the excuse that the Negro Leagues couldn't survive if their best players crossed over. It was used then as an excuse not to integrate but, unfortunately, it was true. Not every player in the Negro Leagues was good enough to make the majors, so some players would have been out of jobs. But that happened anyway once Jackie arrived and others followed. Team owners would also have lost their franchises and investments, and Major League owners would have lost rent money paid by Negro League teams to use their stadiums.

Still, that was no reason not to integrate. Had there been more progressive people around baseball then there could have possibly been a merger of sorts, and teams like the Kansas City Monarchs, Homestead Grays, Pittsburgh Crawfords, Baltimore Elite Giants, and Newark Eagles could have been considered as additions to the American and National Leagues, and then integrated. They could have provided an early expansion, perhaps right after the war when there was renewed interest in the game. That would not only have provided maybe two or four additional franchises, but more jobs for players and more revenue for the game. With some creative thinking, the economic downside could have been turned into a positive, at least in part, had the stigma of Jim Crow not have continued to prevail.

THE ROBINSON LEGACY

By the time the twenty-first century began, Jackie Robinson had finally achieved the renown from baseball that he long deserved. His achievement in breaking the color line was celebrated everywhere. In 1997, baseball commissioner Bud Selig made the unprecedented move of permanently retiring Jackie's number 42. With the exception of players already wearing the number, no big leaguer would ever again take the field with number 42 on the back of his uniform. It was the ultimate honor to a great pioneer. There is little doubt that Robinson persevered and ultimately prevailed through a torturous time. His friend and teammate, Pee Wee Reese, put Jackie's achievement into perspective when he said, "To do what he did has got to be the most tremendous thing I've ever seen in sports."

Yes, Jackie Robinson was a pioneer, an outstanding player and an even more outstanding human being. Ironic as it may seem, however, had the color line been broken by Satchel Paige and Josh Gibson in 1936, and remained broken, much of Jackie's legacy would be lost. There's even a chance that he wouldn't have played at all, and even if he did, he might not be in the Hall of Fame. Remember, Jackie was a twenty-eight-year-old rookie in 1947 and he retired after the 1956 season. During those ten years he had a .311 batting average, hit just 137 homers, never more than 19 in a season, and drove home more than 100 runs only once, in his MVP season of 1949. By numbers alone, this isn't the stuff that makes Hall of Fame careers.

Jackie, of course, also had the intangibles. No fiercer competitor ever graced the diamond. When he was on the bases he was not only a threat to steal (he had 197 during an era when no one stole much), but he was always a major distraction, as well as a catalyst on a great Brooklyn Dodgers team that dominated for a decade. He still might have done all that and fallen short of the Hall had he not been the first.

There's also no guarantee that Jackie would have come up sooner if Satch and Josh had broken the color line in 1936. After an outstanding career at UCLA in which he starred in football, basketball, track, and baseball, Jackie took a job with the National Youth Administration and played some semipro football with the Honolulu Bears football club. When the war started, he was accepted at Army Officer Candidate School and was commissioned as a second lieutenant. Jackie ran into problems because of continued segregation and was eventually court-martialed because he was alleged to have violated Jim Crow statutes in Texas. Finally found innocent, he was given an honorable discharge in November 1944.

It wasn't until April 1945 that he signed a $450-a-month contract with the Kansas City Monarchs and was finally discovered by Branch Rickey. Had baseball already been integrated and the same wartime scenario for Jackie prevailed, the 1945 season would have been his first in the minor leagues. So it's doubtful he could have reached the majors before 1947 anyway, and he still would have been a twenty-eight-year-old rookie. By that time, there might well have been several dozen African-American players who were better than Jackie already in the majors and he would have blended into the league instead of standing out. There's always the outside chance that Jackie, an extremely intelligent man, might have decided upon another career course with the majors already integrated and his thirtieth birthday looming. It certainly could have happened that way.

Under those circumstances, it's not a stretch to say that had baseball been integrated in 1936, Jackie Robinson would not have the same legacy today, not even close. Branch Rickey called his signing of Jackie Robinson the "Great Experiment." He felt that if it failed, the major leagues would not have been integrated for perhaps another ten years. At first glance, that seems hard to believe, but then again, old ways sometimes die hard. However, had an owner found the courage to sign Satchel Paige and Josh Gibson in the 1930s, it might have been called the "Daring Experiment." Baseball would have had two great stars and the major leagues could have been integrated a full decade earlier, as they should have been, and almost everyone could have ultimately profited. Remember, there was never a written rule. This whole shameful history of America's national pastime was based solely on a *gentlemen's agreement* that should never have been made.

Thanks, But No Thanks

The All-America Football Conference was organized in 1944 and began play as a professional football league in 1946 with eight teams to rival the older, more established National Football League, which at the time was comprised of just ten teams. The AAFC would play for four years before financial problems fueled by competition for players caused its demise. But the NFL, not the most stable of leagues at the time, saw an opportunity to expand and sharpen its own product. So the older league took in three AAFC teams, franchises from Cleveland, San Francisco, and Baltimore, then dispersed the other top AAFC players among its other established teams. It was the beginning of NFL expansion and pointed pro football toward the modern era. Of course, the NFL always thought it was vastly superior to the AAFC and when it took in the three teams it suddenly found it got more than it bargained for. It got the Cleveland Browns.

But what if the Cleveland Browns and other AAFC teams hadn't come into the NFL?

*   *   *   *   *

Professional football was still suffering from growing pains at the beginning of World War II. The National Football League began play in 1920 with all the teams grouped into one division, and under that system, the team with the best record was declared champion. There were some great early players like Jim Thorpe, Red Grange, and Bronko Nagurski, but the game was very different. In 1933, when it became clear that a championship game was important to the fans, as well as an economic necessity, the league split into two divisions.

As the NFL slowly stabilized, there were several attempts by various groups of people to start rival leagues. One started in 1926, another in 1936, and a third in 1940, each called the American Football League and each lasting just two seasons before going out of business. But the NFL survived—shifting, adding, and subtracting franchises to comply with the tenor of the times. Then in 1946 the All-America Football Conference arrived. Maybe the new owners felt they wouldn't be jinxed if they stayed away from the name American Football League. At any rate, they also felt there would be an economic and sports boom after the war ended and their league would have a chance to succeed.

The AAFC's Western Division had teams in Cleveland, Los Angeles, San Francisco, and Chicago. In the East there were New York, Buffalo, Brooklyn, and Miami. Many of the teams played in major venues such as Municipal Stadium in Cleveland, the Los Angeles Coliseum, Kezar Stadium in San Francisco, Soldier Field in Chicago, Yankee Stadium in New York, and the Orange Bowl in Miami. There was ample opportunity for big crowds, and before long, it became apparent that the AAFC also had a super team.

THE CLEVELAND BROWNS DWARF ALL OTHERS

The very first AAFC came was played on September 5, 1946, in Cleveland and the crowd of 60,135 at Municipal Stadium—the

114

largest crowd ever to see a pro game to that time—left happy. The Browns demolished the Miami Seahawks, 44-0, to set the tone that would carry over for the next four seasons, at least on the gridiron. This was a team that would totally dominate the new league, playing a brand of football that many felt was so good that a reasonable facsimile wasn't even seen in the NFL. The architect of this success was Paul Brown, who was hired as the Browns' coach while still in the navy and on leave from his head coaching position at Ohio State. He was coaching at the Greta Lakes Naval Training Station when the Cleveland club offered him a personal services contract that would pay him $1,000 a month. He decided to take the position and immediately began the job of assembling his first professional team.

Two of the things he did immediately would pay dividends: he hired a pair of national scouts to scour the country for top players, and he brought in former Northwestern All-American quarterback Otto Graham, who was also in the navy at the time. When Brown heard that the new league would also have a "gentlemen's agreement" to bar black players, he immediately said to hell with that, and quickly signed fullback Marion Motley and lineman Bill Willis, a pair of African-Americans who would not only break the color line in the AAFC, but would also become cornerstones of the team and eventual Hall of Famers. Coincidentally, the NFL also signed two black players that year, Kenny Washington and Woody Strode, the first African-Americans in the league since 1933.

Brown began building his team around players who had been in college before entering military service. He looked for men who had matured during the war and who were not only talented, but ready to dedicate themselves to the philosophy he would teach them. They included pass receivers Mac Speedie (a perfect name for a receiver) and Dante Lavelli, as well as tackle/placekicker Lou

"The Toe" Groza. Before Paul Brown was finished, his team had stars at almost every position.

But that wasn't all. Brown was an innovator. He had a quarterback who was ahead of his time, a precision passer who had great field vision and natural leadership, as well as the ability to stay cool under pressure. Motley was a bruising fullback and both Speedie and Lavelli were as good a receiving duo as any in the NFL. With this group of stars, Brown developed an offense built around a passing game that was more sophisticated than the football world had ever seen before. It featured the hook or come-back pattern, and a wide variety of sideline pass plays. The offense also put players in motion, ran a power sweep, and kept the defense honest with Motley's strength and great running ability.

The Browns compiled an impressive 12-2 record in the AAFC's inaugural season, with one of those wins coming before another record crowd of 71,134 fans in Cleveland as they beat the Los Angeles Dons. In the first ever AAFC championship game, the Browns topped the Eastern Division champs, the New York Yankees, 14-9. An 18-yard Graham to Lavelli pass provided the winning margin, and Graham (who also played defense) intercepted a New York pass to seal the deal at the end.

That's the way it was for the four years in which the AAFC existed. The Cleveland Browns won every year, including a perfect season in 1948. They went 14-0 and then won the title game over the Buffalo Bills, 49-7, in what could arguably be called the greatest (and mostly forgotten) season any professional football team ever had. Paul Brown kept adding to his strong nucleus and the Browns compiled an incredible four-year record of 52 wins against just 4 losses with 3 ties, an amazing .881 winning percentage. The next best team was the San Francisco 49ers at 39-15-2. No team in any other professional league has ever been that dominant over a similar period of time.

Despite all this, the All-America Football Conference still wasn't considered by many as the big time. The NFL continued to look down upon it, and almost right from the start, the league had off-field problems that signaled trouble.

MERGER OR EXTINCTION

It has never been easy for a new professional sports league to succeed. The same thing has been tried in baseball (the Federal League early on, and something called the Continental League later that never got off the ground), in basketball (the American Basketball Association), and even hockey (the World Hockey Association). The only way these leagues ever worked is if there was some kind of merger with the older, established league. So the AAFC was a calculated gamble right from the start.

By 1947, the league was obviously putting a credible product on the field and attendance was good, but there were already problems. For one, the Miami franchise had been replaced by the Baltimore Colts. There were also problems in Chicago, where the Rockets couldn't compete with the established NFL Bears and Cardinals. The league also tried to trump the NFL by playing weekday games, an experiment that failed, and they soon had to begin playing on weekends.

Then there was the signing war. The economics of the time were very different from today, but no matter what the dollar figures, a bidding war will always be a financial strain. The first NFL star to sign with the new league was Chicago Bears tackle Lee Artoe, who jumped leagues for $15,000. There were other cross-league signings as well, and the spike in salaries caused by the competition set both leagues back by millions of dollars. All told, some 100 former NFL players joined the AAFC and 44 of the 60 players who participated in the 1946 College All-Star Game signed with the new league. So the AAFC teams were spending a lot of money to improve the product. As it turned out, they were spending too much.

"The men who had signed with the AAFC received all the publicity during the All-Star training camp," said Pat Harder, a rookie who signed with the NFL that year. "It was as if we had two different camps, an NFL camp and an AAFC camp."

So there was a definite divide as the two leagues warred. At this time, the NFL was not significantly more stable than the AAFC. They were nowhere near the level of Major League Baseball, for example, when it came to a smoothly run professional sports league. Still, they had a history and that gave them an advantage. By 1948, postwar fan interest was waning somewhat and a few players were beginning to defect to the NFL. At the same time, a number of AAFC franchises were not in good shape. The Dodgers merged with the Yankees in an attempt to keep one of the teams solvent. The Chicago Rockets were not only a 1-13 team, but on their third owner in three years. They also lost their star halfback, Elroy "Crazylegs" Hirsch, to a fractured skull. The team was then sold again, and the fourth owner changed the name from the Rockets to the Hornets. Then, before the 1949 season began, Hirsch jumped to the NFL Los Angeles Rams because they offered him more money.

Finally, it became apparent that something had to give. The NFL called a meeting and decided they would offer to take three AAFC teams into their league—the Browns, the 49ers, and the Colts. The players from the other teams would be divided among the other NFL teams. The AAFC could fight back no longer and the deal was signed on December 9, 1949. What would the NFL be getting? The Browns and 49ers were the two best AAFC teams and allowed in on that basis. It also didn't hurt that the Browns already had a huge fan base. The Colts were let in because Washington Redskins owner George Preston Marshall felt they would create a natural rivalry with his team. The odd part was that the AAFC on the whole had an average attendance of 38,310 a game, while the NFL was averaging 27,602. But the deal was done and the All-America Football Conference was history.

WHAT REALLY HAPPENED

As soon as the merger was announced, much of the talk centered on the Cleveland Browns. The Browns obviously represented the cream of the AAFC crop, with some even surmising that their total dominance was instrumental in the newer league's demise. There was just not enough competition and the Browns being the annual league champion had become a foregone conclusion. Once the merger was announced, NFL execs and coaches quickly grew very tired of hearing about the Cleveland Browns. The older league had enough of a collective arrogance to believe that while the Browns may have dominated the AAFC, the team shouldn't dare to think they would do it against the big boys of the NFL.

"The worst team in our league could beat the best team in theirs," said Redskins owner George Preston Marshall. Elmer Layden, who was the NFL commissioner when the AAFC was formed, quipped, "What league? Let them get a ball first."

In 1949 Bert Bell had taken over as NFL commissioner, and he decided it would be great to put the Browns to the test immediately. When he drew up the schedule for the 1950 season he penciled in the Browns to open against the NFL's 1949 champions, the Philadelphia Eagles, and he set the game in Philadelphia on September 16, a Saturday night just before the regular schedule of Week 1 Sunday games. It would be a showcase encounter and the time for the Browns to get their comeuppance for all football fans to see.

As the game drew closer, even Eagles coach Earle "Greasy" Neale didn't seem impressed. Of the Browns, he said, "All they do is throw the ball."

At game time, some 71,237 fans were at Philadelphia's Municipal (later JFK) Stadium to watch this epic clash. Pro football had the center stage event it had craved and everyone soon learned that the Browns were more than ready for their debut into the world of so-called big time football.

"For four years, Coach Brown never said a word [about the NFL]," Otto Graham would say. "He just kept putting that stuff on the bulletin board. We were so fired up we would have played them anywhere, anytime, and for a keg of beer or a chocolate milkshake. It didn't matter."

Cleveland still had its great core group of offensive players. In fact, the addition of Dub Jones to team with Speedie and Lavelli gave Graham yet another target, and there wasn't a single running back in the NFL at the time with the power of Marion Motley. Yet when the Eagles scored first on a field goal to make it 3-0, many thought the rout would soon be on. Only they had the wrong team. As soon as the Browns got the ball, Graham went to work.

He completed a couple of short sideline passes to Jones, who promptly came back to the huddle and told his quarterback he was ready. He meant that the man covering him was coming closer and cheating toward the sideline. On the next play he faked the out, then ran straight down the field and was on the receiving end of a 59-yard Graham touchdown pass. Groza's extra point made it 7-3. When the Eagles marched down to the Cleveland six-yard line, Coach Brown sent the 232-pound Motley in at linebacker, where he smothered three straight Philly running backs. Suddenly, the Eagles knew they were in a game.

Graham then proceeded to take the Eagles defense apart. He threw a 26-yard TD pass to Lavelli, and then hit Speedie from 12 yards out to make it 21-3. Two more scores made the final 35-10. The game proved the complete destruction of one of the NFL's best. No one would ever say a negative word about the Cleveland

Browns again. They were too busy trying to find a way to stop them. Coach Brown didn't gloat or say I-told-you-so, but he admitted the game meant a lot.

"It was the highest emotional game I ever coached," he said. "We had four years of constant ridicule to get us ready. I think today we were the best football team I've ever seen."

The Eagles, a team with stars like running back Steve Van Buren, quarterback Tommy Thompson, receiver Pete Pihos and center/linebacker Chuck Bednarik, didn't make excuses. Tackle Bucko Kilroy said, after the game, "Man for man, they were just a better team."

Greasy Neale wasn't as gracious at first. He said, afterward, "[Paul] Brown would have made a better basketball coach because all they do it put the ball in the air."

Just to prove a point, when the two teams met later in the season Paul Brown directed his quarterback to keep it on the ground and they beat the Eagles, 13-7, without completing a single pass. The only pass Graham threw was nullified by a penalty. It took some twenty years or so for the proud Eagles coach to admit what really happened on that September day.

"I knew ten minutes after the game started that we couldn't stop them," Greasy Neale said.

From there, the Browns rolled. They finished the regular season as Eastern Division champs with a 10-2 record and then met the Los Angeles Rams for the NFL title. In a great battle, the Rams led 28-20 at the end of the third quarter. Five minutes into the final quarter, Warren Lahr intercepted a Bob Waterfield pass and the Browns began driving. After converting on two fourth-down plays, Graham hit Rex Bumgardner in the end zone from 19 yards out. The kick made it 28-27. The Browns then got the ball back at their own 32 with just 1:50 left in the game. Graham drove his team downfield and with just 28 seconds remaining, Groza booted a 16-yard field goal to give the Browns the championship, 30-28.

From there, the Browns became something of a dynasty. They won the Eastern Division title six straight years and added two more national titles, ending their run in 1955, when Otto Graham retired. He had quarterbacked his team into ten straight championship games in two leagues, winning seven titles. Years later, he described one of his best assets as a quarterback. "I could throw a pass to a spot as well as anyone who ever lived," he said. "But that's a God-given talent. I could never stand back and flick the ball 60 yards downfield with my wrists like Dan Marino does."

The Cleveland Browns represented the best the AAFC had to offer. The San Francisco 49ers, another team that came into the NFL, wouldn't make a real mark until years later, but was always a solid representative. So when plans were drawn up for a new football league in 1944, it wound up affecting the history of professional football. But it also could have turned out differently.

What if . . .

THE NFL HAD REFUSED TO MERGE?

The eminent scientist, Sir Isaac Newton, once said that every action has an equal and opposite reaction. While sports isn't exactly science, there is some relevance in this old axiom in that if one thing changes, everything that comes next could also change. By absorbing three AAFC teams in 1950, the older league created an action that caused an unexpected and opposite reaction. The Cleveland Browns came in and dominated the NFL, and history went on from there. But if the merger hadn't occurred, if the Cleveland Browns—and the two other AAFC teams—never got the chance to play in the NFL, it certainly would have initiated a sequence of events quite different from those that actually took place.

Let's say the NFL decided to try to break the AAFC financially. The older league had mostly established teams in 1949, with only one weak sister, the New York Bulldogs. Otherwise, the teams are all familiar to longtime football fans: the Eagles, Steelers, Giants, Redskins, Rams, Bears, Cardinals, Lions, and Packers. A couple of them have changed cities, but they all continue to play today. So it isn't inconceivable that the NFL might have felt it best to wait out the struggling league, let it fold, then grab up all the best players to make their league stronger all around. With an improved product that would include the biggest stars from the AAFC, fans would clamor for more football and the NFL could then conduct its own orderly expansion.

Or suppose, instead of dismissing the Browns' dominance with a no-team-can-be-better-than-ours arrogance, a couple of wily football scouts told NFL bigwigs that the Browns were so good they would embarrass the NFL and that they should keep them out as a team at all costs. There certainly could have been an orderly player draft that would get the top AAFC players into the NFL and create a real competition for positions. Again, the NFL would have emerged stronger and could take it from there.

But here's what could have been lost. The Cleveland Browns were a team ahead of their time. The NFL, as a whole, was still focused on running the football rather than throwing it. Paul Brown's innovative passing attack not only befuddled AAFC opponents, but left the Philadelphia Eagles and the rest of the NFL in shock and scrambling to adjust defensively. Many of the NFL quarterbacks threw deep downfield when they passed. Graham worked the sidelines and threw to spots. He admittedly didn't have a cannon for an arm, but he engineered a passing attack that drove defenses nuts. Had he joined another NFL team with a coach who didn't share Paul Brown's philosophy, he might well have been something less of a quarterback and taken several years to adjust. He certainly would not have had ten straight appearances in championship games.

The rest of the Browns' stars may also have had their careers altered. Under Paul Brown, they functioned as a smooth, well-oiled machine. With player dispersal, they would have all had to fit in elsewhere. In some cases it might have worked out as well. Marion Motley, for example, would have been a star fullback on almost any team, unless he joined one with a leaky sieve of an offensive line. But pass receivers Speedie, Lavelli, and Dub Jones were so used to working with Graham that they might not have been the same players with another quarterback.

LOSS OF RIVALRIES

Not having the Cleveland Browns in the NFL would certainly have affected league history in other ways. Even though there were some very good teams in the early 1950s (the Browns actually lost three straight championship games from 1951–53), Cleveland was the benchmark, the team closest to being a dynasty in the early part of the decade when more fans were beginning to notice pro football. Lost would have been the drama of that first game against the Eagles and the first title game with the Rams in 1950, as well as the rivalries that sprang up with the Detroit Lions and the Rams. The Browns would face both of those teams three times in their six title games, and the confrontations were always intense, if not always close. Had it not been for the presence of the Browns, the Western Division Rams and Lions might well have dominated the entire first half of the decade until the Giants rose to prominence in the East. So the Browns helped create a competitive balance between the East and West. As good as the Browns were, both Western Division teams proved worthy adversaries.

But that wasn't all. Project a little further into the future, to 1957, when the Cleveland Browns drafted a running back out of Syracuse University. His name was Jim Brown, and he is still universally regarded as the greatest running back ever to play the game. He averaged 5.2 yards per carry for his nine-year career and never missed a game due to injury. In addition, he gained as many as 1,527 yards in a 12-game season and 1,863 yards in a 14-game season. The Pulitzer Prize–winning sportswriter Red Smith once said, "For mercurial speed, airy nimbleness, and explosive violence in one package of undistilled evil, there is no other like Mr. Brown." By the time Jim Brown joined the Browns, Otto Graham had retired, and the team's offense was now built around its 232-pound fullback, who had the power of Marion Motley but combined it with breakaway speed and the ability to fake any defender out of his boots. He was the complete package, and being with Cleveland in the NFL's Eastern Division, it wasn't long before an intense rivalry developed between the Browns and the New York Giants, a team built around defense and its All-Pro middle linebacker, Sam Huff. Had there been no Cleveland Browns in the NFL and had Jim Brown been drafted by another team, maybe one in the Western Division, he certainly would have still been great, but the rivalry with the Giants and Sam Huff, which is now legendary, wouldn't have existed.

Huff, when talking about his rival, once said, "Jim Brown will tell you I never, ever played a dirty game against him. We never had an argument, never a mean word toward each other. Just a great rivalry, just a great challenge to shut down the great Jim Brown. Likewise, he would like to run over the great Sam Huff. It was always man vs. man, attitude vs. attitude. I loved every minute of it."

Besides the classic individual rivalry, football fans would have missed some classic games between the two teams. In 1958, the Browns came into Yankee Stadium for the final regular season game of the year with the Giants. Cleveland had a 9-2 record and the Giants were at 8-3, which meant that New York had to win this game in order to force a divisional tie and then a playoff. It was a snowy, windy day with the field in terrible condition when the two teams went at it. On the very first play of the game Jim Brown showed off his prowess by running 65 yards on the slippery turf for a touchdown. With conditions worsening, the only other scoring in the first half was an exchange of field goals by Lou Groza of Cleveland and Pat Summerall of the Giants. So the Brown had a 10-3 halftime lead.

It was still 10-3 five minutes into the final quarter. Giants receiver Kyle Rote had told quarterback Charley Conerly he felt the Browns were vulnerable to a halfback option pass and that he could get open. After Jim Brown fumbled on the slippery field, the Giants got the ball at the Cleveland 45 and Conerly flipped the ball to halfback Frank Gifford, who began running right. But he suddenly stopped and threw a perfect pass to Rote, who caught it and ran all the way to the six. On third and goal the Giants ran the same play and this time Gifford hit tight end Bob Schnelker in the end zone. Summerall's point after tied it at 10-10. But there was no suddenly death rule then, and if the game ended in a tie, the Browns would win the division.

It came down to this. With seconds left, Pat Summerall had to try a 49-yard field goal as the snow came down harder and the footing became impossible. The ball was snapped and Summerall stepped into it.

"As soon as I hit it I knew it would be far enough," he said. "But from that distance a ball often has a tendency to float, like a knuckleball. As it passed the ten-yard line, I could see that it was inside the left upright. Then it straightened itself out and was okay."

The kick was good and the Giants won in dramatic fashion, 13-10. A week later their great defense really rose to the occasion and they held Jim Brown to just eight yards rushing, winning the game 10-0 and clinching the Eastern Division championship. If the NFL had not taken the Browns into the league, this game wouldn't have happened. Now the Giants had to meet the Baltimore Colts for the title. Guess what? This classic confrontation would also not have happened if the Colts were not one of the three AAFC teams entering the NFL in 1950.

A GAME FOR THE AGES

The 1958 championship game between the New York Giants and Baltimore Colts is still called "The Greatest Game Ever Played." It's also credited—if one game can claim something this grandiose—as the game that really put the National Football League on the sports map. This was a classic between two outstanding teams and it took place on December 28 at Yankee Stadium. It became the first championship game in NFL history to go into sudden death overtime, and it introduced the football world to the next great quarterback, Baltimore's John Constantine Unitas.

Johnny U. was the guy who rallied his team in the final seconds of regulation to set up a Steve Myhra 20-yard field goal that tied the game at 17-17. In overtime, the Giants had first crack but were forced to punt. Then Unitas went to work again, moving his team downfield with clutch passes and his gunslinger mentality. He brought the ball to the one, then gave it to his fullback, Alan "The Horse" Ameche, who bulled into the end zone for the winning score. The Colts were champs in a game where both teams, as well as pro football, emerged as winners.

Unitas, who completed 26 of 40 passes for 349 yards, said afterward, "When I slapped the ball into Ameche's belly and saw him take off, I knew nobody was going to stop him."

What might have stopped the Colts, however, was the All-America Football Conference. Remember, the Baltimore Colts were one of the three franchises that came into the NFL at the merger. However, they weren't *these* Colts. That franchise was brought in to give the Redskins a regional rival, but they were a terrible team. They had been 1-11 in the final AAFC season of 1949 and were 1-11 their first year in the NFL. Then they folded. Three years later they re-emerged, but it wasn't the same team. The NFL sold the assets of the dying New York Yankees franchise to a Dallas group that renamed the team the Texans and began play in 1952. It didn't last. The team was basically out of business by midseason. The NFL took over the franchise and had them play the remainder of their games on the road. After the season they reinstated the franchise with a new owner and put them back in Baltimore as the second incarnation of the Colts.

John Unitas had played his college ball at Louisville and was then drafted in the ninth round by the Steelers in 1955. He didn't impress the coaches and was cut, working construction in Pittsburgh and playing semipro for the Bloomfield Rams, getting the grand sum of six dollars a game. The Colts subsequently invited him to a tryout and he made the team. Then, when starter George Shaw broke a leg in the fourth game of the season, Unitas got his chance. Two years later he was leading the Colts against the Giants.

But what if . . .

Suppose the original Colts franchise that came from the AAFC hadn't folded. The entire scenario would have been different. The team would have had different coaches and another ownership group, and chances are they wouldn't have called upon semipro QB John Unitas. Or consider yet another scenario. Had the NFL not taken in the three AAFC teams, then Baltimore would not have had a franchise in 1950, and if the league wasn't ready to expand, they wouldn't have had the second franchise in 1953. Once again John Unitas wouldn't have been there and the two teams would not have played their epic title game. There is also no guarantee that Unitas would have made it anywhere. He got his break when the Colts came calling. Who knows if anyone would have called if the Colts were not in Baltimore at the time?

OTHER PLAYERS

John Unitas was not the only player whose career could have been affected by the actions of the NFL and the AAFC. All the great players on the AAFC Cleveland Browns team might have had different careers if they ended up in a dispersal draft. Marion Motley and lineman Bill Willis are both in the Hall of Fame, as are Lou Groza, center Frank Gatski, and defensive lineman Len Ford. Had they played with other teams logic says they would have excelled. But perhaps, in a different setting and needing a period of adjustment, a couple of them would have come up just short when it came to Hall of Fame selection.

Then there is the case of Yelberton Abraham Tittle, aka Y. A. Tittle to football fans. Tittle was a quarterback out of Louisiana State University who was drafted in the first round by the Detroit Lions in 1948. That same year, the Chicago Bears also snagged a quarterback named Bobby Layne out of Texas in the first round. If there had been no All-America Football Conference, Tittle might have joined the Lions and eventually locked up the number one quarterback spot. But because of the growing bidding war between the two leagues he decided to sign with the AAFC Baltimore Colts instead. He took over the starting job early in the season and became the league's Rookie of the Year. Now here's how the careers of both quarterbacks could have been affected if the track of the AAFC had changed.

Y. A. Tittle would remain with the Colts for three years, coming with them when they moved to the NFL in 1950. A year later, when the Colts disbanded, Tittle joined the San Francisco 49ers, where he split the QB chores with first Frankie Albert and later John Brodie. After the 1960 season the Niners decided to go with Brodie and traded Tittle to the Giants, where he promptly led them to three straight Eastern Division titles, becoming the first quarterback ever to throw more than 30 touchdown passes in two consecutive seasons. He was also a two-time NFL Most Valuable Player and his work with the Giants was what punched his ticket to the Hall of Fame.

But if the AAFC had not merged with the NFL and maybe lasted another season or two, Tittle's route to the NFL would have changed. He most likely would have been part of the pool of players who would have been looking for NFL jobs and could have ended up anywhere. Chances are good that he might not have found his way in 1961 to the Giants, for whom he was a perfect fit, replacing an aging quarterback named Charley Conerly. Had that not happened, not only might Tittle not be in the Hall of Fame today, but the Giants might not have made it to those three straight NFL championship games. So if the NFL had not taken in the three AAFC teams, the course of its history would again have been altered.

Where does Bobby Layne come into all this? Layne, as mentioned, was a first-round pick of the Bears in 1948. Two years later he was traded to the Detroit Lions for a defensive end named Bob Mann. Layne then set about creating his legacy as a leader and winner, and a great quarterback. He led the Lions into the NFL title game three times in the 1950s and wound up beating Otto Graham and the Cleveland Browns twice. In fact, a former Packers general manager, Ron Wolf, called this one of the best trades in NFL history. "Layne was a Hall of Fame player who turned the Lions' franchise around," he said.

But wait a minute. Didn't the Lions draft Y. A. Tittle in 1948? Yep, they sure did, but Tittle opted for the AAFC. Had he chosen the Lions or had there been no AAFC, then he might have cemented the quarterbacking job, which would have meant the team didn't have to trade for Bobby Layne. Whether Tittle could have accomplished the same thing in Detroit that Layne did is a matter of conjecture. We'll never really know. Both were great quarterbacks and Hall of Famers. But as you can see, if things were different with the AAFC, then three or more franchises could have been affected—the 49ers, Lions, and Giants. And perhaps any other team that might have had Tittle and Layne had things turned out any differently. It's almost like a domino effect—the action and the opposite reaction.

WHAT ABOUT THE AFL?

In early 1960, just ten short years after the three AAFC teams came into the NFL, another group of wealthy investors announced yet another new league. Led by Texans Lamar Hunt and Bud Adams, both of whom were snubbed by the NFL after efforts to start expansion franchises in Dallas and Houston, this group started the eight-team American Football League, which began play that fall. By now, football fans know the story of this fourth league called the AFL. After some growing pains, the league got a solid television contract, signed some big name players like Joe Namath, gave fans an even more wide-open game, and eventually forced the NFL into a full merger a decade later. Even before the merger, there was a championship game between the two leagues that would become known as the Super Bowl. Professional football, arguably the biggest spectator sport in America today, was finally in full bloom.

But the course of the AFL could have easily been altered if a different road map had been charted by the AAFC. For example, suppose the NFL did not take in the AAFC teams, but the AAFC received a new infusion of money and was able to survive into the mid- or late 1950s. If an eight-team AAFC was thriving and beginning to grow, and the price war for players continued to escalate, there would have to have been an agreement, with a good chance that the entire AAFC would have merged with the NFL. If that happened in 1955 or 1957, for example, it's very doubtful that the AFL could have started so soon after (in 1960). And if the NFL took in an eight-team league in the mid-1950s and then continued to grow and expand, it's doubtful they would have wanted to take in another complete league (the AFL had expanded to ten teams at the time of the merger).

What might have happened, if the AFL had formed in 1960 or even a few years later, is that they could have had a partial merger. Maybe only a handful of AFL teams would have been taken into the NFL, with the others forced to disband. Sound familiar? But again, if the AFL had formed in the 1960s and hadn't merged with the NFL, certain innovations might have taken longer to arrive.

For example, the AFL was the first league to use a stadium clock to keep game time, so fans always knew how much time remained. In the NFL, officials on the field kept the clock. The AFL also installed an optional two-point conversion after touchdowns, put the players' names on the backs of their uniforms, introduced a more wide-open, exciting passing game, and made it a point to sign more African-American players, even scouring small black colleges often neglected by the NFL at the time. All these innovations soon became part of professional football once the merger was announced in 1966.

There's little doubt that these things would have happened eventually. And there's also little doubt that the NFL would be just as large and successful as it is today. But change the history of the All-America Football Conference and the timing might have been different. So would the careers of many players, including some of the best ever, and some great moments in pro football history would either never have occurred or have turned out differently.

Arnie and Jack Who?

First there was Arnie, then there was Jack, and now there is Tiger. Of course, to say that the whole history of professional golf in America can be traced to these three figures is rather simplistic. Golf is a sport with a long and deep-rooted history. But it is also a sport that was once mainly the domain of wealthy people who could afford to join country clubs and play at elite golf courses. Even when the likes of Ben Hogan and Sam Snead were winning tournaments and carving out their legacies, the public at large paid little attention. Prize money was small and many pros had to struggle just to eke out a living by swinging a golf club. Then along came Arnold Palmer, the charismatic Everyman with the gun-slinger mentality. It was Arnie and his huge following, dubbed Arnie's Army, who began putting golf on the map. Shortly afterward Jack Nicklaus arrived, a chubby blond-haired youngster with a ton of talent. He first challenged Palmer, then surpassed him. It was these two golfers who are credited with putting golf on the professional sports map and paving the way for golf to become the multimillion dollar enterprise it is today, and for perhaps the most extraordinary talent ever to pick up a golf club—Tiger Woods.

But what if Arnold Palmer and Jack Nicklaus were just mediocre golfers?

★   ★   ★   ★   ★

It's said that every great athlete needs a great rival to bring out the full extent of his talent. This is especially true in individual sports where performers cannot become immersed within a team. Would Muhammad Ali have had quite the same legacy if not for Joe Frazier? How about Pete Sampras without Andre Agassi, or John McEnroe without Bjorn Borg and Jimmy Connors, or Sugar Ray Leonard without Thomas Hearns? You can go on and on. It's often the rivalry that not only brings out the best in the player, but also piques the interest of the fans, which is why you often hear the names Palmer and Nicklaus mentioned in the same breath.

Arnold Palmer and Jack Nicklaus emerged in the late 1950s and 1960s not only to challenge each other, but to revolutionize the sport of golf and help bring it to the masses. They were helped, of course, by the advent of television and by some other rising stars such as Lee Trevino, Gary Player, and for a brief time, "Champagne" Tony Lema. But it was really Arnie and Jack who transformed the sport and hastened its rise as a spectator sport, a television sport, and a sport that the many new fans suddenly felt they, too, could play. The duo's talent and popularity also led to a rise in prize money and the creation of additional tournaments, as well as making golfers viable as commercial spokesmen and athletes who could lend their names to the valuable merchandising markets.

WHY ARNOLD PALMER?

Arnold Palmer was born in Latrobe, Pennsylvania, on September 10, 1929. His father, Milfred "Deke" Palmer, worked at the Latrobe Country Club for more than fifty years as the golf professional and course superintendent. That gave young Arnie a leg up on the sport from the beginning. He received his first set of golf clubs when he was just four, and by the time he was eleven, he was already caddying at the club and playing well enough to beat the other caddies. As he grew and matured, the broad-shouldered teen had the build of a football player, yet continued to concentrate on golf, the game he had already grown to love. Before long, he was dominating the sport in western Pennsylvania, winning high school championships and then the first of five West Penn Amateur titles by the time he was seventeen.

Subsequently, Palmer attended Wake Forest University, left to spend three years in the Coast Guard, then returned in 1954 and won the U.S. Amateur Championship that year. He turned professional in the fall and by 1955 had joined the pro tour. Proving himself quickly, he won the Canadian Open that year, won twice more in 1956, and the year after that came out on top four times. By that time, people were beginning to take notice of this rugged-looking kid from Pennsylvania who didn't have a classic golf swing, but hit the ball hard and almost never played it safe. With Arnie, it was all or nothing, and his aggressive style soon began attracting more and more fans. Even so, he still needed a big win to make the jump to the upper echelon of his sport. That came in the 1958 Masters, one of golf's four major tournaments. In fact, to some, the Masters is the most prestigious of them all.

Unlike the U.S. Open, which takes place at a different course each year, the Masters is always held at the Augusta National Golf Course in Augusta, Georgia. Palmer, playing with his usual verve, held off a strong field in the '58 tourney while shooting rounds of

70-73-68-73 for a four under par 284 and a one-stroke victory. An eagle on the 13th hole in the final round, when he took a gamble with his second shot and hit the green pin high, helped clinch the victory while showing the large crowd his go-for-broke mentality. For the win, Palmer received the largest purse of his career—$11,250. The two players tied for second received just $4,500, and the following two earned just $1,968. That's one of the things Arnold Palmer would help change. In fact, Palmer wound up the leading money winner for the 1958 season with a total of $42,607.50. Twelve years earlier, in 1946, the great Ben Hogan was the top earner with $42,556.16. If that's all the leading money winner earned—and it hadn't changed much in a dozen years—imagine what the pros who finished down the list earned. Not very much.

ARNIE'S ARMY IS BORN

Once Arnold Palmer began winning tournaments his following grew quickly. It wasn't only that he won, it was more the way he won that suddenly made him the most popular figure on the links. As mentioned earlier, he didn't have a classic golf swing, à la Sam Snead. He sometimes looked more like a weekend duffer. But he always swung hard and hit the ball extremely well, and he was a risk-taker. He didn't think about and calculate the odds of making a particular shot, he just went for it. At the same time, he always wore his emotions on his sleeve. As he followed each shot intently, the gallery could see immediately by the look on his face whether it pleased him or not. Good round or bad, he kept going for it, taking chances and looking to mount a charge when he trailed on the leader board.

Before long, tournament organizers began noticing a new phenomenon. The crowds that followed Palmer around the golf course were much larger and more vocal than those following other golfers. When they continued to come, they were dubbed "Arnie's Army," and they marshaled their forces at every tournament in which their favorite son played. By 1960, Palmer had already won thirteen PGA tournaments, including a second Masters earlier in the year, when he arrived at the Cherry Hills Country Club in Denver for the U.S. Open. That tournament is still talked about today by those who saw it.

After three rounds, Palmer was seven strokes behind the leader, Mike Souchak, who had a 208. Having a bite to eat with some friends before the final round, Palmer said, "I may shoot 65. What would that do?"

"Nothing," said a golf writer at the table. "You're too far back."

Palmer is said to have snapped, "The hell I am. A 65 would give me 280, and 280 wins Opens."

That afternoon, Palmer more than practiced what he preached. On the opening hole he belted a gargantuan, 346-yard drive that rolled within 20 feet of the hole. He got his birdie and then went on to birdie six of the first seven holes. He finished the first nine in just 30 strokes and then shot a 35 on the back nine for his predicted 65. Sure enough, his 280 was good enough to win the tournament. It was a record comeback and solidified his reputation, not only among the admiring throngs of Arnie's Army, but also among golf fans everywhere who would begin following each tourney to see if he'd mount another of his increasingly famous charges.

Though he would win 62 PGA tournaments, the sixth most in history (Tiger Woods having passed him early in 2008), Palmer didn't stay at his peak as long as other golfers. His most productive period was from 1960 to 1963, when he won 29 tournaments. And his seven majors are well below Nicklaus's record of 18, and were won in the span of just six years. But Palmer happened at just the right time, when golf was finally being televised more often and millions of people at home became a de facto part of Arnie's Army.

That still wasn't all. After he won his first Masters in 1958, Palmer became Mark McCormack's first client. McCormack is considered one of the godfathers of sports agents and he saw something special in young Arnold Palmer. He would later say there were five things about the golfer that made him want to represent him. One was that Arnie had a kind of "Brando swagger" about him. Then there was his modest background; he wasn't a kid of privilege. Third was the way he played the game, the go-for-broke mentality of the gunslinger or swashbuckler, something rarely seen in golf at the time. Fourth was the fact that he never seemed to win easily, but was never beaten, either, until the tournament was over. And finally there was his Everyman quality, his affability and easy ways with words. He was friendly to his fans, chatted with the galleries, and was an athlete with whom the common man could identify.

So in a way, it was really the emergence of Arnold Palmer that put professional golf on the map and had more sponsors and corporate entities looking closely at the sport. And then, Arnie suddenly had a rival.

THE NICKLAUS FACTOR

Jack Nicklaus was born on January 21, 1940, which made him eleven years younger than Arnold Palmer. He was introduced to the game by his father at a young age and was a natural, shooting exceptionally well even during his days as a caddy. He attended Ohio State University, where he became a golfing all-American, then won the United States Amateur Championship in 1959, at the age of nineteen. He won it again in 1961 and the year after that turned professional, just as Arnold Palmer was solidifying his reputation as the best and most charismatic golfer on the circuit.

Nicklaus didn't have any of that charisma at first. Whereas Palmer was often described as being built like a blacksmith, the young Nicklaus was quite chubby, with a bulging belly that earned him the unflattering nickname of "Fat Jack." Later, he would slim down and become universally know as "The Golden Bear" for his shock of blond hair. When he first appeared on the scene he was, in all aspects, the anti-Palmer. Shy, overweight, yet clinical in his approach and with a textbook-perfect swing, young Nicklaus soon showed he could really play the game. The first year he turned pro, 1962, the inexorable link with Arnold Palmer was forged.

Their first showdown came at the U.S. Open, which was played that year at the Oakmont Country Club in Oakmont, Pennsylvania. Palmer had won his third Masters in April and was the favorite, among both the odds makers and the fans. The tournament turned out to be a golf fan's (and television audience's) dream. At the end of three rounds, Palmer (who was tied for the lead) led Nicklaus by two strokes. During the third round the gallery swelled to 24,492 fans, the largest gallery in the history of the Open. And in the final round, the golfers—king and heir apparent—waged a real duel down the stretch.

Nicklaus finally drew even with Palmer after 67 holes. With five holes remaining, both golfers had par the rest of the way and each missed a birdie putt on the 18th green. So after 72 holes, they were tied at 283 and that meant a head-to-head, 18-hole playoff the next day. It was high drama for a sport that was known for its gentlemanly conduct.

With Arnie's Army cheering for their hero on every shot, it was the young Jack Nicklaus who took a one-stroke lead on the opening hole, then opened it up to a four-stroke advantage after six. Palmer was unable to mount a charge and shot a 74. Nicklaus came in at 71 and was the U.S. Open Champion. The King had been beaten but a rivalry was born. Always one to tell it as he saw it, Arnie said, when the tournament ended, "Now that the big guy's out of the cage, everybody better run for cover."

Palmer's opinion of their rivalry boiled down to a very basic analysis, but an accurate one, and it is one of the reasons their rivalry was so intriguing. "Jack navigates more by brain," Palmer said. "I go more by heart. Intellect versus instinct. Jack versus Arnie."

Jack Nicklaus would have a long, distinguished, record-breaking career. He would win a record 18 majors, the last coming in 1986 when he would take his sixth Masters title at the age of 46. He is now widely regarded (with Tiger Woods already nipping at his heels) as the greatest golfer in history. Perhaps his most important contribution to the game was coming along at just the right time to join with Arnold Palmer at a point where golf was just beginning to show up on the sports map. Arnie and Jack—with a little help from their friends—were the two guys who really made it happen. They were both outstanding golfers who would continue to be national celebrities well into their senior years. But what might have happened if Palmer and Nicklaus didn't have the mantle of greatness from the beginning? What if they were just solid, but not spectacular, pros who won only occasionally?

COULD ANYONE HAVE TAKEN THEIR PLACE?

Both Arnold Palmer and Jack Nicklaus were the perfect duo coming together at just the right time and not only creating a great rivalry, but also an interesting contrast that made it easy for fans to take sides and not so easy to debate—at least in the early years—who was the better golfer. Palmer was Everyman—with a hint of danger about him, and he played that way, challenging the course, himself, and other golfers to come get him. Nicklaus was the pudgy kid who looked like he ate too much and had been pampered, but he had the perfect golf swing, hit the ball longer than anyone, and still had a feathery touch on the greens. He was a technician, and right from the start Nicklaus showed he would be one of the best. He was reserved, at least at first, a bit shy and always self-effacing. Palmer, on the other hand, was friendly and outgoing, his emotions always on his sleeve, playing to and interacting with the galleries. He even had a unique way of hitching his pants as he walked up the fairway or prepared to swing.

So it's really no wonder that these two gave their sport a tremendous boost when they came on the scene. Suppose, however, they had the same qualities described above with one big difference. Neither was a particularly great golfer, just middle of the pack pros who won a tournament every couple of years and otherwise scratched for a living as working professionals. Not only would neither have achieved the fame, fortune, and great legacy they have today, but without their emergence, the progress of the entire sport would have been set back for maybe ten years or more, and its pace might well have been slowed for years after that.

As one story put it, "Had Palmer not also been a winner, all his charismatic charm would have been little more than an interesting sidebar to golf." That's true, since sports is all about winning and all the color and personality in the world doesn't matter unless there is talent to match. There were a number of other fine golfers emerging about the same time that Arnie and Jack came on the scene. A couple of them also had unique personalities, but for various reasons, it's doubtful if they could have carried the day in quite the same way.

Probably the most charismatic of the golfers to appear at about the same time as Palmer and Nicklaus was Lee Trevino, known as the "Merry Mex" in honor of his Mexican heritage. Trevino was born in Dallas, Texas, in 1939 and began playing on the PGA Tour in 1967. A self-described golf "hustler," Trevino was especially tough to beat when he went against another golfer head-to-head. But he was pretty good in tournament play, too, and was named Rookie of the Year by *Golf Digest* magazine when he made his debut. Trevino was another guy who would joke with the crowds and always show an exuberant personality.

He was also the winner of six majors, taking the U.S. Open, the British Open, and the PGA title twice each. He never won the Masters, but in 1971 he beat Nicklaus in an 18-hole playoff to take the U.S. Open, after telling people the one-on-one matchup was tailor made for him since he was, at heart, a hustler. It was that kind of playful braggadocio that endeared him to the people. The problem was that Trevino just didn't win often enough. He was a winner only 29 times on the tour and never showed the dominance of Palmer and Nicklaus.

Trevino was still at his peak when he won the PGA title in 1974. A year later, he was struck by lightning while on the course at the Western Open and he suffered back and spine injuries. He later needed surgery to remove a damaged disk from his back and after that was periodically hampered by back problems. Though he continued to play well for another decade or more—he won his second PGA title in 1984—he never quite recaptured his early '70s form and consistency. Without Palmer and Nicklaus, Lee Trevino would have been one of the very top golfers of the day, but without enough of the right stuff to have the same effect on the game.

Then there was Gary Player, the only foreign-born player in the group. Player was born in Johannesburg, South Africa, in 1935 and won the British Open in 1959, the year after Palmer won his first Masters. He took the Masters in '61, the PGA in '62, and his only U.S. Open in '65. So Player, who would win nine majors, was competing on a pretty even field with Palmer and Nicklaus in the early 1960s and then with Jack in the 1970s. In fact, there was a time when the trio was referred to as "The Big Three." Player was quiet and gentlemanly, a consummate sportsman who was very friendly with both Arnie and Jack. They even did a golf show on television together. But without Arnie and Jack, Gary Player would not have raised the bar of U.S. golf the way the other two did.

For one thing, Player spent a great deal of time competing abroad. He won the South African Open 13 times and the Australian Open on seven occasions. His nine majors—two more than Palmer—certainly amount to an outstanding achievement. But he won just 24 times on the PGA Tour because of his commitments around the world. So he wasn't always a regular in the United States and didn't have the kind of personality to grab a crowd and not let go. He was the perfect complement to Palmer and Nicklaus, but without them might have been something less in the eyes of the public. Much of his popularity came on their coattails.

Finally, there was Tony Lema, who is now largely forgotten because his life was tragically cut short. Lema was born in California in 1934, turned pro in 1957, and struggled for his first few years. He began to put it all together in 1962, and on the eve of his first PGA Tour victory at the Orange County Open in October 1962, he told the press corps he'd buy them all champagne if he won. After that, he was forever known as "Champagne" Tony.

Champagne Tony won three tournaments that year, lost out to Nicklaus by a stroke at the 1963 masters, then won the British Open in 1964. He seemed poised to take his place alongside Arnie and Jack as not only a top golfer, but as a charismatic and popular figure. Lema loved playing to both the crowds and the press, and his skills on the links were quickly beginning to make his fun-loving persona more attractive. But it wasn't to be. After the 1966 PGA championship, both Lema and his wife were killed in the crash of a private plane. It was a tragic loss for the Lema family and for golf. In fact, Johnny Miller, who would win a pair of majors in the mid-1970s, said that at the time of his death, Champagne Tony Lema was the most popular golfer on the circuit with the exception of Arnold Palmer.

So the surge in popularity that characterized the PGA Tour and golf throughout the 1960s and beyond was started by the appearance of two men—Arnie and Jack. Had they not arrived when they did, and had they not both won often and become rivals, the ascension of golf as a major spectator and TV sport would definitely have been delayed. There was no one else who could have filled the void if Palmer and Nicklaus had just been mediocre pros. The hottest golf chatter then would probably have gone back a generation and continued to be about Ben Hogan and Slammin' Sammy Snead, the pair who dominated the game before Arnie and Jack, but at a time when golf's popularity was much more limited and television wasn't there to spread the game to the masses.

NO ARNIE'S ARMY

Arnie's Army was unique to golf and somewhat unique to the world of sports. Never before had so many people flocked to see an athlete in an individual sport such as golf, where they had to walk the course with their hero and couldn't just sit in the stands eating hot dogs and drinking beer. It's doubtful that any other golfer at that time could have inspired the kind of huge fan interest that Arnold Palmer did. Had Jack Nicklaus come along without Arnold Palmer preceding him, he might have been just as great in the long run, but there certainly would not have been Jack's Army following his every move.

Just look at the attendance figures from the 1962 U.S. Open, the one in which Jack defeated Arnie in an 18-hole playoff. Not only did the third-round crowd of 24,492 spectators set an attendance record for a single day, but the attendance for the first three days alone was a record 62,300, topping the previous year's mark of 47,975. There's no way of knowing just how many of those fans were members of Arnie's Army, but there's little doubt that it was Palmer who brought a lot of them out because they knew he always had a chance to win. And once he began bucking heads with

Nicklaus, the young challenger, the crowds increased, with the majority still pulling for their hero.

So it's safe to say that had Arnold Palmer been just a mediocre golfer, attendance wouldn't have been nearly as great, and the reason is simple: There would not have been an Arnie's Army, Jack Nicklaus's talent notwithstanding.

THE RIVALRY

As mentioned at the beginning, any great athlete will always shine more brightly if he has a rival, someone who brings out the best in him and allows him to produce memorable moments. Arnie and Jack might have been rivals for a relatively short time, but because the rivalry flared brightly and caught the public's fancy their names will always be thought of in the same breath when it comes to the growth of their sport. Their duel at Oakmont in 1962 was one of those memorable moments and it came at just the right time.

Golf is a sport where rivalries can be difficult because there isn't a lot of match play, and in tournament play anyone can win. If the rivals are tied or very close going into a final round and happen to be playing in the same foursome, then you can have a direct confrontation. An 18-hole playoff is even better, because then the two are side by side, with fans holding their collective breaths on nearly every shot.

But let's face it, if Arnie and Jack had been mediocre there would have been no rivalry and their names would never be mentioned together unless they were on a list of middle-of-the-pack golfers who seemed to be on the PGA Tour forever. It's the same with Tiger Woods today. He's the best and most popular golfer of his time, maybe of all-time, and yet all people are hoping for is a real rival to step up. Phil Mickelson has provided that excitement on occasion, but he's been too inconsistent to regularly challenge Woods, and the fact that the two have yet to develop a full-fledged rivalry has been disappointing to fans and media folk alike.

With Palmer and Nicklaus it happened. Unfortunately, Arnie's prime didn't last nearly as long as Jack's and, in time, the Golden Bear outdistanced him, both in victories and certainly in winning major tournaments. Had the rivalry lasted longer, the sport might have grown even faster. Maybe it was fellow star Lee Trevino who best explained the difference in the two golfers.

"[Jack Nicklaus] was the first to bring in course management," Trevino once said. "He could go to a course and tell you within one stroke what [score] was going to win. He used to set his sights on that because he could shoot it. He was the only player I know who, if he decided he wanted to win a tournament, could go out and do it. No one will ever be as popular as Arnold Palmer and no one will ever come close to Jack as a player."

Not only does that explain the difference, but also why their rivalry was so important to the game and its fans. The golfing world was lucky that the two came along at about the same time and that both were capable of playing sensational golf. Mediocrity would have ended it all before it began.

TELEVISION, PRIZE MONEY, AND THE ARNIE-JACK CONNECTION

If you were to question what would have happened if Arnold Palmer and Jack Nicklaus had just been mediocre golfers, every TV producer, equipment manufacturer, tournament organizer, and corporate merchandiser from those days would probably cringe. Had both men not been outstanding golfers all those entities would have lost a great deal of money. The reason is simple. They all climbed aboard Palmer's broad shoulders and Nicklaus's combination of power and finesse, as well as both their wills to win. All of golf and those associated with it profited by the presence of these two stars.

The irony for years was that, while golf was considered a sport for the wealthy, for people who could afford to join swanky country clubs, those who played it for a living struggled. As Gene Sarazen, a champion from a much earlier era, once said, "The life of a professional golfer is precarious at best. Win, and they carry you to the clubhouse on their shoulders. Lose, and you pay the caddies in the dark."

For years, the guys on the PGA Tour struggled. Many had to work as teaching pros at golf or country clubs and then go out on tour when time and schedule would permit. They couldn't live by just traveling from tournament to tournament full-time. Leading up to his win in the 1958 Masters, Palmer had earned a total of $2,008 in five lesser tournaments that he didn't win. Even back then, when everything was a lot less costly, it was tough to survive on that kind of money, especially if you had a wife and family. Remember, none of the pros flew from tourney to tourney in private jets. They often drove, sometimes two or more carpooling to save a few bucks. They had to pay for food and lodging, and pay their caddies, as well. Winning relatively small amounts of money for finishing back in the pack didn't leave much, if any, after expenses were paid.

Doug Ford, a touring pro who won the 1957 Masters, always traveled in a motor home to keep transportation and living expenses down. That was one way to try to beat the game besides doing it on the golf course.

It all began changing with Arnie and Jack. More spectators meant more money, and the presence of Palmer and Nicklaus drew the people in like a magnet. Higher television ratings mean more advertising money, and these two golfers brought the ratings up. Suddenly, advertisers saw that Arnold Palmer could sell their products. They hired him. Nicklaus, too, then Trevino, and eventually others. Yet Arnold Palmer probably was the main man. Even today, well into his seventies, Arnie still appears as a commercial endorser. He's still known and recognized by everyone, and still extremely popular. Nicklaus has never been as outgoing, but he's just as recognizable and has also had his share of endorsements.

When Jack defeated Arnie in the 1962 Open, the purses were still modest. Palmer was the tour's leading money winner that year with $81,448.33. In 1972, ten years later, Nicklaus was the leading money winner when he pocketed $320,542.26. That's quite a difference. And when the dollar leader is making that much, those behind him are making more, too. The money gradually increased. By 1982, Craig Stadler led in earnings with $446,462. Then it suddenly jumped as the sports explosion continued and athletes everywhere were earning bigger bucks. In 1992, Fred Couples led with $1,344,188, and by 2002, Tiger Woods earned $6,912,625. In 2004, Vijay Singh went over the $10 million mark and Woods did the same thing a year later.

The sky may be the limit now with all the top professionals earning big money, living well, and traveling in style. It would be naïve to say it wouldn't have happened anyway, because all sports have followed a similar ascending dollar curve, but if Arnie and Jack hadn't come along at just the right time, prize money and all that went with it would definitely have been delayed. Without an Arnie's Army to get the ball rolling, television would not have jumped so quickly, and without a guy like Arnold Palmer and his agent showing that golfers could be effective commercial spokesman, that end of the business also would have taken much longer to develop.

THE PRO-AM AND CELEBRITY TOURNAMENTS

Golf has always been a major recreational activity for other celebrities, such as entertainers and politicians, as well as athletes from other sports. Because golfing celebrities loved to rub elbows with the pros, many of them began putting together their own tournaments, beginning in California, where the weather was warm all year round. Bob Hope and Bing Crosby were among the first to organize these events. They were made for television spectaculars, giving viewers a chance to see their favorite celebrities play some golf, as well as the top pros. And in the late 1950s and early 1960s, that meant Arnold Palmer and Jack Nicklaus were leading the way. They were joined by greats of an earlier time like Hogan and Snead, as well as other young pros on the tour. The result of these celebrity Pro-Ams was that many more Americans decided that they also wanted to play golf, and soon more accessible courses were being built around the country.

Others celebrities who had tournaments named after them during this period were Glen Campbell, Jackie Gleason, Andy Williams, Ed McMahon, and Sammy Davis, Jr., and as with every other innovation that moved the sport forward at this time, Arnie and Jack were in the forefront, the most requested and most popular pros, the engines that helped make it all work. Take them out of the equation and the Pro-Am might not have gained the popularity it did at the time.

Once the sport really took off and more corporate sponsors became involved, the celebrity Pro-Am slowly disappeared, replaced by corporate buying rights. By 2006, nearly every PGA Tour event had a corporate sponsor's name instead of a celebrity's or the name of the city in which the event was held.

PERSONAL ACHIEVEMENTS

Arnold Palmer and Jack Nicklaus have remained successful celebrities long after the end of their prime playing careers. Both have designed golf courses, with Nicklaus's company going all over the world. Nicklaus Designs has more than two hundred golf courses to its credit. Palmer remains a busy corporate spokesman, is a skilled and licensed pilot and sits on the boards of a number of corporations.

While Nicklaus still tends to maintain a lower public profile, the fascination with Arnold Palmer has not dimmed throughout the years. He was once described as "a man with a down-to-earth common touch that has made him one of the most popular and accessible public figures in history."

That's quite a tribute but one that undoubtedly would not have been spoken had Palmer not been a star. If he had been a mediocre golfer the public simply would not have had the chance to know him. But Palmer came to the fore, followed by Nicklaus, and they took the entire sport of golf with them.

Trotting to Chicago

There was something new and different when the National Basketball Association prepared for its 1950–51 season. For the first time in the league's brief history, three teams would have a black player on their rosters. It certainly was an important addition.

Baseball had integrated three years earlier, in 1947, when Jackie Robinson opened the season with the Brooklyn Dodgers, but baseball had been all white for more than half a century. Basketball didn't represent quite the same situation and for a number of reasons. For one thing, the court game didn't have the same long history as baseball; basketball leagues had come and gone for years, but nothing was permanent until shortly after the end of World War II. The National Basketball League (NBL) had begun in 1937 and integrated in 1942. The Basketball Association of America (BAA) began in 1946 and slowly absorbed most of the NBL teams. But it wasn't integrated for the first five years of its existence. Finally, the black players began to trickle in.

There was, perhaps, a better way. What if the Harlem Globetrotters had become part of the NBA?

★   ★   ★   ★   ★

The sport of basketball has a long history, though not as long as baseball and football, and certainly not as stable. While the other two sports had standardized rules by the early twentieth century, the court game went through a much longer period of change and flux. Major League Baseball was already set in its two-league format by 1903 and the National Football League was started in 1920, yet a professional basketball league that would profit enough to remain in business didn't begin until 1946, and still had to go through a decade of growing pains before it really stabilized. Basketball certainly can't be called a Johnny-come-lately sport, but it did have to feel its way through more than its share of tough times.

For example, the pros in the 1920s had to barnstorm, looking everywhere for games, playing for several teams at once and earning very little money. The rules changed from arena to arena, if there was a real arena. Sometimes games were played in dancehalls or even in basements. The early backboards could be made of wood or wire mesh, and sometimes there were no backboards at all, just a long pipe with a basket on the end of it. Some courts were open; others were surrounded by a wire cage or by a big net so that the ball couldn't go out of bounds. The rules continued to change and frequently differed from college to professional teams. Partly because of the lack of standardized rules and a standard court, early attempts to form professional leagues never worked. Even in the 1930s, organized league games were played only on weekends because the so-called pros had to work during the week to make a livable wage. They made next to nothing as professional basketball players. Some were even ashamed to admit they played for money, because the pay was so anemic.

As with baseball and football, basketball in its earliest days was divided along racial lines. Blacks rarely played on the same teams with whites, a situation that led to the rise of the two best all-black basketball teams in history. The New York Renaissance Five, known as the Rens, were formed in 1922 by Bob Douglas, who owned the Renaissance Casino Ballroom in Harlem. The home games were actually played on the dance floor at the Casino, and after the game everyone would stay around and dance. But the Rens played legitimate basketball, barnstorming across the country and beating most of the teams they faced.

From 1932 to 1936, they won 473 games and lost 49. In 1933–34 alone they won 127 times, losing just seven, and compiled an incredible 88-game win streak in the middle. Like other barnstorming teams of that era, the Rens sometimes played two or three games in a single day. They had set places to stay in Chicago and Indianapolis, and sometimes traveled 200 miles to get back after a game because they were denied hotel rooms in so many towns and cities. The Rens played a crisp game, with sharp passing and a lot of ball and body movement. They were the equal of any of the white barnstorming teams of the day, such as the Philadelphia SPHAs and Original (New York) Celtics. The Rens had star players like Clarence "Fats" Jenkins, Wee Willie Smith, Bill Yancey, James "Pappy" Ricks, and Charles "Tarzan" Cooper. The team finally disbanded in 1948 and was elected, as a unit, to the Basketball Hall of Fame in 1963.

Then there were the Harlem Globetrotters. The team was organized by twenty-four-year-old Abe Saperstein on the South Side of Chicago in the late 1920s, and originally named the Savoy Big Five after their first home, the Savoy Ballroom. The Savoy was located above a movie theatre and featured dances with some of the best bands of the day. When business declined, the owners decided to put some basketball games in the building to draw new crowds and agreed to sponsor Saperstein's team. Like the Rens, the Savoy Big Five played games before dances, but before long the arrangement soured and Saperstein, without a "home court," began forming another team he intended to take on tour. He called his team the New York Globetrotters and they began play in January 1927.

Soon the team was piling into an old Model T Ford and touring the Midwest. It wasn't until 1930 that the name "Harlem" was added to their moniker. Saperstein apparently decided to use Harlem as their de facto home because that section of Manhattan was widely thought of as the center of African-American culture at the time. He also wanted the team to have more of a mystique, and that was part of his way of "marketing" them. Ironically, the Trotters wouldn't play a single game in Harlem until 1968, but their fame spread long before that.

The first major star on the Trotters was 6'4" Inman Jackson, who was an extremely skilled center and also enjoyed showboating. Once the Trotters began adding comedic routines to their repertoire in 1939, Jackson was the first pivot man to initiate many of the fancy moves that would later be taken over by Reece "Goose" Tatum, then Geese Ausbie and Meadowlark Lemon. The team also always had a ball-handling or dribbling star, perhaps the two most well known being Marques Haynes and Curly Neal. These two elements would always play a central role in every Trotters team through the years—the ace dribbler and the clown and showman in the pivot.

The comedy began almost by accident. During one game in 1939, the Trotters opened up an enormous 112-5 lead over a totally overmatched opponent. Since they had clearly won the game, some of the players began showing off their individual skills and entertaining the audience with feats of ball-handling wizardry. Using their skills, they began improvising comedy routines and the crowd loved it. Seeing the reaction of the fans, Abe Saperstein told his players that any time they could grab a big lead, he would allow the showboating and comedy, and that's how the element of entertainment crept into the team's game and would eventually become its showpiece attraction.

Like the Rens, the Trotters played serious basketball at first and were an extremely competitive team. Like any other kind of business, the Trotters were professionals and Abe Saperstein quickly realized the value of entertaining. With Marques Haynes shouldering the dribbling role and "Goose" Tatum taking care of pivot plays, the Globetrotters became a national and then international attraction in the 1940s. Their comedic routines made people laugh, but in the 1940s and '50s, the Trotters also continued to be one of the most competitive basketball teams in the land.

By that time many collegiate basketball teams were already integrating, with black players slowly finding their way into major programs, mostly in the big cities of the North. Because professional basketball continued to be unorganized and not under any single governing body, there was no "gentlemen's agreement" regarding blacks as there was in baseball. But the Rens and Trotters continued as all-black super teams while most of the other top professional teams remained all white.

THE TOURNAMENTS

With no all-encompassing professional basketball league, it was almost a given that someone would come up with an idea to find and crown a world champion. Leave it to Arch Ward, a sportswriter and later sports editor of the *Chicago Tribune*. Ward first came up with the idea for baseball's annual All-Star Game beginning in 1933, and a year later created football's College All-Star Game, in which top collegians would play the defending National Football League champion. In 1939, he proposed the first World Professional Basketball Tournament, with the best pro teams in the country competing. Naturally both the Rens and Trotters entered, hoping to prove themselves as top teams no matter who the opposition might be.

Not surprisingly, the Rens and Trotters wound up meeting in a semifinal that year. The two clubs fought hard, and in the days of slowdown basketball, there wasn't a lot of scoring, but when the smoke cleared the Rens had come out on top by a 27-23 count. They then moved on to the final where they met the Oshkosh team, champion of what was then called the National Basketball League, a professional league located mostly in the Midwest that had no black players at the time. Maybe that gave the Rens a little more impetus, because they topped Oshkosh, 34-25, to become the tournament's first champions.

A year later it was the Trotters' turn. Once again playing against the cream of the crop, the Trotters avenged their loss to the Rens by beating them, 37-36, in a quarterfinal squeaker. When they reached the finals, they defeated football legend George Halas's Chicago Bruins in a hard-fought overtime game, 31-29. Led by tournament MVP Sonny Boswell, the Trotters followed the Rens as the best in basketball. The question everyone was asking at that time, however, was whether there would ever be one stable professional league where the best players could showcase their talents.

THE NBL INTEGRATES PRO BALL

The National Basketball League began in play 1937, essentially in the Midwest, but began expanding in the 1940s and continued play right through the war years. It wasn't always easy to keep it going and the players didn't make a ton of money, but before long the league began signing some outstanding athletes. In the beginning, the NBL wasn't integrated, but things changed in 1942.

Many of the NBL teams were sponsored by manufacturing companies, which was another way to try to keep franchises solvent. Two of the league teams in 1942–43 were the Toledo Jim White Chevrolets and the Chicago Studebakers. Both had lost players to the war effort and had to fill their rosters. In this case, there was no single pioneer black player, à la Jackie Robinson. There were ten of them. Toledo signed four African-American players and the Studebakers added six. Bill Jones, who played at the University of Toledo, recalled how easy it was when he joined the Jim White Chevrolet team.

"I was already playing professionally prior to signing with Toledo," he said, "but those were independent teams with no league affiliation. There was a better feeling in the NBL—it was a true league. I had played with many of these players before [in college and pro leagues] and we all knew each other. When I got to Toledo, I did not have any problems with fans, teammates, or opponents. Integration was not a big deal because I had already gone through it at the University of Toledo."

Sid Goldberg, who owned the Toledo team, knew he had to sign the black players in order to survive. "I went to the league and told them that I didn't know what they would do, but if they wanted me to stay in [the league] I was going to use blacks," Goldberg recalled. "Some of [the owners] didn't relish it, I suppose, because they thought it would bring problems. But I don't think any of them objected."

In reality, there were few problems. Bill Jones, who had also been with the Trotters, said, "There was never any bench jockeying like in baseball. We never had problems on our own team. Players on the court, for and against, were fine."

Johnny Jordan, the Studebakers' head coach, who also had former Globetrotters on his team, decided to sign them based on their talent rather than need. He said, "There was no strife [on the team].

157

All the blacks were treated well by players and fans. People knew the Globetrotters were great ballplayers. They were well received."

Though the NBL wasn't on par with Major League Baseball, it was nevertheless a professional sports league, one that integrated almost without a whisper. Dick Evans, a white player on the Studebaker team, which is considered by many the first fully integrated team in pro sports, remembers not being criticized or questioned, even by his friends.

"I never remember anybody saying, 'How can you play with those guys?' because we had a lot of respect for them. And people who saw the games thought it was great. [The black players] were just like us. Some good guys and some were wise guys. They were just like we were. I had some good friends [among] the blacks and some I didn't do nothing with. That's normal with any group of people, a church group or a group out of school."

Unfortunately, the Toledo team folded quickly and Chicago folded after the season. That's how unstable the NBL was at the time. A year later, there was only one black player in the league, Willie Smith, a former Ren, who started at center for the Cleveland Chase Brass. Once the war ended and the league began growing again, more black players were offered contracts. Rochester Royals owner Les Harrison signed a former Long Island University star, "Dolly" King, while the Buffalo Bisons (soon to become the Tri-Cities Blackhawks) inked William "Pop" Gates, a star with the Rens. Youngstown followed suit by signing Bill Farrow.

By 1946–47 a second pro league had formed, the Basketball Association of America (BAA) and they began play without a single black player, despite the success the rival NBL had in integrating their league. Apparently, there was some kind of "gentlemen's agreement" in place, at least with some of the new owners. The NBL continued on its course. When Rochester's Les Harrison encouraged Ben Kerner and Danny Biasone to bring expansion teams into the league he also told them of his plan to sign black players. "I said, 'Will you take a chance? We're breaking the color line. Will you accept it?' They both said yes." Kerner's team was Buffalo, which lives on today as the Atlanta Hawks. Biasone brought the Syracuse Nationals, now the Philadelphia 76ers. So the NBL continued to integrate. Only the league wouldn't survive much longer.

HERE COME THE RENS

Perhaps the most liberal achievement of the NBL occurred in the 1948–49 season. By that time, the BAA had absorbed the four best NBL teams—the Fort Wayne Pistons, Rochester Royals, Indianapolis Krautskys, and Minneapolis Lakers. The problem was that while the NBL had the better teams and better players, the BAA was in the larger cities and had the bigger arenas. Then when the NBL Detroit Vagabonds disbanded on December 17, after compiling a dismal 2-17 record, the franchise was awarded to Dayton, Ohio. To finish the season, the NBL brought the New York Renaissance team in to play as the Dayton Rens. Pop Gates was the coach and the team finished at 14-26 for a combined 16-43 mark. In fairness to the Rens, the team had aging players and lacked the size of other teams, but they were competitive and made history as the only all-black franchise in the annals of major league sports.

It was later learned that Bob Douglas, the owner of the Rens, wanted to bring his team into the new BAA as a separate franchise in the fall of 1947. He had the support of close friend Joe Lapchick, the coach of the New York Knicks, but the request was denied. So the Rens finished the next year in Dayton and finally disbanded after many successful, history-making seasons.

As for the NBL, it also folded after the 1948–49 season. The remaining six teams were absorbed into the BAA which, at the beginning of the 1949–50 season, was renamed the National Basketball Association. And in its first season it was still an all-white league.

THE COLOR LINE FALLS

The all-white credo didn't last long. Things changed on April 25, 1950, at the NBA draft in Chicago. After the teams had completed the first round and began choosing a second time, it was finally the Boston Celtics' turn. Owner Walter Brown had a quick conference with his thirty-two-year-old coach, Arnold "Red" Auerbach, then stepped to the podium and announced: "Boston takes Charles Cooper of Duquesne."

Chuck Cooper was an All-American forward who just happened to be black. Someone quickly asked Brown if he was aware of that fact and the Celtics' owner snapped, "I don't give a damn if he's striped, plaid, or polka-dot. Boston takes Chuck Cooper of Duquesne."

That wasn't the end of it. Seven rounds later the Washington Capitols selected Earl Lloyd out of West Virginia State, an all-black school. That summer, the New York Knicks bought the contract of Nat "Sweetwater" Clifton from the Harlem Globetrotters. So when the 1950–51 NBA season started, there were three African-American players taking the court in the NBA. Four years after the NFL had integrated, and three years after Major League Baseball, the NBA color line was down, and it would stay down.

In many ways, this was a much easier integration than Jackie Robinson's had been. Sure, there were some incidents at hotels and restaurants in certain cities, but there were few problems among the players. With baseball, many of the players were from the South and had lived with segregation all their lives. The majority of NBA players had come out of collegiate programs, many of which were already integrated, and most of the whites and blacks had played against each other in pickup games and other venues. The integration of the NBA was once described as "an under-the-radar" process that ultimately proved every bit as important as Jackie Robinson's debut with the Brooklyn Dodgers. Perhaps the reason it took the extra years was simply a kind of malaise, not enough people speaking up and standing up. That feeling may best be explained by a comment made by Fred Scolari, who was a guard with the Washington Capitals in the NBA's inaugural season of 1949–50, when there were still no black players. Scolari was once asked if any of the white players noticed.

"We should have," he said. "The talk always came this way. The Minneapolis Lakers would play the Globetrotters in a series every year, and we would watch the game and then question whether those kids would be good enough to play in the league. I played against a guy in a Denver AAU [Amateur Athletic Union] tournament, a fella named [Ermer] Robinson, a great, great player who eventually played with the Globetrotters because he couldn't come in the league, I guess. I played against him and he was certainly good enough to play. Eventually, Sweetwater Clifton proved it, and you could look around now. But you look back on things and wonder, 'How did that ever happen?' But it did."

As of 1950–51, it had finally ended. The black players didn't come flooding in during the early years of the 1950s. It was more of an increasing trickle. Some even claim there was an unspoken quota system in place for a while. It wasn't until the later '50s and early '60s when a rush of talented players (Maurice Stokes, Elgin Baylor, Bill Russell, Wilt Chamberlain, Oscar Robertson, Walt Bellamy, and others) came in and began to transform the game. But there may have been a way to hasten the integration of the NBA while improving the product at the same time. That way involved the Harlem Globetrotters.

What if . . .

THE TROTTERS WERE ALWAYS THERE?

If one person was taken aback when the NBA originally drafted Chuck Cooper and Earl Lloyd it was Abe Saperstein, the owner of the Harlem Globetrotters. In fact, Eddie Gottlieb, the coach of the Philadelphia Warriors and a friend of Saperstein, said immediately upon hearing the Celtics call out Chuck Cooper's name, "Uh-oh, Abe's gonna go crazy."

It wasn't that Saperstein didn't want to see the NBA integrated. Rather, ever the businessman, he was protecting hearth and home. The Globetrotters by that time had become the biggest draw in the business, with fans flocking not only to see their talent, but their comedy routines. In fact, for years the NBA would use them in doubleheaders, even into the 1960s, allowing them to play an exhibition game before the NBA contest to hype the gate. No wonder Saperstein wanted a monopoly on the top black talent.

The Trotters had already beaten the Minneapolis Lakers twice, in February 1948 and again in February 1949. The first time the score was 61-59, and the second time 49-45. The Lakers were the best team in the NBA by then and had 6'10" George Mikan, the NBA's first great big man, at center. Minneapolis would win the next five contests between the teams, from 1940 to 1952, and one more in 1958, but there was little doubt that the Trotters could play with them. In fact, after their first meeting, Lakers general manager Max Winter said, "Little did we realize that it would turn out to be one of the most memorable basketball games of all time."

That it was, with the Trotters' Ermer Robinson hitting a buzzer-beater for the winning basket. At that point, it would have been interesting if someone in the NBA hierarchy had a bright idea: Why not try to bring the Trotters into the league as a franchise, put them into a big city like Chicago, and let the crowds come? Their drawing power was enormous, they played solid basketball, and whenever they had a big enough lead they could take to entertaining the fans with their great ball-handling wizardry. It would seem the perfect marriage for a still-young league looking to make its mark and one that had just taken the important step of welcoming black players. Plus, in 1950–51, there was no NBA franchise in Chicago.

Could this have worked and, if so, what would it have meant to the Trotters, the NBA, the game of basketball, and other black players? It's an intriguing question, and there was precedent for such move. The New York Rens had become the Dayton Rens for the final part of the 1948–49 NBL season and it didn't cause a major uproar. If, just two or three years later, the NBA reached out to the Globetrotters, they could have easily pointed to the acceptance of the Rens in the NBL. So for argument's sake, suppose the details were worked out and in 1950–51, the NBA added a team in the Western Division, the Chicago Globetrotters. The Trotters had started out in Chicago, so in essence they would be coming home. They'd also have a major arena waiting, the Chicago Stadium, which was built in 1929 and could hold between eighteen to twenty thousand fans for basketball, depending on how many standees were allowed. With the Trotters' popularity, putting them in the Chicago Stadium and immediately creating rivalries with the two top division teams, Minneapolis and Rochester, could have created a real showcase for the fledgling NBA.

THE SAPERSTEIN FACTOR

Dealing with Abe Saperstein might have been the biggest obstacle to bringing the Trotters into the NBA. He was a businessman and a good one, and if he figured his team could make more money by traveling and entertaining fans, and just helping to hype the NBA gate in doubleheaders, he might have refused any offer. The NBA might well have had to make a special arrangement with Saperstein, maybe giving his team a percentage of the gate over the average league attendance. For example, if the average league attendance was 8,500 fans then, but Trotters games drew 11,300, the team would have received a percentage of the 2,800 fan differ-ence. Perhaps there could simply have been a special arrangement with the gate at Chicago Stadium. In any case, Saperstein most likely would have driven a hard bargain.

Saperstein undoubtedly would have had some other questions, as well. For example, if the Trotters became an NBA team they would have to participate in the NBA draft, meaning Saperstein could no longer sign players independently. So if he saw a player he thought would be a perfect Globetrotter, there would be no guar-antee he could get him, especially since the league had now inte-grated. And that would beg another question. How long would it be before writers, fans, even other league members would clamor for the Globetrotters to begin drafting white players? Otherwise, they could be accused of reverse discrimination. If, indeed, the Trot-ters did begin drafting white players, the team would lose some-thing of its identity and eventually become just another NBA team.

Saperstein would have had to decide what to do if he ever pulled his team out of the league and began traveling again. One possible solution would have been to create an "alternate" Harlem Globetrotters team that could barnstorm and entertain fans while leaving the Chicago Trotters (with the "Globe" out of the name) to play in the NBA. From a business standpoint, Saperstein would then have both an NBA franchise and a popular barnstorming team to entertain. In other words, he'd have the best of both worlds. And that would also solve the problem of the draft. There would be no reason to keep the NBA Trotters an all-black team.

FAN AND PLAYER ACCEPTANCE

Having the Globetrotters accepted as an NBA franchise probably would not have been a problem. For starters, the team would have been extremely competitive. Their games against the Lakers attest to that. George Mikan, for one, obviously admired the Trotters as basketball players and would have relished the challenge of meeting them on a regular basis.

"There was no clowning around when we played," Mikan said. "[Saperstein] had an excellent group of guys. They had Marques Haynes, who could dribble the ball. Goose Tatum, who was quite proficient as a pivot man. Babe Pressley, who guarded me, and a guy named Ermer Robinson who made the shot that beat us in 1948. There was a lot of cheering from both sides and that was quite a day for everyone."

Marques Haynes echoed Mikan's comments about the talent level of the team. "All [the Globetrotters] were great talents and proved their abilities against the NBA teams, including the Lakers. We beat them a number of times and, of course, they beat us. During those years we had the best talent in the world when it comes to black players."

So mutual respect on the court wouldn't have been a problem, and real basketball fans would have appreciated the game the Trotters brought with them. The lessons learned in the NBL tell us that racial incidents at games would have been almost nonexistent. When the NBA did integrate, the first blacks—Lloyd, Cooper, and Clifton—had no real problems with hecklers and there was little or no racial baiting. It was clearly not the same kind of situation that Jackie Robinson suffered through his first years with the Dodgers. Had the Globetrotters come into the NBA at that time, they would undoubtedly have become immediate fan favorites in Chicago, and because the team originated there in 1926, the players would have been claimed as native sons.

As a bonus, had the Trotters come in as a team, the NBA would have been hailed as the most progressive professional sports league in the country and lauded by civil rights activists who wanted to see the old ways end. So having the Trotters as a franchise could have had some far-reaching implications that would have been felt a long way from the simple dimensions of the basketball court.

Had the NBA made the move and reached an agreement that would have brought the Trotters to Chicago as a new franchise it would have balanced the league. At the time, there were six teams in the East and only five in the West. Though teams would come and go over the next few seasons, and then begin moving to reach larger venues and a larger fan base, the Trotters would have been a huge positive to the NBA of 1950–51.

In fact, if the NBL had been able to survive and had kept the Rens as a franchise, they might also have tried to add the Globetrotters to the mix. Some of the same problems would have existed, such as the demand to integrate the black teams. The NBL is the league that set the precedent for integration, and Bill Jones, who helped integrate the NBL in 1942, always felt a special affinity for the old league.

"I am proud to be a pioneer because of the fellows that I played with," he said. "Very little recognition has been given to the National Basketball League. People have not properly recognized it today. The league was ahead of its time in the integration and utilization of black basketball players."

By staying all-white until the 1950–51 season, the NBA was actually being reactionary in its thinking. Many college basketball teams had already been integrated and the NBL followed suit. In fact, William Himmelman of Nostalgia Sports Research found that seventy-three black players had taken part in mostly white professional basketball leagues before 1950, including those who played in the Chicago World Championship Tournament from 1939 to 1948.

"It's a very impressive, long list," Himmelman said, "and having talked to many in the past, I know how proud they were of it and how upset they were that everyone looks at Cooper and Lloyd as the Jackie Robinsons. They were more the Pumpsie Greens, who was the last of the major league baseball players to integrate a team."

All these things considered, it's almost hard to believe that the NBA and its BAA predecessor that began in 1946 kept blacks out for five years. The color line was destined to fall, because visionaries like Red Auerbach, who was a rookie coach with the Celtics in 1950, were determined to put the best basketball teams they could on the floor. If the NBA had made an effort to get the Globetrotters into the league they could have righted a lot of wrongs very quickly, and it would have worked. The basketball climate was right.

THE TROTTERS AND THE GAME

The game of basketball was very different back in 1950, slower and more deliberate. There was no 24-second clock and the jump shot was still in its infancy. Many players continued to use the old two-hand set shot. Teams moved much more slowly, stalled when they had a lead, and generally kept scores down. Had the Trotters come into the NBA in 1950, they certainly could have hastened the changes in the game that finally came in the later 1950s, and given fans a much more pleasing product.

As it was, the NBA of the early 1950s was a stodgy, slow game and not a good product for the fans, who often got more excitement from watching a college game. Collegiate doubleheaders at Madison Square Garden in New York were often sellouts, while the NBA Knicks had trouble filling the building. The Globetrotters' flair and energy on the court made them attractive to the NBA, since they added the entertainment factor that was sorely lacking from the games. If the team had a permanent home in Chicago, though, the ball-handling wizardry of Marques Haynes and sleight of hand pivot work of Goose Tatum might have indeed helped change the face of the game.

Unless the rules changed, though, even the Trotters would have been stifled. On November 22, 1950, the Lakers and George Mikan met the Fort Wayne Pistons, whose strategy from the outset was obvious: hold the ball as long as you can, and if you stall on the offensive end, then Mikan can't score at the other end. It came down the final seconds when Fort Wayne's Larry Foust made a game-winning basket. Final score: Pistons 19, Lakers 18. It was the lowest-scoring game in league history. What a yawner.

Often, in those days, when a team got the lead they would simply sit on it, stall, and almost force the opposition to commit a foul in trying to get it back. That strategy probably reached its zenith in a 1954 playoff game between the Syracuse Nats and the New York Knicks. When it ended, free throws outnumbered field goals, 75-34. The next year, the 1954–55 season, the league finally wised up and introduced a new rule—the 24-second clock. It was simple. Whenever a team got the ball on offense, they would have 24 seconds to take a shot or lose the ball on a violation.

The rule changed the game. The coach who really jumped on it was Red Auerbach of the Celtics. This was still a couple of years before he would draft center Bill Russell and further change the game, adding artistry to the faster tempo. But once the 24-second clock arrived, Auerbach told his team to run and fast break every chance they had. The result was that the Celtics became the first team in history to average more than 100 points a game (101.4) for the season, six better than the Lakers, who had the most talent in the league.

With the Trotters in the league, those running the NBA might well have seen the need for this rule change sooner. Obviously, the Trotters were great athletes, and besides being outstanding ballplayers, they had their comedy routines, which had sharpened their skills even more. They had speed and quickness, and they worked together extremely well. If they were allowed to run via the 24-second clock there's a good chance they could have dominated the league or at least been easily in the upper echelon. Their style of play could have become a prototype for other teams. Red Auerbach, after all, was already figuring it out. When he drafted Bob Cousy out of Holy Cross in 1950, he found a guard who could do a lot of the same things as Marques Haynes.

Many of the early 1950s team ran set plays, single and double-screens that would free up a shooter. In some ways, setting these screens, or picks, was like the Green Bay Packers' sweep in football. Teams practiced these set plays incessantly, and if executed properly, defenses couldn't stop them from getting a screened shot. Though it took precision execution, it also made for boring, predictable basketball. The Trotters, more than any other team, would have had the ability to freelance and improvise. With the 24-second clock in place to speed up the process, they could have pushed the NBA towards the game that the Celtics eventually developed.

Had the Trotters come into the NBA, the game could have changed in yet another way. Without them, the color line fell in 1950–51, but if they had been in the league and showing the diverse skills that would change the game, chances are more African-American players would have come into the league more quickly. Scouts would have made an effort to check out the black colleges and look for players probably never even considered as NBA prospects—the kind of players that the Harlem Globetrotters would seek and always find all those years.

So while there was little doubt that the NBA was integrating and would continue to integrate, the presence of the Harlem Globetrotters, or Chicago Trotters as they might have been called, would have still made for a huge story. It would have portrayed the young NBA as the most progressive professional league in terms of race relations and set an example for the entire country. The draw of the Trotters also could have sped up the development of the entire league in terms of both a fan base and the style of the game.

On the downside, had Abe Saperstein agreed to allow his team to become part of the NBA, much of the world would have been deprived of seeing the great show that continues to be put on by the Globetrotters to this day. It could have worked both ways if Saperstein had put together a second team, outside of the NBA roster, to carry on the entertainment and comedic side of the Trotters. He might well have decided to do that even if his primary players were locked in to the league schedule. Over the years, there have been copycat teams putting on similar shows. So someone certainly would have taken up the mantle of the Trotters and that tradition would also have continued.

But it really could have worked if enough people thought outside the box. The NBL had shown the way by bringing in the Rens for part of a season and putting them in Dayton. By 1950, the Globetrotters were already a huge attraction and the Rens had disbanded, so they were the logical choice. It's a "What-If" that could have been a plus for everyone—the NBA, the Trotters, professional sports, and, perhaps most importantly, America, by helping to bring the races closer together at a critical time in the country's history.

The Magic Number

Hockey has always been considered one of the big four of team sports, sitting alongside baseball, football, and basketball. In its purest form, it's a beautiful game that requires great skills to play well, and a tough, physical sport not for the faint of heart. It also has a long and colorful history that mirrors those of the other sports. And like baseball, football, and basketball, hockey has expanded in this era of big money. As of 2007, the National Hockey League had 30 teams. Unfortunately, in many ways the sport now lags behind the other three, both in revenue and popularity. It doesn't have a national television contract and in the eyes of many doesn't play well on the small screen. Then there was a disastrous work stoppage in 2004–2005 that wiped out the entire season. Many feel that hockey's rapid expansion has been ill advised and the sport could have been better served by growing more slowly. The NHL is the only league that began expanding by doubling in size in one year, a very ambitious undertaking. Could the sport have more today if it also had less? Could be.

For example, what if the National Hockey League had stopped its expansion at twenty teams?

★   ★   ★   ★   ★

This is a tough case to sell for the simple reason that we're in an era when everything in sports leads to more. Athletes are bigger, faster, stronger, and making more money than ever because there are more teams, more cable television outlets, new stadiums and arenas, higher ticket prices, huge merchandise sales, and all kinds of corporate sponsorships. It would be very difficult today for a league not to expand, to seek new cities and franchises, new ways to bring in additional fans and revenue. That's simply the nature of the modern beast.

As of 2007, Major League Baseball, the National Basketball Association, and the National Hockey League all had 30 franchises, while the National Football League had 32. So the four so-called major sports leagues were all about the same size. In each case, expansion essentially began in the 1960s and continued from there. But the four all did it in different ways, sometimes absorbing part or all of a rival league (the NFL and NBA) or just adding and moving franchises (MLB and the NHL). Baseball, football, and basketball were relatively stable at the time they began their expansions. The one exception to smooth and logical expansion was hockey.

THE ORIGINAL SIX

Here's a bit of the back story. The NHL was originally formed in 1917, and in the early years, franchises came and went, similar to what occurred with the NFL and even the NBA. By 1942, however, the league had stabilized into six teams located in Montreal, Toronto, Boston, New York, Detroit, and Chicago. Hockey, back then, was also essentially a Canadian game, with a very large majority of the players, even those playing in the four American cities, coming from north of the border.

As for the six teams, they all had big stars that diehard fans knew well. The Montreal Canadiens were hockey's equivalent of the New York Yankees, having won more Stanley Cups than any other team. Toronto's Maple Leafs, the other Canadian franchise, were next. Forgetting about the early years, in just the twenty-five seasons between 1942–43 and 1966–67 when there was only a single division of six teams, the Canadiens won ten Cups and the Leafs captured nine. The Detroit Red Wings won five times and the Chicago Black Hawks once, while both the New York Rangers and Boston Bruins failed to capture a single championship. But it was a tight, highly competitive and stable league with loyal fans who knew almost all the players, not only those from their hometown teams, but the opposition's as well.

There was also a great tradition, a mystique that separated hockey from the other sports back then, especially in Canada, where many of the players grew up playing on makeshift outdoor rinks in the winter. Some parents would even flood and freeze their backyards so their kids could skate and practice their stickwork and shooting. The competition was ferocious because everyone knew there was only one National Hockey League and just six teams with available roster spots. So nearly every young boy in Canada at that time hoped he could make one of the teams, still known today as the Original Six.

TRADITION AND TOUGHNESS

There was also a tradition of toughness that, in the eyes of most fans, separated hockey players from other athletes. Back then, none of the players wore helmets unless they were recovering from a head injury. Fans not only knew what the players looked like, but could see their facial expressions and feel their emotions during a game, something that created a real intimacy between fan and player. When the Canadiens' great forward Maurice "Rocket" Richard began one of his patented rushes up ice, it wasn't only his speed and puck-handling skills that turned the fans on. It was the look on his face, his eyes flaring wide open in anticipation and a don't-try-to-stop-me-attitude reflected in his whole demeanor.

Even his opponents knew he was special. Glenn Hall, a Hall of Fame goaltender and one of the best of his generation, has never forgotten the look on the Rocket's face as he would bore in for a shot. "What I remember most about the Rocket were his eyes," Hall said, in later years. "When he came flying toward you with the puck on his stick, his eyes were all lit up, flashing and gleaming like a pinball machine. It was terrifying."

Would anyone say that about Wayne Gretzky, Mario Lemieux, or Sidney Crosby today, guys who maybe played the game with more skill and precision than the Rocket, but not with the same white-hot passion?

Then there was Eddie Shore, a defenseman who started his career with the Regina Capitals of the Western Canada Hockey League in 1924–25. Shore moved on to the league champion Edmonton Eskimos the next year, and when the WCHL folded in 1926 his contract was sold to the Boston Bruins. He scored 12 goals as a rookie, at a time when defensemen rarely scored, and immediately showed he was a different kind of player. Shore was big, tough, and mean and, during a period in which the NHL was still trying to stabilize and find an audience in America, was the right man at the right time.

"In order to succeed, the league needed a superstar of extraordinary dimensions," said the Rangers' Frank Boucher. Eddie Shore turned out to be that man. He's often credited, even today, as the guy who put professional hockey on the American map almost single handedly, and the stories about him are legendary. It's said, for instance, that no one ever hit as hard or was hit harder in return than Eddie Shore.

"He was bruised, head to toe, after every game," recalled Milt Schmidt, who was his teammate with the Bruins for four years. "Everybody was after him. They figured if they could stop Eddie Shore, they could stop the Bruins. Most people [back then] would skate down the side. But Eddie always went down the middle of the ice and people bounced off him like tenpins."

Remarkably, Shore would average 50 to 55 minutes a game on ice, unless he was in the penalty box, and played through almost every kind of injury imaginable. He once had his leg cut so severely by a skate that he took fourteen stitches. Told by a doctor to stay off the leg and not play for several games, Shore was out there the next time the puck dropped, playing his customary 50 minutes. He not only popped all the stitches, but finished the game with his pants soaked in blood. Another time most of his ear was severed in a fight. He not only took the ear to the hospital himself, but refused anesthesia and watched in a mirror as the doctor sewed the ear back on.

Then there was the time he missed the train to Montreal for a game the next night. It was already snowing in Boston but Shore was determined to reach his destination in time for the game. He hired a cab to take him, but when he felt the driver wasn't making good enough time he took the wheel and wound up crashing the cab in what had become a blizzard. He then hiked through the deepening snow and ferocious wind to a farmhouse and persuaded the farmer to hitch up a sleigh to take him to the nearest train station. The trip took Shore twenty-two hours in bitter cold and with no sleep. He arrived an hour before the puck was dropped, played his full shift, and scored the game's only goal. That, in essence, was Eddie Shore.

There are no Eddie Shores today. There really can't be because of the way the game has evolved. Still, stories about Shore and other great early players became part of hockey's folklore, at least until the league began to grow quickly and new teams began springing up in warm-weather climates and other nontraditional hockey sites where the traditions often did not follow.

SUPERSTARS AND ALL KINDS OF NICKNAMES

With just six teams in the NHL for such a long period of time, it's apparent that only the best of the best could make it. Through the 1940s, '50s, and '60s there was a huge influx of superstars that fans flocked to see. And because there were just six teams, every team played the other some fourteen times a year in the days of the 70-game schedule. Fans became almost as familiar with the visiting players as those who played for the home team.

The names of the elite players from that era seem endless: Rocket Richard, his brother Henri, Jean Beliveau, Bernie Geoffrion, Doug Harvey, Jacques Plante, Gordie Howe, Ted Lindsey, Terry Sawchuk, Frank Mahovlich, Tim Horton, Johnny Bower, Glenn Hall, Bobby Hull, Stan Mikita, Tony Esposito, Rod Gilbert, Andy Bathgate, Gump Worsley, Rod Gilbert, Eddie Giacomin, Brad Park, Bobby Orr, Phil Esposito, and many others. The list goes on. The majority are Hall of Famers and part of the game's elite. Each had his own personality, and because they played without helmets and came into all the league's cities so often, the fans knew them all.

They also had classic nicknames, as did most players in the league. It was part of their identification. Maurice Richard, of course, was "The Rocket," and his younger brother, Henri, was "The Pocket Rocket." Bobby Hull was "The Golden Jet." There was "Boom Boom" Geoffrion, "Gump" Worsley, "Terrible" Ted Lindsay, "Cyclone" Taylor, "Punch" Imlach, "Fast Eddie" Giacomin, "Elbows" Nesterenko. Those kinds of nicknames rarely exist today. Sure, they may have been a product of the times, but they also gave the players and the league a strong sense of identification and helped make all those players stand out.

Players also tended to stay together longer, playing not only on the same team, but on the same forward line. The center and two wings could often be identified by the nickname of their line, another element the game no longer has today. For example, in the late 1940s and early '50s, Gordie Howe, Ted Lindsay, and Sid Abel of the Detroit Red Wings were the Production Line. And they produced, finishing 1-2-3 in league scoring in 1949–50. In the early 1960s, the Rangers' Rod Gilbert, Jean Ratelle, and Vic Hadfield were called the GAG Line, which stood for "Goal-A-Game." Chicago's Ken Wharram, Doug Mohns, and Stan Mikita were known as the Scooter Line for their speed, and played together long enough for each to score 20 or more goals in five straight seasons. These were all outstanding players, and because they stayed together, they helped give the game its identity in the years that they played.

PRE-EXPANSION INNOVATIONS

Some of hockey's changes began before expansion. As with other sports, it evolved slowly. There was a time when the great Gordie Howe, still considered by many the greatest player ever, said that getting 20 goals in a season was akin to hitting .300 in baseball. No more; not even close. Rocket Richard was such an explosive scorer that he once notched 50 goals in 50 games. That was the longtime record. Now it's long gone. The game of the 1940s and early '50s was a close-checking, defensive-minded game with scores of 2-1, 3-2, and even 1-0 not that uncommon. Still, the fans loved it.

One major change came in the late 1950s. For years, the blades on all hockey sticks were completely straight. Then, during a European tour of Rangers and Blacks Hawks players, Rangers star Andy Bathgate began experimenting with a curved blade on his stick. He showed the stick to Chicago stars Bobby Hull and Stan Mikita and they both began using it. The curved stick enabled players to shoot harder and made the puck move a bit when it whipped off the end of the curve. They could also control the puck better. Though the NHL eventually put limits on the degree of curve allowed, many players soon used it and scoring immediately picked up. In the hands of a great shooter like Bobby Hull, the curved blade became a real weapon, and for a time, the Golden Jet was the most explosive scorer in hockey.

In 1966–67, the last year before expansion, the Boston Bruins unleashed an eighteen-year-old defenseman on the rest of the league. Hockey fans could tell that Bobby Orr was special the first time they saw him just by the way he glided around the ice, handled himself with older players, and always seemed to be in the right place at the right time. Before long, hockey had perhaps its most innovative player of the last half century. There are no ifs, ands, or buts about it: Bobby Orr changed the game.

Until Orr came along, defensemen stayed at home, on their end of the ice. Their job was to check and defend, stop the opposing forwards from scoring, and when they did get the puck, they would simply look for one of their own forwards and pass it out. Rarely did they venture beyond mid-ice, and they rarely scored. Doug Harvey, considered by many the best defenseman in hockey between the late 1940s and early 1960s, never scored more than 9 goals or had more than 44 assists in a single season. In fact, there were many years in which he had just 3 or 4 goals and maybe 25 assists. Most other defenders played the same way. Then along came Orr.

He was Rookie of the Year and a second-team All-Star his inaugural season, then simply took off. Like most defenseman, Orr could check and defend, and he could take the puck away from forwards better than most. When he got the puck, though, instead of just dumping it off, Orr would rush it up ice with the skill and verve of a Maurice Richard. Once into the opposition's territory, he was as deadly as any forward, and a real sharpshooter. He began scoring unlike any defenseman before him, and he was still quick enough to get back if the other team took possession of the puck.

For six straight seasons beginning in 1969–70, Bobby Orr would score more than 100 points. He led the league in scoring twice, something no other defenseman has ever done, and helped the Bruins win a pair of Stanley Cups. Orr once scored an amazing 46 goals in a season . . . amazing because he was a defenseman. But he scored 37 on two other occasions and 33 on another. He also had 102 assists one year and 139 total points. His career was eventually shortened by a chronic knee problem that required multiple surgeries, but while he was at his peak he showed everyone a new way to play his position, and those who followed would also become more offensive minded than defenders of the past. But no one has ever done it quite like Bobby Orr, a player many still consider the best ever.

Something else occurred beginning in the late 1950s that would have a lasting effect on the game, something good for the players, but not necessarily for the fans. For years, many would say the most dangerous job in sports was that of a hockey goaltender. He would stand in front of the net and have to stop a cold, hard rubber puck that could be propelled at speeds approaching 100 miles per hour. Indeed, there were goaltenders who suffered nervous breakdowns or had to take time off because their nerves were completely shot. They had pads to protect them, a large goaltender's stick, and a catching glove, but for years, their faces were exposed for all to see, and for the puck to hit.

Finally, in 1959, Montreal's all-star goalie Jacques Plante donned a protective mask after taking an Andy Bathgate shot to the cheekbone. Once healed, his coach, Toe Blake, persuaded him to honor tradition and remove the mask, which he did. But the following season he wore it again, and slowly other goaltenders got wise and followed suit. It has now long been standard equipment. The last time a goalie appeared in an NHL game without a mask was Andy Brown in 1973.

It went the same way with helmets. Players traditionally didn't wear them unless protecting an injury. In the 1970s, though, more players began to appear with helmets and then face masks. By 1979–80 the league had passed a rule that all new players had to wear protective helmets. Those who had started in the league without one could finish their careers that way. The last player to appear bareheaded in game was Craig MacTavish, who retired after the 1996–97 season. Another long tradition, part of the old game, was gone, and with it, a great deal of the fans' ability to identify with the players.

EXPANSION

Hockey was already changing when the 1966–67 season began, though the league still consisted of the Original Six teams. By comparison, baseball had already expanded from the longstanding 16 teams to 20, and had plans in place to grow even more. The National Football League was comprised of 15 teams, but already had a merger in place with nine American Football League teams. So, they were in essence a 24-team league and would grow to 26 by the time of the full merger in 1970. The NBA, which had started later than the other leagues (in 1946), had just 10 teams in 1966–67. But they were in two divisions and additional expansion plans were already in place. By 1970 the NBA would grow to 14 teams.

It's no wonder then that the NHL, with a single division of six teams, felt like everybody's little brother. They couldn't even have a championship series between the winners of competing divisions like the other sports. They had to choose a champion among the same six teams that were playing each other repeatedly all season long. At the time, the league also didn't have a network television contract, and there were rumors that the Western Hockey League, considered a minor league, was about to declare itself a major league and demand to play for the Stanley Cup. That led the NHL to undertake its first expansion since the 1920s.

In the 1967–68 season, the NHL took the unprecedented step of doubling in size, adding six teams and putting them together in a separate division. The new teams were the Philadelphia Flyers, St. Louis Blues, Minnesota North Stars, Los Angeles Kings, Oakland Seals, and Pittsburgh Penguins. Each new team was allowed to draft twenty players from the original six franchises. It would take several years for these expansion teams to be competitive, but the league felt they could weather that storm. And they didn't stop there.

The Buffalo Sabres and Vancouver Canucks joined the league in 1970, followed by the Atlanta Flames and New York Islanders between 1972 and 1974. Then the Kansas City Scouts and Washington Capitols joined in 1974. So in just seven short years the NHL had tripled in size, from six to eighteen teams. Part of the reason for the rapid expansion was the formation of a rival league in 1972, the World Hockey Association (WHA). As soon as this maverick league pirated away some top NHL players, like Bobby Hull, and coaxed Gordie Howe out of retirement so he could play alongside two of his sons, the NHL knew it had to continue to grow and put franchises in new places.

Soon, however, there were signs of instability. In 1976–77 the California Seals moved to Cleveland and became the Barons, while the K.C. Scouts were relocated to Colorado, where they were renamed the Rockies. The Barons would last just two years in Cleveland and then would merge with the Minnesota North Stars. When the WHA folded in 1979, four teams—the Quebec Nordiques, Hartford Whalers, Winnipeg Jets, and Edmonton Oilers—were allowed into a growing NHL.

But the addition of more teams, including those from the WHA, didn't give the NHL the stability it needed. The Hartford Whalers would eventually become the Carolina Hurricanes, the Quebec Nordiques morphed into the Colorado Avalanche after the Colorado Rockies became the New Jersey Devils, and the Winnipeg Jets would wind up as the Phoenix Coyotes. Then, after a fairly stable period in the 1980s, the league went expansion crazy again, adding nine more franchises over a ten-year period. Teams coming in included the San Jose Sharks in 1991, then the Ottawa Senators and Tampa Bay Lightning in 1992. Also in 1992, the Minnesota North Stars relocated to Texas as the Dallas Stars. The Mighty Ducks of Anaheim joined in 1993, along with the Florida Panthers. Next came the Nashville Predators in 1998 and the Atlanta Thrashers in '99, followed by the Minnesota Wild and Columbus Blue Jackets in 2000. There were the 30 teams, but it wasn't an easy expansion.

What did it all mean to this old, tradition-filled sport, this ice sport that thrived in cold weather suddenly having franchises in Florida, California, Dallas, and Phoenix? Did the NHL, in its haste to keep up with the growth patterns of the other major sports, grow too quickly and without thinking about the final consequences? Though NBC does air a Game of the Week and a substantial amount of the Stanley Cup Playoffs, the sport is still lacking a meaningful network television contract right now. And how many of the league's long-standing traditions have been lost? What if NHL expansion had gone a bit more slowly and paid a bit more homage to the Original Six?

THE TALENT POOL WOULD BE BETTER

By 1997, the NHL had already expanded to 26 teams. The league had two reigning superstars slowly coming to the ends of their careers—Wayne Gretzky and Mario Lemieux—great scorers considered among the best that ever played. There were already concerns that the rapid expansion had diluted the talent pool and made the product something less than it had been.

"I do not think the current talent pool is capable of supporting four more teams," said Craig Button, director of scouting for the Minnesota North Stars. He was looking then at the NHL's inpending continued expansion to 30 teams. "To fill these rosters, it's not going to be done by bringing in high-quality people. I think the league will remain competitive, but the competition will be at a different skill level."

Another who echoed the same feeling was Jimmy Devellano, who was senior vice president for hockey operations with the Detroit Red Wings. "When the league went from 21 teams to 26 (from 1990 to 1993), it was the European market that allowed us to expand. We're not going to get very many more players from there than we already are."

European players began coming years before. They came from the Scandinavian countries, then Eastern Europe, and finally from Russia. Many of them could certainly play the game well. There were those who felt that while many of these foreign players contributed to the game, they also took away some of the traditional identification. Many didn't speak English (or French as in parts of Canada), and it was often difficult to pronounce their names. If they played great hockey and helped their teams win, they were certainly cheered. But it also made it easier for some fans to turn away if their teams weren't winning.

Craig Button felt that the Russian pool was also shrinking. "There are 275 million people in Russia," Button said, "and there are just 40,000 kids 18 and under playing organized hockey there. But when it was the Soviet Union, they produced some of the world's best players. They had an incredible sports system that took kids at a young age and said, 'You're going to play hockey,' . . . and they developed them."

The first wave of former Soviet players came to the NHL with outstanding puck-handling techniques and playmaking skills that reminded older fans of an earlier era in the NHL, pre-expansion, when puck control was more important. Today's game has an emphasis on speed, as well-conditioned athletes race up and down the ice, going full out for short shifts, and while there is still plenty of hitting, longtime fans continue to question the overall skill level of the average player and wonder if the game would be played on a higher level if there were fewer teams. More isn't always better.

There are signs that the talent pool is reviving, especially in the United States. In a recent NHL entry draft, a record 30 percent of the players selected were from the United States. And, amazingly, despite competition from baseball, football, basketball, and even tennis, there are more American kids playing hockey than ever before, with over 14,000 youth hockey players in the warm weather of Southern California alone. So this traditionally cold-weather sport is apparently making inroads in areas where you never have natural ice, but there are enough rinks to support solid youth programs.

Whether the overall talent will catch up with the number of teams is still a question. Remember, when there was just the Original Six, every team in the league had huge stars supported by other very good players, and the teams that had more of them would wind up with the best record. Today, there simply aren't enough of those kinds of stars to go around.

HAS LOSING THE "MYSTIQUE" HURT?

It's apparent that nothing stays the same in sports. Things change, the game evolves, the equipment gets better, there are new rules designed to spark fan interest, and there is a continuing flow of players with the hope that there will be enough of those special few that make people want to see them in person. As mentioned earlier, hockey always had a special mystique, maybe because it was a small league with a great many colorful and talented players. Here's how longtime hockey writer Red Fisher of the Montreal *Gazette* put it some years ago. Fisher began covering hockey and the Montreal Canadiens way back in 1955.

"The mystique is gone," he said. "I don't see the mystique. I don't feel the mystique. After all, the Rocket and the Pocket and Beliveau and Geoffrion and Moore and Harvey and Plante and Dryden and so on, they've retired. The mystique simply disappeared into the mist in the 1980s."

Fisher, of course, was referring to the beloved Montreal Canadien teams that dominated the NHL for so many years. There are, however, more people who feel that the further the Original Six recede into history the more the special mystique of the game will be lost. Some league officials believe that everything today hinges on marketing and that history doesn't really matter. But just as a love of baseball is often passed down from generation to generation, the old time hockey fan will tell his son, daughter, niece, and nephew, and then even his grandchildren about the game he knew and what it was like, and that should mean something.

Former goaltender turned analyst Glenn Healy, who played for both the Rangers and Toronto Maple Leafs in the 1990s, feels the tradition of the Original Six should be maintained.

"They're an essential fabric of the league," Healy said. "The better the Original Six teams do, the better the league does. That's the reality. When [the Rangers] won the Cup in 1994, there were three generations of Ranger fans waiting to see a Stanley Cup. It mattered to those fans whether we won a Cup."

Peter Chiarelli, who became the general manager of the Boston Bruins after starting out with the Ottawa Senators, said he felt something special in coming to an Original Six city. "There is definitely something special about [the Original Six teams]," he said. "You can feel how deep-rooted the history is. It's quite powerful."

He also felt there was a correlation between the health of the Six and the overall health of the league. "Those teams are the first building blocks and it's important to have those initial blocks stable and sturdy and steady," he said.

The Six certainly don't dominate anymore. The last to win a Stanley Cup were the Detroit Red Wings in 2001–2002. Before that, the Rangers won in 1993–94, their first since 1940, and the Canadiens last won in 1992–93. Otherwise, it has been expansion teams who have hoisted the Cup recently. The Bruins haven't won since 1971–72; the Maple Leafs not since 1966–67; and the Blacks Hawks haven't taken home the hardware since 1960–61. It is parity? Most likely. Dynasties are hard to come by these days, and the problems in Boston and Chicago have resulted in a fan drop-off. Detroit is also having problems because of the overall economy of the city and surrounding area. So in that sense, not all of the Original Six are strong and sturdy.

Another Hall of Fame player, Mike Gartner, who saw time with both the Rangers and Leafs, believes that the Original Six can still contribute their particular mystique to the league.

"All of them carry something the other teams can never get—and that's tradition," Gartner said. "That can be both a positive thing for their franchise to build on and it can be an anchor around their neck when things don't go well."

Could the loss of this mystique have been averted? It's difficult when a league goes from six teams to thirty teams so quickly. The only thing that might have kept some of this mystique in the NHL was a slower and more controlled expansion. If the NHL, as it came into a new city, took the time to acquaint the fans with the traditions of the sport and of the Original Six, then some of the old mystique may have been retained and possibly transferred to the new franchises. The new venues should have been chosen carefully, with the fan base educated before the team actually arrived. The league should have made sure it was stable at 12 teams before moving on to 14 or 16, and it probably should have stopped at 20 to maximize talent, demand, and exposure.

Still, it's hard to ignore some of the financial considerations that made rapid expansion attractive. That's another fact of life in modern sports. Back in 1997, when the league was going through its final rapid expansion, each new team had to pay an estimated $75 million just to join the league. Adding just two teams to the already existing 26 at the time would give each team about $5.7 million. That kind of money could go a long way toward paying and keeping top stars, which probably made expansion difficult to resist.

The call for newer and larger arenas also cost the league tradition and mystique. The Montreal Forum may well have been the most famous hockey arena in the world, and it was closed on March 11, 1996. Also gone are the Olympia in Detroit, Chicago Stadium, the Boston Garden, and the old Madison Square Garden in New York. Of the arenas that housed the Original Six during their heyday, only Maple Leaf Gardens in Toronto remains. In most cases, the newer arenas lack the intimacy of their predecessors as well as the memories and traditions. In other words—the mystique.

Even current NHL Commissioner Gary Bettman acknowledges there was something special about the days of the Original Six. "I think that this is a game so steeped in history and tradition and has such a strong culture, there is always this special status, star quality, that those teams have throughout the league among hockey fans, no matter how well they're playing. Fans, no matter what market it is, no matter how old or how new, they always want to see an Original Six team."

But the fans can't have a desire to see something they know nothing about. Perhaps more care should have been taken to preserve their legacy. Though there are now six teams throughout Canada, giving fans of this still hockey-crazed country more opportunities to watch their national sport, there is less of the great rivalry that marked the Montreal Canadiens and Toronto Maple Leafs. The two teams simply don't play enough. Perhaps it was former Montreal defenseman Terry Harper who captured best what has been lost when he said, "To me, the Leafs and Canadiens were more than just two hockey teams. It was a way of life. The Canadiens and the Leafs were all that you cared about in the winter."

Now that's mystique.

MARKETING MISTAKES

Even before the lockout of 2004–2005 the NHL was experiencing major problems. The players wanted salaries commensurate with other sports, but many of the teams couldn't afford to pay the freight and there was talk of a salary cap, which the players' union vehemently opposed. The NHL said that its clubs were spending about 76 percent of their gross revenues on players' salaries, which was higher than any other major sport, and that the teams had collectively lost $273 million dollars during the 2002–2003 season. More franchises were losing money and several had already declared bankruptcy. Attendance was down in a number of cities and the league did not have nearly the television revenues of other sports. This was all part and parcel of a rapid expansion.

As one story described the NHL, "The league may be overexpanded, under-financed and poorly marketed." A statement like that doesn't speak of stability. Ironically, hockey had been shown on ESPN, the largest sports network in America, for a time, but after the strike, the league chose a lesser known cable network to air its games. After that, there was the feeling that ESPN wasn't giving the sport equal news time with other sports and, because so many people looked to ESPN for their sports news, the lack of hockey information being put forth was hurting the sport, giving fans the perception that the National Hockey League was no longer viable. Right or wrong, true or false, cases like this pointed up the lack of a strong marketing effort.

Though attendance was bouncing back, as of 2007 there were empty seats in Chicago, New Jersey, Washington, Long Island, St. Louis, and Nashville. There was also the feeling that many people who purchased season tickets were simply not showing up for a lot of the games.

David Carter, the executive director of the University of Southern California's Sports Business Institute, said this about the league in 2007: "The National Hockey League is going to continue to go through peaks and valleys and I don't think it's constructive for anybody to focus on the significant upticks or hand-wring too much over any of the shortcomings. In the macro sense, the league is coming back. In a micro sense, looking market to market, there are certainly challenges."

It is no secret that the league is losing ground in both non-traditional markets and even in some longstanding hockey towns. The Nashville Predators, for example, have a smartly run franchise, an entertaining team, and some exciting young stars. But they're still having trouble filling the arena. It's a nontraditional market where maybe a little more tradition is needed. And even some of the older teams that aren't winning are losing fans.

In early 2007, the Predators hosted the Anaheim Ducks. At the time, Anaheim had the best record in the league and the Predators the second best. But when hockey's two best teams met there were fewer than 12,000 fans paying their way in to see the game.

If it had been Montreal and Toronto back in the '50s or early '60s, or the Rangers and the Bruins, tickets would have been as scarce as people on the moon.

There are some who feel that perhaps up to six NHL teams will be lost in the next decade if the league doesn't do something to right itself. Hockey has worked in some nontraditional, warm-weather markets, but in some ways it's a different game there. A fan in Florida or California or Texas could never empathize with a guy like Eddie Shore walking through a blizzard and asking a farmer to hitch up a sleigh so he could reach Montreal in time to play a hockey game. To those fans, that's a world away. Yet perhaps if those same fans knew more about the old traditions they would come to appreciate having a special game in their own backyards.

If you look closely at some of the league expansion and franchise movement, you have to question the ultimate wisdom of it all. Winnipeg and Quebec City were both expansion teams. Despite playing in Canada, it was decided the franchises weren't working and they were moved to Phoenix and Denver. It worked in Denver, but hockey in the desert hasn't gone over too well. A second team in Minneapolis has worked, but a second team in Atlanta, as well as teams in Nashville and Columbus, are questionable. Some feel that two franchises in Southern California are one too many and that hockey is ultimately not going to fly in Florida. It all smacks of over-expansion, the wrong markets, and the lack of a plan to allow new fans to learn about the grand old traditions that have been the National Hockey League.

COULD IT HAVE WORKED?

There's little doubt that hockey had to expand. Six teams in a single division certainly weren't enough. But it could have been done a lot differently, slower and more carefully, with more attention paid to the great traditions of the game and continued homage to the superstars who helped make the game and the world of the Original Six great.

If the league had gone to eight teams, then ten, it still could have split into two divisions, made the new teams more competitive quickly, and worked to establish the sport in the new cities. And while there certainly must have been pressure for hockey to follow the other sports and become a coast-to-coast league, expansion into warm weather climates should have been studied and explored thoroughly, with the best venues chosen and then prepared for this new sport that was going to be played on ice. The league also should have made sure that with each expansion, the new teams were stable and the entire league viable. There should also have been a way to allow new fans to meet the legends of the game, and maybe even see them skate on the ice—without helmets.

If the league stabilized and was successful with 16 or 20 teams perhaps they should have stopped then and there. The NHL could have been a tighter league and concentrated on having successful franchises in the best cities for the sport they could find. They also could have kept more of the old traditions alive. This doesn't mean not allowing the game to evolve. All sports go through growth and change. But hockey was always a bit different, and that difference is what created the mystique, and that mystique is one of the things that has been lost. That cannot be emphasized too strongly.

On January 1, 2008, the NHL presented a special game. The Buffalo Sabres hosted the Pittsburgh Penguins. What was special was that the game was held outdoors, in Ralph Wilson Stadium, the home of the NFL Buffalo Bills. The rink was set up in the middle of the football field and more than 71,000 fans showed up to watch. When it began snowing midway through the game, the fans loved it even more. This was old time hockey, and many remembered the days they played on outdoor rinks or in backyards, shoveling the snow away so they could skate on the ice beneath it.

If you listen to some of the comments from people at the game you'll get a strong sense of what the NHL has lost during the years.

". . . in Buffalo this game is more than a mere event. It is a celebration of the city, its hockey culture and its Northerness," wrote Erik Brady in *USA Today*. "In much of the USA, hockey doesn't matter. Here, where mothers lace their kids' skates in the dark at dawn on chilly winter mornings, little matters more."

Chuck Maryan, who watched the game on TV from Louisiana, immediately thought of his days growing up in 1960s suburban Buffalo. He remembered stamping down the snow with his brothers and then spraying at least thirty coats of water over it for ten days. They made their own backyard rink and then would skate all day. And when their father hung a floodlight on their basketball hoop, they'd skate much of the night, as well.

"Looking back," Maryan said, "I see now it was really all about family."

Buffalo banker Jon Braun, who went to the game with several family members, also recalled growing up with a backyard rink in the suburbs around the city. He played hockey there and at the houses of friends, who also made rinks. One of them was Kevyn Adams, who now plays for the Chicago Blackhawks and won a Stanley Cup in 2006 with the Carolina Hurricanes. Three years ago Jon Braun moved into a new home and had a backyard rink built to his specifications.

"I wanted my kids to have what I had," he explained.

Steve Champlin, another longtime resident of Buffalo who once worked for the Bills and is now director of football administration for the Indianapolis Colts, remembered playing home-and-home series with neighbors on backyard rinks some forty years ago. He said that backyard rinks were a lot of work, but always a labor of love.

"What I remember," he said, "is how much fun it was—and how cold."

That, in essence, really captures what hockey is and should be. That doesn't mean it can't be played in California or Florida, or any other place that is willing to embrace the sport and its traditions. A smaller, tighter National Hockey League with the great traditions intact would probably have been more successful and ultimately more profitable. It was really too much, too soon.

The NHL could have done it better.

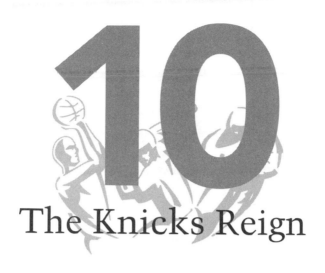

The Knicks Reign

The 1969–70 season was special for the National Basketball Association, and for good reason. The great Bill Russell had retired at the end of the previous year, thus ending the amazing run of the Boston Celtics. With Russell at center, the Celts had won an incredible eleven championships in thirteen seasons, making them arguably the greatest dynasty in the history of sports. Now, the league would crown a new champion. The question was, Which team would rise to the top? When the smoke cleared everyone had the answer. It was the New York Knickerbockers, one of the NBA's original teams, claiming their first title. And in winning, the Knicks unveiled a very different game from the one the Celtics and Russell had employed all those years. It was a game based on an amazing exhibition of teamwork, intelligent basketball, and defense. At the hub of the attack was a burly center out of Grambling by the name of Willis Reed. But he had plenty of help—from Clyde, Dollar Bill, Jazzy Cazzie, Fall Back Baby, and DeB. What they had in common with the Celtics was the first name of their coach. The Celts had Red Auerbach and the Knicks had Red Holzman. However, this great team would not become the next NBA dynasty.

But what if a healthy Willis Reed had led the Knicks to four more titles?

★   ★   ★   ★   ★

The National Basketball Association was still in the process of growing up when Bill Russell came along. The Boston Celtics drafted the 6'9" center out of the University of San Francisco prior to 1956–57 season. Russell, who had led the Dons to a pair of NCAA championships, would show the rest of the NBA and basketball fans everywhere something they had never seen before. The man with the vision to draft Russell was Celtics coach Red Auerbach. Auerbach never liked the slow, deliberate game of the early NBA, which had started as the Basketball Association of America (BAA) only ten years earlier in 1946. It was a game of get a lead, stall, and foul . . . and it was dull. When Auerbach drafted the speedy Bob Cousy out of Holy Cross before the 1950–51 season, he knew he wanted his teams to run, contrary to the general league philosophy. Then once the league adopted the 24-second rule in 1954–55, nothing could stop the Celtics, especially when Auerbach saw Bill Russell as the final piece to the puzzle.

Russell was a defensive and rebounding machine. He would block shots—often flicking the ball to a teammate instead of just smacking it away for effect—and when he got a rebound, he would immediately look for the outlet pass to start a fast break. With the ball-handling and passing ability of Cousy to trigger that break, the Celtics immediately became lethal. Russell joined them after leading the United States Olympic basketball team to a gold medal in the 1956 Games, and the following spring, the Celtics won their first championship. They lost in the finals to the St. Louis Hawks the next year, when Russell was hurt, but then won in ten of the next eleven years—including eight in a row—losing only when Wilt Chamberlain and his Philadelphia 76ers managed to top them in 1966–67.

By the 1968–69 season, Bill Russell was aging and the team finished fourth in the regular season with just 48 wins. But in the playoffs they turned back the clock and beat the Knicks, the 76ers, and finally the Lakers (now with Wilt Chamberlain) in seven games to claim their eleventh title. After it ended, Russell—who was by then also the team's coach—announced his retirement as a player, officially ending an era of domination that hasn't been seen since in any sport. But what next?

THE GAME OF THE LATE '60s

By the latter part of the decade, the lessons of the Celtics hadn't gone unnoticed. In addition, there were more talented players coming into the league who could effectively play the running and free-lance game. It was a talent parade that began in the late 1950s, with players like Elgin Baylor, Oscar Robertson, Jerry West, Hal Greer, Lenny Wilkins, John Havlicek, Dave DeBusschere, Gus Johnson, Walt Frazier, Dave Bing, Sam Jones, and many others arriving shortly. It was also an era of great centers. Following Russell, there was Wilt, then Nate Thurmond, Walt Bellamy, Jerry Lucas, Zelmo Beatty, Willis Reed, Wes Unseld, and, in 1969, Lew Alcindor, who would soon become Kareem Abdul-Jabbar. So the players just kept coming and the game kept getting faster.

Yet despite the talent everywhere, no team could beat the Celtics as long as Bill Russell stood tall at center. So after Russell left, there was immediate speculation about which team would claim the title. Would it be the physical Baltimore Bullets, with their run-and-gun, fast-breaking style that featured center Wes Unseld and guard Earl "The Pearl" Monroe? Or would it be the Lakers, with their trio of superstars—Elgin Baylor, Jerry West, and now Wilt? They were two of the likely candidates. There was also curiosity about the most talked about rookie to come along in years, 7'2" Lew Alcindor, who had a storied career at UCLA and would be joining the young Milwaukee Bucks. And then there were the New York Knickerbockers.

One of the NBA's original franchises, the Knicks had never won an NBA title, but had come on strong at the end of the 1968–69 season. Until they were beaten by the more experienced Celtics in the playoffs, there were some who felt the Knicks had become the best team in the league, and with the New Yorkers, there was a real emphasis on the word *team*. Under Coach Red Holzman, the Knicks began playing a game that was not like most others. The question was, could they sustain it from start to finish in 1969–70?

BUILDING A TEAM TO SEE THE BALL

It had already been a frustrating ride for longtime New York hoop fans. The Knicks had won a few division and conference titles in the early 1950s, but could never take home that elusive championship. The '60s had been even worse. The team finished last in the Eastern Division every year from 1960 to 1966, and along the way there were some ignominious defeats. In November of 1960, they were beaten by the Lakers as Elgin Baylor torched them for 71 points. On Christmas Day, the team was destroyed by the Syracuse Nats, 162-100, their worst loss ever. If that wasn't enough, on March 3, 1962, playing on a neutral court in Hershey, Pennsylvania, Wilt Chamberlain and the Philadelphia Warriors beat them, 169-147. What made this high-scoring donnybrook memorable was the performance of the man they called the Big Dipper. All Wilt did that night was set an NBA record by scoring

100 points and, once again, the Knicks found themselves on the wrong side of history.

Things finally began to change in 1964, when the team drafted a 6'9" center out of Grambling named Willis Reed. Though he played for a last place team, Reed was the NBA Rookie of the Year, averaging 19.5 points a game and grabbing 1,175 rebounds. A year later, a trade brought 6'11" center Walt Bellamy to New York. Big Bells had come into the league in 1961–62 and immediately averaged 31.6 points and grabbed 1,500 rebounds for the expansion Chicago Zephyrs. The Knicks' brass envisioned him as the answer to Russell and Chamberlain, and to make room for him, Reed was moved to power forward. They also traded for 6'4" sharp-shooting guard Dick Barnett, and made Princeton All-American Bill Bradley a territorial draft pick. Instead of joining the Knicks, Bradley opted to go to England as a Rhodes Scholar, leaving the team and hoping he'd return in two years. In 1966, their first pick would be All-American Cazzie Russell, who had been a huge star at Michigan and was an explosive scorer.

Despite these changes, the team still wasn't winning, finishing the season at 36-45 and leaving fans wondering if the denizens of Madison Square Garden would ever produce a winner. The team continued to build, however, and in 1967 their first draft choice was 6'4" guard Walt Frazier out of Southern Illinois, who had led his team to the National Invitation Tournament championship. Shortly after the draft, the Knicks received the news that Bill Bradley had decided to play basketball again after finishing his studies and would also be joining the team.

Perhaps the biggest change in 1967 occurred on December 27, when the team's chief scout, Red Holzman, was promoted to head coach. A native New Yorker, Holzman played at City College under the legendary Nat Holman and then joined the Rochester Royals in 1948. He played with the Royals title team of 1951 and eventually became coach of the Milwaukee Hawks, who moved to St. Louis during his tenure. In 1957, after four years at the helm, he was fired, and a year later he began scouting for the Knicks, working with their various head coaches—Fuzzy Levane, Eddie Donovan, and Dick McGuire. Donovan was the man he said was a real mentor.

"Talking to Eddie really helped me," Holzman would say, "I learned a lot from him. We both try to play team defense and team offense. Eddie was always a great defensive coach."

That's the kind of team Holzman wanted. Shortly after he took over, he began preaching his theories in no uncertain terms. At Knicks' practices you could always hear his voice ringing out, "See the ball! See the ball, damn it!" Holzman began working toward installing a pressing defense that he hoped would drive opponents to distraction. Under his guidance, the team won 28 of its final 42 games to finish with a winning mark at 43-39. The rookie Frazier was a bit inconsistent, but in a February game he exploded for 23 points, 15 assists, and 15 rebounds, a classic triple-double, prompting Reed to say, "This was a complete game. One guy accounted for most of our points."

Though still a bit rusty from his two-year layoff, Bradley was glad to be back. "I went to the gym at Oxford and I stood there alone," he said. "When I played basketball there and even when I flew to Italy to play there, I always had the feeling I wasn't playing against the best."

Bradley wanted to test himself in the NBA, but he and the rest of the Knicks got off to a sluggish start in 1968–69, despite the exhortations by Holzman to see the ball and find the open man. The problem, it was felt, was the erratic play of center Bellamy, who could look like the equal of Wilt or Russell one night, and the equal of a third stringer the next. In addition, with Bellamy in the middle, the team wasn't getting all it could out of the talented Reed. There was also a sense they still needed another complementary player, someone to complete the picture. Finally, on December 19, with the team struggling at 6-10, the Knicks pulled off a trade that will forever be remembered as the turning point in franchise history.

In what can be construed as a stroke of genius, the Knicks sent Walt Bellamy and guard Howard Komives to the Detroit Pistons in return for 6'6" forward Dave DeBusschere. The trade did three very important things for the Knicks and for the kind of team Red Holzman wanted to create. For starters, it rid them of Walt Bellamy, who just didn't fit in with Holzman's team concept. Second, Bellamy's exit allowed Willis Reed to move back to center, his natural position.

"Since that trade, I feel like a new person," Reed would admit after the deal was done. He had always considered himself a center. A happier Reed would be an even more productive Reed, and he was the guy who would become the fulcrum of the team's success, the captain.

The final plus coming out of this daring deal was the acquisition of DeBusschere, a hard-working, hard-rebounding, and solid scoring forward who would do the dirty work on defense and whatever else was needed to win.

Drafted by Detroit as a territorial pick out of the University of Detroit in 1962, the athletic DeBusschere was also signed by the Chicago White Sox and actually got to pitch a few games in the major leagues. He kept up the dual career until after the 1965 baseball season, and then gave up the diamond for the hardwood. The season before, the Pistons had made the twenty-four-year-old DeBusschere their player-coach, showing just how much they thought of his basketball acumen as well as his talent. Now he was with the Knicks.

The night after the trade was completed, the Knicks played the Detroit Pistons. With the players already having switched sides, the New Yorkers won the game in a rout, 135-87, the 48-point margin of victory their greatest ever. Within a very short time, Holzman knew he had the team he wanted, and the Knicks began fully playing his game.

WHAT HAPPENED NEXT

By the time the 1969–70 season opened, the Knicks were firing on all cylinders. Holzman had decided that Bradley would fit better in the starting lineup as a small forward playing opposite DeBusschere. Russell, who had been starting while Bradley struggled at guard, was better suited to come off the bench and provide a lift with his scoring ability. Frazier, in his third season, had become one of the best defensive guards in the league, with the ability to pickpocket the ball unexpectedly at almost any time. Barnett was also a better defender than people thought and would often take the opposition's best guard to allow Frazier more time to freelance, disrupt the offense, and go for the steal.

The Knicks were far from the tallest team in the league, but there were few tougher frontcourts than Reed and DeBusschere. Reed had extraordinary strength and was an intimidating presence, while DeBusschere, at 6'6", had no problem mixing it up underneath against taller players. They were both outstanding rebounders. Bradley, though not quite equal to the other two as a defender, was an extremely smart player who always seemed to be in the right place at the right time. This was a team that took great pride in keeping the opposition under 100 points.

Offensively, the Knicks were very balanced and had five different players capable of producing 20-point plus games—Reed, Frazier, DeBusschere, Barnett, and Russell. Bradley never quite became the offensive threat he had been at Princeton, where he once scored 58 points in an NCAA consolation game against Wichita State, but was a tremendous passer who could score when the opportunity was there. Reed could do it under the hoop or put in a soft, left-handed jumper from fifteen to twenty feet out. Frazier was a real surprise. He averaged less than 10 points a game as a rookie but had blossomed into a 20-point per game scorer. He could go to the hoop or pull up and hit the jumper. Barnett had a twisting left-handed jumper in which his body looked like a corkscrew. So confident was he in his shot that he would often let it go and say to his teammates, "Fall back, baby," which told them to get back on defense because his shot was going in. DeBusschere was strong enough to convert offensive rebounds, but could also hit long jump shots from the corner. Russell had the deadly jump shot and was the player most capable of getting "hot" to the point where everything he tossed up went in.

Not only did the Knicks have a balanced attack that embraced Holzman's theories of hitting the open man, they were also unselfish and very smart, to the point where the coach would often listen to DeBusschere and Bradley when it came to dissecting the other team's defense. As soon as the season opened, it became obvious that this team was special. The Knicks came out of the chute like gangbusters, winning their first five before losing to San Francisco. After that, they embarked on what would be a record 18-game winning streak, simply defeating everyone in their path. When they broke the record with a win over the Cincinnati Royals, their record stood at a mind-boggling 23-1.

It was as if the rest of the league couldn't figure them out. They were playing a game unfamiliar to every other team, and they had the players that could execute it. The streak came to an end, as they all do, but the Knicks continued to roll. Halfway through the season, they were 33-8 and raised their record to 57-15 before a 3-7 letdown in the final weeks left then with a division-winning 60-22 mark, four games ahead of fast-closing Milwaukee with Alcindor.

By now, the story of the Knicks' playoff run has become part of NBA lore. They had to open against archrival Baltimore, a team that always played them tough, and it went the full seven games, with the Knicks winning the finale, 127-114. After that, they met the young Milwaukee Bucks and beat them handily, in five games. Then it was on to the championship round against Wilt Chamberlain, Jerry West, Elgin Baylor, and the Los Angeles Lakers. This one turned out to be a classic. The two teams split the first four games and then in the fifth, Willis Reed went down with a leg injury. With DeBusschere helping to contain Chamberlain, the Knicks held their lead and prevailed.

After the game it was revealed that Reed had muscle and ligament damage in his leg and would miss game six. Without Reed's presence, Chamberlain erupted for 45 points and the Lakers won easily, 135-113, setting up the seventh and decisive game at Madison Square Garden. The big question was whether Reed would play. Those who knew the Captain and how seriously he took his role of team leader felt he'd find a way to be there. As the teams took their warm-ups there was no Reed. Finally, he limped out and the Garden crowd erupted in cheers, but as he warmed up it was apparent he was dragging his leg and everyone wondered just how effective he would be.

They didn't have to wait long to find out. The first two times the Knicks came down court Reed stayed outside, got the ball, and hit two straight jumpshots. It lifted the entire team. Those would be the only two hoops Reed would get all night. But defensively he was able to use his bulk and strength to lean just enough on Chamberlain to take him out of his game. DeBusschere again helped contain Chamberlain in addition to scoring 18 points and grabbing 17 rebounds. What they did also allowed Walt Frazier to take over on the offensive end, where he produced one of the all-time clutch games in NBA annals, and one that is sometimes forgotten because of Reed's courageous effort. Frazier, often called Clyde (as in Bonnie and Clyde), went out and scored 36 points, coupling it with 19 assists and his usual defensive brilliance as the Knicks won their first championship ever, 113-99.

Willis Reed and Walt Frazier made the all-NBA First Team after the season. And the two were joined by DeBusschere on the all-NBA Defensive First Team. Reed was also the NBA's Most Valuable Player that season, as well as the All-Star Game MVP and Finals MVP. The Knicks didn't have a starter more than twenty-nine years old and were playing a kind of basketball that simply seemed to confuse other teams, even those who seemingly had more natural talent. In the eyes of many, the Knicks were about to take over from the Celtics and become basketball's next dynasty.

But it didn't happen.

WHAT WENT WRONG

Willis Reed was far from the most talented center in the league. He didn't have Russell's speed or rebounding or shot-blocking ability. The same applied when it came to Chamberlain, and he wasn't nearly the scorer Wilt was. He also wasn't as good a rebounder as Nate Thurmond, didn't throw the quick outlet pass like Wes Unseld, and wasn't the scorer that Kareem Abdul-Jabbar would become, and he didn't pass as well as Bill Walton would when he joined the NBA. Still, the burly Reed was a total team player who took his responsibility as team captain very seriously. He was also a guy who believed you had to earn respect in the NBA and that you did it with toughness. Early in his career, he took on half the Lakers bench and came out on top, leaving one opponent unconscious on the floor in front of him. After that, very few players would challenge the captain or seek a physical confrontation.

He was also a natural leader. By limping out onto the court for the seventh game in 1970 despite a serious and painful leg injury, and somehow willing himself to play the mighty Chamberlain defensively, he stood even taller in the eyes of his teammates. There was little doubt that Willis Reed was the axis around which the Knicks revolved, and their success followed. Despite the obvious talents of the other four starters, the Knicks were not a big team, even for the 1970s, and it was Reed who was the equalizer when it came to their shortcomings.

"The courage Willis demonstrated was his faith in us," Bill Bradley said. "His courage is incredible. I had chills before that game. Willis not only played on one leg, he kept Wilt from hitting."

When the 1970–71 season began, the Knicks were once again favorites to win it all. In the days before free agency, good teams tended to stay together. They might tweak with a trade now and then, and give a few rookies a shot to make the club, but teams finishing at or near the top didn't get the best draft choices. With the Knicks, it was hard to see anyone cracking that lineup, because the starting five simply played too well together. When the team got off to a 31-11 start, they once again appeared to be the class of the league. But in the final months they inexplicably became basically a .500 club, finishing the season at 52-30, which was good enough for first place in the newly-formed Atlantic Division. But the 21-19 record over the final 40 games made people wonder if maybe the Knicks weren't as good as they thought. Though Reed's numbers were very close to the previous year, he didn't seem quite the same player in the second half of the season. It may have been the beginning of the tendinitis that would affect his knees. Though the Knicks topped the Atlanta Hawks in the first round of the playoffs, they were then beaten in seven by the Bullets, a team that won just 42 times in the regular season. No repeat title.

At the beginning of the 1971–72 campaign, the real reason for the Knicks' fall from the top surfaced. Reed's left knee was barking right from the beginning of the season because his tendinitis had flared up again. It was easy to see that his mobility was limited. He missed the first two weeks of the season, and when he returned, he injured the knee again. For the year, he played in just 11 games. Amazingly, the team still made it all the way to the Finals after finishing second in their division at 48-34, but lost to Chamberlain, West, and the 69-13 Lakers, 4-1. The ballclub was helped during the season by the acquisitions of guard Earl "The Pearl" Monroe from Baltimore and center/forward Jerry Lucas from Cincinnati. Both took some time to adjust to Holzman's system, but eventually did. Had the captain been healthy, the Knicks might have given the Lakers a run for their money.

In 1972–73 the Knicks bounced back and won a second title. Frazier and Monroe were arguably the best backcourt in the league, while DeBusschere and Bradley continued to excel at forward. Reed played 69 games with Lucas spelling him, but he clearly was no longer a real impact player. He averaged just 11.0 points a game and pulled down only 590 rebounds. Yet he managed to suck it up in the playoffs and lead the team over the Lakers in five games. For his efforts, he was once again named Finals MVP.

But the end was near. The next season his knees limited him to just 19 games, and when it was over he retired, just short of his thirty-second birthday. Even in his last year, when he rarely played, the team was good enough to finish 49-33 and win a round in the playoffs before losing. The next year they dipped to 40-42 and then 38-44. In fact, they wouldn't win a round in the playoffs for the next nine years, and by then all the stars from the two title teams were gone. Yet the question remains: What if Willis Reed had remained healthy? What if he continued to play at his 1969–70 level for another five years? What would that have meant to the Knicks, to the league, and to the style of basketball we see today?

WHAT MAKES A TEAM?

When the Knicks were firing on all cylinders, as they were in 1969–70, they were extremely difficult to beat. Had they continued to do that for the next five or six years, there's a good chance they could have added three or four more titles to their resume, making the team the logical successor to the Celtics dynasty. Remember, the Celtics had thirteen years of a healthy Bill Russell, who continued to play well into his mid-thirties. If Willis Reed had been able to do that for the Knicks, he still would have been playing in 1977–78, just two years before Larry Bird and Magic Johnson came into the league.

While the championship team of 1969–70 is often remembered for the great courage Reed showed in that final game, it should also be remembered for the coach and the other players who made that great run possible. Four of the starters, save Barnett, are in the Hall of Fame, and Barnett had more game than he is sometimes given credit for. Here's a sampling of why this team was able to win and also befuddle so many other talented players and ball clubs along the way. And why they could have continued to win if Willis Reed had remained healthy.

The captain, of course, was the leader and the intimidator. But he was also a guy who once scored 46 points in a game and grabbed 33 rebounds in another. So he could put the numbers up as well as defend—a complete player and true center. If Reed was the engine that made the team run, Walt Frazier was the driver. Today he would be called a point guard, but the smooth and slick Clyde did it all. He was a 20-point scorer, always near the top of the league in assists, and played incredibly tough on the defensive end.

Defensively, he was a riverboat gambler who knew he could help his team as much with a key steal as with a key basket, and he reveled in his defense. His steals would often come in bunches and turn on the Garden crowd, as chants of "DEE-FENCE, DEE-FENCE, DEE-FENCE" rang down on the court.

"I don't believe in contact defense," Frazier once said. "I like to keep them guessing where I am. I have the advantage because my hands are so quick. It's like I'm playing possum; I'm there but I don't look like I'm there. They're relaxed more than if you're up there pressuring them all the time. That's when they get careless."

Frazier made it happen in the seventh game against the Lakers in 1970. The man he picked was the great Jerry West, and Clyde felt it was a turning point. West was bringing the ball up and momentarily slowed his dribble close to the mid-court line. Frazier suddenly jumped across the line, flicked the ball off West's fingers, grabbed it, and went in for a lay-up. He was fouled by West and completed the three-point play.

"West looked bewildered," Frazier would say later. "For that one moment, he was out of control, and you never saw that happen with Jerry. We'd wounded their leader. I knew we had them."

"It's not only that Clyde steals the ball," said teammate Bradley, "but that he makes them think he's about to steal it, and that he can steal it anytime he wants to. He's the only player I've ever seen [whom] I would describe as an artist, who takes an artistic approach to the game."

The trade for Dave DeBusschere gave the Knicks the ingredient they needed to complete the team. DeBusschere was the blue-collar worker, the digger who rebounded and defended. He was up to any physical challenge, and could score points in bunches. Like the other members of the team he was completely unselfish, totally reliable, and always at his best in the clutch. As Atlanta forward Bill Bridges, who battled DeBusschere for years, put it, "There's not one other guy in this league who gives the 100 percent DeBusschere does, every night, every game of the season, and at both ends of the court."

Even though Red Holzman approved the trade that brought DeBusschere to the Knicks, he really hadn't envisioned the kind of player he'd be getting. "I didn't realize he was as good as he was until we got him," the coach said. "I always knew he was an out-standing player, but not this good."

DeBusschere also worked beautifully with Bradley. They set picks for each other, ran backdoor plays, had the ability to slip underneath for easy lay-ups, and set Reed up for his short jumpers. While DeBusschere battled underneath, Bradley was perpetual motion, often running his defender to exhaustion. There were undoubtedly more talented front court tandems in the league, but none who could do so many things or knew each other's moves so well or could work as well with their center and guards. These were five guys who fit like fingers in a glove.

Barnett was the unheralded starter on the first title team. He had a great jumpshot and was a solid defender, a perfect compliment to the others, a quiet guy who is often the forgotten member of the team. When Earl Monroe arrived in 1971–72, the team took on yet another dimension. It's really a shame that the Pearl came at the time Reed was beginning to show the effects of creaky knees, because had he been there when the Captain was in his prime, the team might even have been even better. Add the Pearl to the mix with a healthy Reed and there's even more of a chance the Knicks would have become a dynasty.

In one way, Monroe was the anti-Frazier. He was an offensive force, a dynamic one-on-one player who had more moves than a break dancer. The Bullets were the Knicks' heated rivals for years and Frazier played Monroe in many epic battles.

"I matched Frazier with Monroe," Holzman once wrote. "Ace against ace. If Monroe got 34, Frazier might get 34. The idea was not to allow the Bullets to get a big edge at that one position. They saw so much of each other that Clyde could have played Pearl in his sleep."

Then all of a sudden, they were teammates, and after a period of adjustment, they clicked. Monroe deserves a great deal of credit.

Allowed to control the ball on offense and freelance, as he did in Baltimore, he was capable of averaging 25 points a game. Yet on Holzman's watch, he had to tone his game down, which he did, and also stepped into the defensive role required of him. In the 1972–73 championship season, the Pearl averaged 15.5 points a game. He would average 20 again a few years later when the composition of the team changed, and was truly one of the great players of his time.

"Earl was my biggest nemesis," Frazier recalled. "I used to say, 'Earl doesn't know what he's going to do, so how could I know?' He was just very creative and would make up shots as he goes. But I loved defense and I relished the opportunity to try to stop him. Playing with him was also very exciting. I think that we were the best backcourt ever. People thought that we wouldn't be able to play together, that we would need two basketballs, but we proved them wrong because we won a championship together."

Throw in the bench, which had some key players such as Cazzie Russell and Mike Riordan, and later Jerry Lucas, and this simply was a very great team. They led the NBA in defense five of six years when they were all together, and took tremendous pride in that. What's more, they worked as a complete team at a time when the NBA was pointing toward a different kind of game. And when healthy, they simply dominated.

WHY THE KNICKS COULD HAVE BEEN A DYNASTY

There's an old saying in boxing that says *styles make fights*. In other words, if the styles of two great fighters don't fit together, they could end up in a dull match. The fact that the Knicks played the game with a style that was different from all other teams made for some interesting match-ups. Sure, a pair of run-and-gun teams can put on an offensive show and rack up the points. But when that run-and-gun team came face to face with the Knicks, they found a club diametrically opposite in their approach to the game, which made for some great basketball. All you have to do is look at the Knicks' 23-1 start in 1969–70 to see how they dominated a league totally unprepared for what they unveiled when everyone was fresh and healthy and firing on all cylinders.

If styles make fights, then the Knicks' most difficult opponent and toughest matchup in the years after Debusschere joined the team was the Baltimore Bullets. They were an explosive and crowd-pleasing team with a quintet of talented starters, and while they freelanced and didn't play the same kind of defense as the Knicks, the match-ups were classic. Barnett was matched with Kevin Loughery, a good-shooting guard who would average 20 points a game. Bradley locked horns with 6'7" Jack Marin, a fine player who scored and rebounded a bit better than Dollar Bill, and their battles had an intensity all their own. Center Wes Unseld was undersized at 6'8", but he was exceptionally strong and quick, a fine rebounder who threw a lightning fast outlet pass and gave Reed all he could handle. DeBusschere was matched up with Gus Johnson, who was just 6'5", but had strength to spare. Gus could score and rebound, and had he not been sabotaged by bad knees would probably be in the Hall of Fame. Then there were Clyde and the Pearl. Enough said about the battles between the future teammates.

As one writer described it, "Unseld versus Reed was epic. Gus Johnson versus Dave DeBusschere was as good as it got. Earl Monroe versus Walt Frazier was the pinnacle."

Frazier, when asked to describe the confrontations between DeBusschere and Johnson, said, "Dave was a tenacious player, a good rebounder and defender who could shoot the ball well from the perimeter. I remember vividly those match-ups with Gus Johnson, another powerful man—he had an Adonis body, powerfully built. They used to go to war. They asked no quarter and they gave no quarter. After the game I always remember that DeBusschere was sitting over in the corner resting because he had given it all that he had. Most of the time he came out on top."

And when Dave came out on top, so did the Knicks. As tough as the Bullets were, the Knicks usually found a way to win. They were beaten in the playoffs of 1971, but that's when Reed's knees weren't 100 percent. Despite their great freelancing team, the Bullets apparently didn't think they could win a title because they traded Monroe to New York the following year. It was that extra dimension of defense that usually got the Knicks over the top.

Many of the other teams in the league depended on one or two big stars to get them through while the Knicks always depended on all five. The Lakers of 1969–70 had three—Jerry West, who led the league in scoring; Wilt Chamberlain, who returned from an injury in time for the playoffs and continued to be the league's best rebounder; and the aging Elgin Baylor, who was still good enough to average 24 points a game. Yet the Knicks with their team concept prevailed, even managing to win the fifth game after Reed was hurt, and then winning the seventh when Reed was just a shell of himself.

The early 1970s saw the arrival of very talented and exciting players, but many of them were on teams that freelanced too much and didn't play with the total team concept. In the 1972–73 season, the year the Knicks won their second championship, the stars of the league included Nate "Tiny" Archibald, Kareem, Spencer Haywood, Pistol Pete Maravich, Charlie Scott, John Havlicek, Bob Lanier, Sidney Wicks, Dave Bing, Rick Barry, Elvin Hayes, Dave Cowens, and Lenny Wilkens. A rival league, the ABA, was also operating at the time and using a run-and-gun style with a three-point shot in place, and it featured Julius "Dr. J" Erving as one of its stars. He would join the 76ers a few years down the road and then several ABA teams would be absorbed into the NBA.

Many of the aforementioned stars are in the Basketball Hall of Fame, and if you compare their individual skills with members of the Knicks, especially the front court of Reed, Bradley, and De-Busschere, they were more talented. But they weren't playing the same game and weren't molded into the same kind of team as the Knicks. And many of them never got to taste a championship.

The direction of the NBA in the mid- to late 1970s was toward a showboating one-on-one game that was slowly leaving the team concept behind. Many players coming into the league seemed intent on just showing off their individual skills rather than melding with teammates into perhaps a less exciting but more effective unit. As a result, attendance began to drop off and interest in the league seemed on the wane. It was a stroke of good fortune in 1979–80 that revived it—the arrival of two outstanding collegiate players whose NCAA rivalry had already made national headlines. They were Earvin "Magic" Johnson and Larry Bird.

Johnson, a 6'9" point guard, and Bird, a 6'9" forward, both went to flagship franchises, the Lakers and the Celtics, and they would help revive the league. Not only did their teams win, but both Johnson and Bird knew how to play the game the right way. Despite great individual skills, both were unselfish and always thought of their team first. It improved the level of play and the fans began returning.

Unselfish! Team play! Sound familiar? That was the Knicks, who may have done it better than any team ever. If you look back at the team, the other four starters (using Barnett-Monroe as one) all had normal length careers, staying basically healthy and finally experiencing a natural decline as they approached their mid-thirties. All except Willis Reed.

So let's project. What if Willis Reed had stayed healthy and productive to the age of thirty-six? That would have taken him up to the end of the 1977–78 season. Looking at the ledger, there's no reason to think that a fully healthy Reed wouldn't have propelled the Knicks to a repeat title in 1970–71, when the Bullets beat them early. The following year, they made it to the Finals but lost to the Lakers. This one may have been tough even with a healthy Reed, since the Lakers found the magic that season, going 69-13 with an amazing 33-game winning streak.

The following season, 1972–73, the Knicks won it despite the fact that Willis Reed averaged just 11 points a game during the regular season and clearly wasn't the same player. Monroe and Jerry Lucas were there by then and provided the extra lift, and Reed was the MVP of the Finals. After that, Reed was basically done. The champions over the next three years were the Boston Celtics, Golden State Warriors, and Celtics again. None of those teams were considered among the NBA's best ever. These were not classic Celtics teams, and the Warriors, led by Rick Barry, emerged as surprise winners. It's not a stretch to think that a healthy Knicks team could have beaten all three. None of them played with the same defensive skills and teamwork as the Knicks. All would have had difficulty coping with the Frazier-Monroe backcourt. DeBusschere remained a top rebounder and defender until the day he retired, and Bradley continued to be a smart and steady player. If they had the big man in the middle taking care of business as only he could, it's easy seeing the Knicks winning each year.

If that had happened, it would have been six titles in seven years, and there's only one word that spells: dynasty.

HOW A KNICKS DYNASTY COULD HAVE CHANGED THE NBA

A Knicks dynasty certainly would have been great for New York fans. The team was so revered and loved during the 1969–70 season that they probably could have filled a 50,000 seat arena every night. The people who came to Madison Square Garden then, for the most part, were longtime fans who knew good basketball. Had Reed stayed healthy and the team remained on top, tickets at the

Garden would have been at even more of a premium than they were and for a longer period of time. But aside from the obvious effects in New York, how would a Knicks dynasty have affected the NBA as a whole?

For starters, if the Knicks continued to win with Holzman's "see the ball, hit the open man" philosophy, more and more people would have realized that this was a team playing the game the right way. Whenever something is working in almost any field, there are bound to be copycats. In that sense, it's surprising that no other team came remotely close to approaching the Knicks' style of play during their dominant years, but there may have been a good reason for that.

To copy what the Knicks were doing, a team would need a committed coach who knew how to create and control that kind of game, and he would have to be fully supported by his front office. On top of that, he would need to find the right combination of players. The Knicks wouldn't have been the Knicks if Walt Frazier hadn't turned out to be one of the all-time great guards and one of the best ever defensively. They wouldn't have been the Knicks if the Pistons had not agreed to trade them Dave DeBusschere for Walt Bellamy and Howard Komivies. They wouldn't have been the Knicks if Bill Bradley hadn't decided to return to the NBA after his stint at Oxford. This was a matter of the right guys being in the right place at the right time, under the leadership of Red Holzman, who had the ability to balance this team and make it work.

So in that sense, it would not have been easy for other teams to duplicate the Knicks' style of play with the same effectiveness. However, had Reed remained healthy and had the Knicks won from four to six championships, the message would have been even louder and clearer. At that point other teams might have concluded that the only way to beat the Knicks was to *be* the Knicks, or just like them.

Had the Knicks remained a dominant team (with a healthy Reed) into the latter 1970s, they wouldn't have left much of a gap until the Lakers with Magic Johnson and the Celtics with Larry Bird became dominant. Both teams played a solid, two-way game, but unlike the Knicks they were fueled by star power. Magic still had Kareem Abdul-Jabbar at center and James Worthy at forward. Bird was supported by forward Kevin McHale, center Robert Parish, and guard Dennis Johnson. Still, they were close enough that they could have carried on the tradition.

Other organizations and coaches might also have become more familiar with the Knicks and their system and might have tried to play a similar game. It's hard to say whether the Knicks could have influenced today's game. The NBA today has become pure entertainment, with dancing girls and laser lights almost as important to the presentation as the game, and the game, played by great athletes, has too often become one of spectacular dunks and three-point shots. Many of the subtleties are gone. To basketball purists, that's a shame.

Someone once said that the art of basketball consists not in making repeated spectacular shots but, as in billiards, positioning to get easy ones. That's what the New York Knicks of the early 1970s did. Their game was a beautiful one, a combination of team-work, guile, and a balance of offense and defense. They lit up the Garden and lit up the NBA, and it's a shame they couldn't have done it longer. But with a healthy Willis Reed, they certainly could have.

The Deal's Off

The trade has always been one of the staples of baseball, especially before the advent of free agency. Every team making a trade has a good reason and expects to get the best of the deal, whether it's a one-for-one trade or several players for one or maybe even a multiple-player deal. Usually, the objective is to make a team better, though in some cases it's more important for a team to rid itself of a particular player and, in that case, what they're receiving in return isn't quite as important. In any case, there have been a number of trades that have not only affected the teams involved, but have helped shape or change the course of baseball history, whether it be via a single event or over a period of years. These are all trades in which the trigger was pulled and the players moved.

But what if, at the last minute, the trade wasn't made?

★ ★ ★ ★ ★

There have been a myriad of baseball trades over the years—major deals, minor ones, one-for-one swaps of superstars, one-for-five swaps involving one superstar and prospects, and those little deals that are almost an afterthought, yet wind up affecting the fortunes of one or more teams or players, and sometimes the game itself. In looking at a variety of these trades one may start to wonder why they were made and then how they turned out. There's another side of this coin, as well, that may even be a bit more complex. It's the question of what might have happened if the trade *wasn't* made, if the offer was on the table and the team or teams didn't pull the trigger. Here are some deals which would have changed baseball if they *hadn't* been made.

WHAT IF THE NEW YORK GIANTS HADN'T TRADED AMOS RUSIE FOR CHRISTY MATHEWSON?

Nothing could have stopped Christy Mathewson from being a great pitcher. He was not only one of the earliest stars of the game, he was a college man at a time when most major league ballplayers were rough-and-tumble guys with little education or sophistication. The man they called Matty, or Big Six, was born in Pennsylvania in 1880, began pitching at thirteen, and then attended Bucknell College, where he starred in both baseball and football. He eventually signed a pro contract to pitch for the Taunton, Massachusetts, club in the New England League and made his professional debut on July 21, 1899. It was at Taunton that Mathewson added another pitch to go with his fastball and curve.

He saw a left-handed teammate throw the ball by turning his hand in the opposite direction of the curve and snapping his wrist as he let the pitch go. "He could never tell where it was going," Matty said, "so it was no use to him in a game. It was a freak delivery, but it fascinated me."

Mathewson perfected the pitch, which was dubbed the "fade-away," the same pitch that is called the screwball today, and it made him even better. The next season he was a dominating 20-2 at Norfolk of the Virginia League when, in late July, the New York Giants came calling. Maybe the Giants threw him in against the big boys too soon because Matty, who just turned twenty, was 0-3 with a 5.08 earned run average. At season's end, the Giants returned him to Norfolk, and here's where the story becomes intriguing. Following the rules of the day, the Cincinnati Reds were able to draft Mathewson off the Norfolk roster and, as soon as that happened, the Giants began having second thoughts. They began looking almost immediately for a way to get the young pitcher back.

They didn't have to look far. On their roster was a veteran right-hander named Amos Rusie, who has been one of the best pitchers of the 1890s. Some old timers even said that Rusie was the fastest pitcher ever, faster than Walter Johnson and Lefty Grove, two acknowledged flamethrowers from baseball's early days. At a time when pitchers threw often, Rusie had records of 33-20 in 1891 with 337 strikeouts, and 32-31 the following year. Then, in 1893, the mound was moved back from fifty feet to its present sixty-feet, six-inch distance and Rusie became even better because his curveball became more effective. In the following three seasons, he won 33, 36, and 23 games for the New Yorkers, making him one of the real pitching stars of the day.

By that time, however, Rusie was also feuding with Giants' owner Andrew Freedman over fines assessed in 1895. The hurler wanted the money back, and when the owner refused, Rusie sat out the 1896 season. Could you imagine a player doing that today, with millions of dollars at stake? Rusie returned the next year and once the owner gave him the go-ahead to pitch, he compiled an impressive 28-10 mark. The next season he won 20 once more, but late in the season he felt something pop in his shoulder when he fired a pickoff throw to first. Back then, they called it a dead arm. Today it might be diagnosed as a torn rotator cuff or torn labrum. Rusie had no choice but to sit out the next two seasons and hope his arm would return to normal. At the end of the 1900 season, Rusie was just twenty-nine years old, so there was no reason to think that he couldn't still pitch.

On December 15 of that year, the Giants announced that they had reacquired young Christy Mathewson from the Reds in exchange for . . . Amos Rusie. In a sense, both teams were taking a chance. Mathewson was just twenty years old. Sure, he had promise, but no one can predict that a twenty-year-old will be great, with very rare exceptions. As for Rusie, he had already won 246 games while losing just 173. The Reds were hoping his strong right arm would come back and hopefully, at his age, he could win another 150 games for them.

It didn't happen. Rusie never again found the magic. He tried to pitch in 1901, appeared in just three games, threw 22 innings with an 0-1 record, and realized his arm was shot. He had no choice but to retire. Though he never won another major league game, he was still elected to the Hall of Fame in 1977 for his pre-1900 work. Mathewson, however, went the other way. He became one of the greatest ever, beginning with a 20-win season in 1901. Two years later he began a string of three straight 30-victory campaigns. In 1908, he was 37-11 with a 1.43 ERA, and a year later was 25-6 with a microscopic 1.14 earned run average. He would end up with thirteen seasons of 20 or more victories and would tie Grover Cleveland Alexander for the most wins by a National League pitcher, 373. Mathewson was so good that in 1936 he became one of the first five players elected to the newly opened Baseball Hall of Fame.

But what if the trade had never been made and the Cincinnati Reds insisted on keeping Christy Mathewson? Would he still have been great? Without a doubt. Would he have been *as* great? Probably not quite. Maybe even more importantly, his legacy, and that of the New York Giants and their feisty manager, John McGraw, could not have been the same.

In 1902, John McGraw became manager of the Giants and would remain at the helm for thirty years. McGraw was a fiery competitor cut from the same mold as a later Giants manager, Leo Durocher. He also loved the old style of baseball from the so-called dead-ball era, especially the hit-and-run, and he loved Christy Mathewson. They were, in a sense, an odd couple—the hard drinking, hard cursing, fiery, win-at-all-costs McGraw, and the pitcher who was quiet, intelligent, soft spoken, but incredibly talented. Each thrived with the other.

The Giants won 106 games in 1904, but there was no World Series that year. The next season they won 105 and then met the Philadelphia A's in the Series. Mathewson set a record by throwing three complete game shutouts as the Giants won the championship in five. From there, the New Yorkers had winning teams every year through 1914, taking three more pennants as Mathewson became a major star. McGraw surrounded him with other top players, and the team played the game with a hell-for-leather style, the way McGraw felt it was intended to be played.

Had Cincinnati not made the trade and decided to hold on to the talented youngster, things would have been very different. Because the cream always rises, Mathewson would have won his share of games, but not 373 of them. From 1906 through 1914 the Reds fielded losing teams. Not once did the ball club finish above .500. Nor did they have many top players, stars who would have played even better with Mathewson on the mound. If you take away just five wins a year for ten seasons, Mathewson is still a Hall of Famer with 323 wins to his credit. Take away an average of eight wins a year and suddenly he's below that magic 300-win mark. Could it have happened that way? Absolutely, unless the Reds improved.

That's the other side of the coin. With a stud like Christy Mathewson at the top of the rotation, Cincinnati might have made more of an effort to build a better ball club, which would have afforded Mathewson more wins, but never as many as he won with the Giants. If the trade was never made, the Giants wouldn't have been quite the dominant team they were in baseball's early days. Though the ball club had some other stars and another Hall of Fame pitcher in "Iron Man" Joe McGinnity, they would have surely missed Mathewson's great talent. McGraw's legacy would probably be intact, but he might not have attained that exalted position as one of baseball's greatest managers, and he certainly would not have had as many victories behind the bench.

In a final irony, Mathewson actually ended up back with the Reds. After suffering his first losing season in 1915, he was switched to the bullpen the next year. On July 20, 1916, he was traded to the Reds with two other future Hall of Famers, outfielder Edd Roush and third baseman Bill McKechnie, in return for Reds manager Buck Herzog and outfielder Red Killefer, a .248 career hitter. The Reds essentially wanted Matty to manage, which he did until the middle of 1918, when he joined the armed services and served as a captain on the Western Front. He inhaled some poison gas there and after returning to the States was diagnosed with tuberculosis. He died in October 1925 at the age of 45.

The Reds would have had an additional benefit if they hadn't traded him. They wouldn't have had to face a pitcher who went 64-18 against them over the years, including 22 wins in a row at once point. They definitely should have thought twice before pulling the trigger on that one.

WHAT IF THE CINCINNATI REDS HAD NOT TRADED FRANK ROBINSON TO THE ORIOLES FOR MILT PAPPAS?

This was one of those trades that could be classified as a "block-buster." It involved a superstar player who appeared to be in the prime of his career and a very good pitcher who had proved himself a consistent and solid double-digit winner. When all was said and done, it turned out to be one of the worst trades in history for one of the teams, and a great one for the other.

The superstar, of course, was Frank Robinson, who had come to the Reds by way of Beaumont, Texas, a twenty-year-old rookie who promptly won a starting job in the outfield. While playing on a team that would tie the then record of 221 home runs in a season, Robinson also hit his share and tied a rookie record (since broken) with 38 home runs. Five years later, Robby led the Reds into the World Series, producing an MVP season with a .323 batting average, 37 homers, and 124 RBIs. By that time, he was considered to be in the same category as the league's great superstars—Willie Mays, Henry Aaron, and Roberto Clemente. A year later he was even better, hitting a robust .342, with 39 home runs and 136 runs batted in, and it's hard to get much better than that.

But by the middle 1960s, things were changing. In 1965, the now veteran Robinson had been joined on the Reds by the likes of Pete Rose, Tony Perez, Deron Johnson, Vada Pinson, Tommy Harper, Gordy Coleman, and Johnny Edwards. The team even had a pair of 20-game winners in Sammy Ellis and Jim Maloney, but finished only fourth to the Dodgers at 89-73. Then, sometime after the season ended, Cincy GM Bill DeWitt began talking trade with the Baltimore Orioles. The player he was thinking about dealing—Frank Robinson.

The Orioles in 1965 were an up-and-coming third-place team that finished at 94-66. The team's star was third baseman Brooks Robinson, a sensational fielder and solid hitter who had 18 homers and 80 RBIs in '65, but he wasn't a real slugger. Big Boog Powell at first had 17 homers and would hit more, but he still hadn't reached his prime. At the same time, the team had five solid young starters—Milt Pappas, Steve Barber, Wally Bunker, Dave McNally, and Jim Palmer. So the Orioles were looking for a big bat and felt they had pitching to give. The Reds had plenty of hitting, but were looking for another pitcher to slot in behind Ellis and Maloney. It seemed like the right scenario to make a swap.

On December 9, the trade was made. Frank Robinson would be sent to Baltimore in return for Pappas, reliever Jack Baldschun, and utility outfielder Dick Simpson. Robinson and Pappas were the key pieces and there was an immediate outcry from many Cincinnati fans who couldn't understand why Robinson, a five-tool player of enormous talent, would be shipped out. DeWitt's answer was simple and terse. Robinson was "an old thirty," he said. In Pappas, the Reds were getting a twenty-six-year-old right-hander who had been in the majors since he was nineteen and had already won 110 games, including a pair of 16- and 15-win seasons. So Cincy thought they could be getting another potential 20-game winner. With a surplus of hitting on the club, they felt they were obtaining what they'd need and wouldn't miss Robinson that much.

As it turned out, Robinson was far from an old thirty. He went over to Baltimore and not only became the Orioles' best player, but the team leader as well. In 1966, he became the first player to win a Most Valuable Player award in both leagues and also won the Triple Crown of hitting with a .316 batting average, 49 big home runs, and 122 runs batted in. The Orioles not only won the pennant, but went on to win the World Series as well. Robinson would end up sparking his team to four pennants and a pair of World Series titles over his first six years in the American League. The guy who was an old thirty would play ten more years after his trade and finish with 586 home runs, a .294 lifetime batting average, and 204 stolen bases. He is not only considered one of the all-time greatest players—a first-ballot Hall of Famer—but also became the first African-American to manage in the big leagues when he became the player-manager of the Cleveland Indians in 1975.

As for Pappas, well, it didn't work out so well for Cincinnati. He was just 12-11 his first year in Cincy, and while he went 16-13 in 1967, the Reds traded him to Atlanta early in the 1968 season. For that handful of victories and no pennants, they had traded away Frank Robinson. Why?

One reason may have been the breakout season of third baseman Deron Johnson. In 1965, the twenty-seven-year-old had 32 home runs and led the league with 130 RBIs. Unfortunately for the Reds, he was not close to being the five-tool player Robinson was and he soon fizzled. Robinson, apparently, felt there was another reason. In his autobiography he mentioned that when Pete Rose joined the team in 1963 and took the second base job from the popular incumbent, Don Blasingame, the only players on the Reds who befriended Rose were Robinson and center fielder Vada Pinson, another African-American. This distanced the two stars from other players on the team. He also noted that "some writers were reporting that Vada Pinson and I formed a 'Negro clique . . . that is gnawing at the morale of the club.'" Robinson noted that there were groups of two or three white players who hung out constantly and were never singled out for forming a clique.

Because of Robinson's immense talent, there would seem to be a secondary reason for the Reds making the deal. Whether it was tied to some latent racism is tough to say. Cincy wouldn't bounce back until 1972, when they had added players like Johnny Bench and Joe Morgan and would become known as the Big Red Machine. The aging Robinson certainly could have continued to contribute to that team. But what if the trade hadn't been made? How would it have affected the two teams and the career of Frank Robinson?

Cincinnati had several down years after the trade before bouncing back and becoming one of the best teams of the early and mid-1970s. Pappas wasn't much help, but Robinson could have been. Once Sparky Anderson took over as manager and Bench and Morgan joined Rose, Perez, Dave Concepcion, and the other top hitters, this was a powerful team. Robinson would have brought more respectability to the ballclub in the late 1960s and would have helped substantially in the early 1970s. He probably would not have been around for the '75 and '76 championship teams. Had he stayed, however, he most likely would still be remembered as the greatest player in team history despite the presence of those top stars of the '70s.

Instead, he forged an even greater legacy in Baltimore. He was able to play on the big stage sooner and more often, helping his team to the World Series in 1966 and then three years in a row from 1969–71. Those Orioles teams were among the best of their era and Frank Robinson was their leader. Had he not joined the Orioles and become a familiar figure in the American League, he also might not have had the chance to manage the Indians in 1975, and thus there might not have been a black manager in baseball until quite a few years later. The trade definitely proved a benefit to Frank Robinson.

As for Milt Pappas, his career might well have benefited had he remained in Baltimore. The Orioles continued to pitch well and would have had a very solid team in the late 1960s even without Frank Robinson. Pappas still could have contributed. He didn't do well in Atlanta and was traded again to the Cubs in the middle of the 1970 season. In each of the next two years, he won 17 games, going 17-7 with a 2.77 ERA in 1972. But after a subpar 7-12 season in 1973, Milt Pappas retired at the age of thirty-four with 209 career victories. Had he stayed in Baltimore he might well have won more.

WHAT IF JACK HAMILTON HAD NOT BEEN TRADED TO THE CALIFORNIA ANGELS IN JUNE OF 1967?

At first glance, this seems like one of those minor trades that wouldn't have altered the destinies of either team involved. In a swap of journeyman pitchers, the New York Mets sent right-hander Jack Hamilton to the California Angels in return for left-handed pitcher Nick Willhite. The deal was made on June 10, 1967, between two teams that were essentially out of the pennant race. Neither player stayed with his new team for very long. Hamilton moved on to Cleveland in 1969, went to the White Sox before the season ended, and then retired with a 32-40 lifetime record. Willhite finished the season with the Mets and was never heard from again.

Just taking those few facts the next logical question is, What could have really changed if this trade was never made? There is an answer, however, a very dramatic one. If the trade were never made, then Jack Hamilton would not have been on the mound for the Angels in an August 18, 1967, game against the first place Boston Red Sox. He wouldn't have been pitching in the fourth inning when the young Red Sox star Tony Conigliaro came to the plate, and his high inside fastball wouldn't have crashed into Conigliaro's face, effectively ending a career that already seemed headed in the direction of Cooperstown. That's how a seemingly insignificant trade can alter the destiny of a team, a player, and the game itself.

Who was Tony Conigliaro? In 1967, he was one of the brightest young stars in the game playing for one of baseball's best teams. Tony C., as he was called, was born in Revere, Massachusetts, on January 7, 1945, so he was a natural to play for the Red Sox. He was tall (6'3") and handsome, and had the look of a star. When he joined the Red Sox in 1964, he was just nineteen years old. Though he missed six weeks of the season to injuries, he still managed 24 home runs with a solid .290 batting average and already had the word "star" written all over him.

When he slammed 32 home runs the next season, he became the youngest player in baseball history to lead the league in four baggers. By the time the Red Sox were in a pennant race in 1967, the twenty-two-year-old Conigliaro was already a star and a fan favorite at Fenway Park. It was really a case of local boy makes good, with the promise that it would only get better. When the Red Sox hosted the Angels on August 18, Conigliaro had played in 95 games that year, was hitting .287 with 20 homers and 67 RBIs, and was the primary supporting player to the team's veteran star, Carl Yastrzemski. In the fourth inning, Conigliaro stepped in to face Hamilton, who had only been with the Angels for a little more than two months.

Crowding the plate as usual, Conigliaro seemed to freeze as Hamilton threw one inside. It was not a pitch thrown intentionally at a batter's head, but Tony C. simply couldn't get out of the way. He went down hard and had to be taken from the field on a stretcher with a broken cheekbone and severe damage to his left eye, and he didn't play again that season. So severe were his injuries that he also missed the entire 1968 season, and many doubted that he would ever play again. But he returned the following year and managed to hit 20 home runs and drive in 82 runs in 141 games. A year later, playing in 146 games, he clubbed 36 home runs and drove home 116 runs. It was his best season yet and fans felt the real Tony C. was back. Only he wasn't.

His comeback was made all the more remarkable when it was later revealed that the vision in his left eye was still seriously impaired, with some saying he was legally blind in the eye. The Sox must have known something because, in an act of irony, they traded him to the Angels in a two-for-three deal prior to the 1971 season. No other major players were involved. Tony C. played just 74 games for the Angels that year, hitting only four home runs. By then, his vision had deteriorated to the point where he could no longer continue, and he retired on the spot. An attempted comeback with the Red Sox in 1975 lasted just 21 games, but he did hit his final two home runs, giving him 166 for his short career. Sadly, tragedy continued to stalk him. In 1982, just after auditioning for a broadcasting job with the Sox, he suffered a severe heart attack that left him so incapacitated that he needed constant care until his death in 1990 at the age of forty-five.

Had Jack Hamilton not been traded to the Angels, there is no telling what kind of heights Tony Conigliaro could have scaled. Orioles pitcher Jim Palmer, for one, thinks they could have been considerable. Said Palmer, "He might have been the guy to break Ruth's and Aaron's records. With his swing, in that ballpark, there's no telling how many he would have hit."

Unfortunately, a single pitch changed all that. But it wouldn't have happened if either the Mets or Angels had said no to what seemed like a meaningless a trade just two months before.

WHAT IF DENNIS ECKERSLEY HADN'T BEEN TRADED TO THE OAKLAND A'S FOR THREE MINOR LEAGUERS?

If it were not for this trade, baseball might not have seen one of its greatest closers in action. Dennis Eckersley was actually traded four times, and if one of the first three hadn't been made, baseball history would definitely have been altered. Finally, on April 3, 1987, Eckersley was shipped from the Chicago Cubs to the Oakland A's for a trio of minor leaguers. Eckersley was thirty-two years old then and considered one of those starting pitchers who was beginning the long descent into mediocrity and retirement. He was coming off a season and a half of shoulder tendinitis and also admitted to having a drinking problem. The best remedy for the Cubs seemed to be to get rid of him and his $3 million salary. But as the old expression goes—you never know.

Coincidentally, the man who would become known simply as "The Eck" was born in Oakland on October 3, 1954. He was just twenty years old when he arrived in Cleveland and promptly shut out the A's, 2-0. He would go 13-7 that year and be named American League Rookie of the Year. Two years later, in 1977, he threw a no-hitter against the Angels, but the Indians must have been disappointed with his 13-12 and 14-13 records in those seasons, since they traded him to Boston prior to the 1978 campaign. That year, he became the first Red Sox pitcher in seven years to win 20 games (20-8) and it seemed as if he'd finally found a home.

After following up with a solid 17-10 year, he then produced four mediocre seasons in which he was an aggregate five games under .500, and early in the 1984 season, the Sox shipped him to the Cubs. Trade number two. He was 10-8 the rest of the season in Chicago, then was 11-7 in 1985 before tendinitis once again slowed him toward the end of the year. When the ailment returned the next season and he finished at 6-11, the Cubs had seen enough. Plus they also knew that Eckersley was drinking excessively. To them, he had become just another failed starter—damaged goods in several ways, so the trade was made.

It's hard to say why the A's agreed. The reason must have had to do with the dynamics of baseball. Most teams are always looking for arms and maybe they felt that as a former 20-game winner and still just thirty-two years old, Eckersley had a shot of regaining his winning form. It was worth the chance as long as they didn't have to give up too much. What they didn't know was that, on his own, Eckerley had spent six weeks at the Edgehill Newport treatment center in Rhode Island and was now able to deal with his problems. So he reported to Oakland with a clean bill of health and an optimistic outlook.

The A's were going to give Eckersley a shot at their rotation when closer Jay Howell came down with a sore arm. The team decided that the Eck, with his good fastball and slider, might be able fill the role temporarily. He closed for a good bit of the season and wound up with 16 saves in 54 games, only two of them starts. The A's liked what they saw, kept him in the closer's role the next year, and that's when he really emerged, saving 45 games with a 2.35 ERA. He gave up a dramatic home run to Kirk Gibson in game one of the World Series that year, but as a closer, he was on his way. The next year he saved 33 games and had a 1.56 ERA, and in 1990 he saved 48 with an incredible 0.61 earned run average. He had become almost untouchable.

The secret to his success was a simple one. It's called strike one, strike two. As a closer, Eckersley almost always threw strikes, putting hitters in an immediate hole. In 1992, he became just the second reliever in history to record more than 50 (51) saves in season. He was so good that year that he not only won the Cy Young Award, given to the best pitcher in the league, but was also named the American League's Most Valuable Player.

Even better, the Eck wasn't a flash in the pan. He pitched for the A's until 1995, when he was forty years old, then pitched another two years for the Cardinals and a final season with the Red Sox. With the Cards in 1997 and approaching his forty-third birthday, he was still good enough to record 36 saves. When he left the game, he was third all-time in saves with 390, and had 197 victories, most of them as a starter. His accomplishments would result in his being elected to the Baseball Hall of Fame.

If this trade was never made, Dennis Eckersley would probably have remained a mid-level starter for another few years, but might never have had the chance to become a closer. In fact, had Jay Howell not been injured, even the A's might not have given him that chance. His ascension to that role not only made him a superstar in the second half of his career, but it showed all of major league baseball the value of having a ninth-inning closer who could shut the door on the opposition and get those crucial final three outs. That in itself helped changed the game, as the one-inning closer slowly became the norm. At the time the A's decided to use him primarily in the ninth inning, many teams still used their closers for two or more innings in certain situations. After the Eck, very few did.

The Eck was also the guy who usually shut the door in all the close games. Had he not become the best closer in baseball there's a good chance the A's would not have made three straight World Series appearances from 1988 through 1990. It was only because the Cubs and A's agreed on a trade that baseball fans got to see one of the best closers in history and his new team was able to ride his strong right arm all the way to the Fall Classic.

WHAT IF THE NEW YORK YANKEES HADN'T TRADED LEW BURDETTE TO THE MILWAUKEE BRAVES IN 1951?

There have always been trades that come back to haunt the team that made them. Even with the New York Yankees, a franchise that has always had a reputation throughout the years for making good trades, you can find a blemish or two, but perhaps none worse than the one they made on August 30, 1951. On that day, they sent a twenty-four-year-old right-hander who looked like he might be a career minor leaguer to the Boston Braves, along with $50,000, so they could acquire a thirty-four-year-old veteran, four-time 20-game winner Johnny Sain. The Yanks were driving for their third straight American League pennant and wanted some veteran insurance for the stretch run, and they always seemed to have the ability to pick up the right guy who would help them win. The pitcher they gave up was named Selva Lewis Burdette, and six years later the Yankees would come to regret pulling the trigger on this one, and in a big way.

At the time it was made, it seemed like one of those typical Yankees trades. They were getting a proven pitcher, a crafty curveballer who had won 100 ballgames for the Braves beginning in 1946. He and lefty Warren Spahn formed a great, one-two pitching punch, and when the Braves took the National League pennant in 1948, they were so good that someone coined the saying, "Spahn and Sain, and pray for rain." Johnny Sain was 24-15 that year, leading the senior circuit with 314.2 innings pitched and 28 complete games. Though he was not having a good year (5-13) when the Yanks dealt for him, the Braves had also fallen to a .500 team. The Yanks were sure Sain would help them, and he did. He was 2-1 in seven games down the stretch and over the next two seasons went 11-6 and 14-7 (with a 3.00 ERA) swinging back and forth between the rotation and the bullpen as the Yanks won again, so he was a valuable pickup. Everything about it said good trade.

After a 6-6 season in 1954, Sain's star began to set. A year later, the Yanks traded him to Kansas City and he retired at the end of the season, eventually forging a second career as one of the game's best and cagiest pitching coaches. He worked for seven different teams over a three decade span, including the Yankees, where Jim Bouton called him "the greatest pitching coach who ever lived." Sain himself once said, "Pitching coaches don't change pitchers. We just stimulate their thinking."

While Sain was carving out a second career after retirement, what about Selva Lewis Burdette, now called just plain Lew? The year after the trade he was mostly in the minors again. But in 1952 he stuck with the big club, appearing in 45 games, all but nine in relief, and he had a 6-11 record. Nothing much to write home about. A year later, the Braves moved the franchise to Milwaukee, where the team, as well as the twenty-six-year-old righthander, was reborn. The Braves finished second to the Dodgers with lefty Warren Spahn still their ace. Spahnie had a 23-7 record that year, but right behind him was Lew Burdette at 15-5. Burdette was still a swing man, making just 13 starts in 46 appearances, but he completed six of those games and still managed eight saves out of the bullpen. He was proving to be both valuable and versatile.

Over the next few years Burdette and the Braves got better. Lew was essentially a starter now, and in 1956 he went 19-10. The following year he was 17-9 and helped the Braves win the National League pennant. Waiting to meet them in the World Series was none other than the New York Yankees, Burdette's former team. What he proceeded to do in the Series made history. After Whitey Ford beat Spahn in the opener, 3-1, Burdette took the hill against Bobby Shantz. He gave up single runs in the second and third, but nothing after that as the Braves won, 4-2. The Yanks took Game 3 and the Braves evened things in the fourth, winning 7-5 in 10 innings, as Spahn went all the way. Now it was Burdette and Ford in game five.

The game was close; Ford was great, but Burdette was even better. He allowed the Yanks seven scattered hits and won the game, 1-0. The Yanks came back to win game six, which meant the two teams were going to a seventh and deciding game. Warren Spahn was unavailable and the Braves once again turned to Burdette, who would be pitching on just two days rest.

"I'll be all right," Burdette said. "In 1953 I once relieved in 16 games out of 22. I'm bigger, stronger, and dumber now."

His joke notwithstanding, Burdette went out and did it again, shutting out the Yankees for a second time, once again on seven hits, as the Braves won, 5-0, and were world champs. Lew Burdette has come closer than anyone to duplicating Christy Mathewson's three shutouts in the 1905 World Series. He gave up just two runs in 27 innings. The Yankee castoff had come back to nearly single-handedly defeat the Bronx Bombers in the World Series. Had they not traded him to the Braves, the Yanks would have surely won the series, that is, if the Braves were in it at all.

The Yanks got a measure of revenge the following year when the two teams met again. This time they beat Burdette in two of the three games he pitched, including Game 7, but he had become a 20-game winner that year and one of the stars of the National League. Burdette would win 21 the next year, then 19 and 18 over the next two seasons. He was a mainstay of the great Braves teams that featured Spahn and Henry Aaron during the 1950s. If the Yanks hadn't traded him, the Braves would have been hard-pressed to find another like him and might well have suffered as a team. As it was, they won two pennants and finished second five times. This was an exciting team that would have lacked a little punch if they hadn't had Selva Lewis Burdette.

There's another footnote to the Lew Burdette saga. In 1959, Pittsburgh left-hander Harvey Haddix pitched one of the greatest games in baseball history. He threw 12 perfect innings against the Milwaukee Braves, retiring 36 batters in succession. Why 12 innings? Because the game was still tied at 0-0 at that time! And guess what? Haddix didn't win. The Braves got a run in the thirteenth to break through and win 1-0. The pitcher who prevented Harvey Haddix from perfection? Lew Burdette. This time he pitched 13 scoreless innings to shut out the Pirates. If the trade hadn't been made, chances are Haddix would have had a nine-inning perfect game.

Lew Burdette was always fidgety on the mound, touching his cap, his face, his shirt. For years, he was suspected of loading the ball up, throwing an illegal spitter, which he denied, saying the spitter was too hard to control.

"I'd love to use it, if I knew how," he said. "Burleigh Grimes (the last legal spitball pitcher) told me five years ago not to monkey around with it, but to let them think I threw it. That's what I've done."

This was a good short term trade for the Yanks, a great long-term trade for the Braves, and a trade that cost the Yankees a World Series.

WHAT IF LEW BROCK HADN'T BEEN TRADED FOR ERNIE BROGLIO?

This is another trade that changed the face of the National League for almost a decade and, in a sense, was similar to the Frank Robinson for Milt Pappas trade. On June 15, 1964, the St. Louis Cardinals traded former 20-game winner Ernie Broglio, who had won 18 more in 1963, to the Chicago Cubs in return for a struggling young outfielder named Lou Brock. It was actually a three-for-three deal, but Brock and Broglio were the reason the trade was completed, the two centerpieces. This is a trade that would have ramifications for both teams during the ensuing decade.

Right-hander Ernie Broglio had joined the Cardinals in 1959 as a twenty-three-year-old rookie. The team was in a rebuilding mode and the rook went 7-12. He seemed to find himself the next year as he compiled a 21-9 record and 2.74 earned run average. The next two seasons he was a .500 pitcher, going 9-12 and then 12-9, but in 1963 he put together another solid year with an 18-8 record and 2.99 ERA. By that time, the Cards were back to being a force in the National League, finishing second to the Los Angeles Dodgers with a 93-69 record.

Their longtime star, Stan Musial, had just completed the final year of a great career, but there was plenty of other talent, including Bill White, Dick Groat, Ken Boyer, Curt Flood, and Tim McCarver. On the mound, young Bob Gibson had an 18-9 mark, vet Curt Simmons was 15-9, and Ray Sadecki 10-10, which made Broglio's 18-8 record a big part of the team's success. In 1964, it was apparent that the Cards would again be contending for the pennant. Gibson, Simmons, and Sadecki were all pitching well, but Broglio was struggling. The Cards felt the team needed something, another sparkplug at the top of the lineup. Broglio was the guy deemed expendable.

Meanwhile, in Chicago, a young outfielder named Lou Brock was struggling to find his way. He had had a four-game cup of coffee in 1961 at the age of twenty-two, and then played in 123 and 148 games in 1962 and '63. His numbers were not startling. He batted .263 and .258. He had 9 homers in each of the years but just 35 and 37 runs batted in. Though he had a world of speed, he didn't seem to know how to fully use it, stealing just 16 and 24 bases during those two seasons, and when he hit just .251 in the first 51 games of 1964, the Cubs felt he could be moved. The team already had the big three bats of Ernie Banks, Ron Santo, and Billy Williams. What they needed was more pitching.

So the deal was made, and at first it wasn't a very popular one in the Cardinals clubhouse. "Everybody loved Ernie," said catcher Tim McCarver. First sacker Bill White added, "We thought we had given up too much. Brock was not a good fielder, he struck out too much, and he made a lot of mistakes on the bases."

One of Brock's problems was that he felt, as an outfielder, that he had to hit with power. Manager Johnny Keane told him to relax, concentrate on reaching base, and then steal. He gave him the green light to run anytime, and suddenly, Brock was transformed. He not only proved himself to his new teammates, he was the spark that drove the Cards to overtake the Phillies in the final weeks of the season and then defeat the Yankees in the World Series. Brock hit .348 in 103 games for the Cards and ended the season with a .315 batting average, 14 homers, 58 runs batted in, and 43 stolen bases. He also scored 111 runs. He then showed his ability to play on the big stage by hitting .300 in the Series with a homer and 5 RBIs. It was an All-Star worthy performance.

From there, Lou Brock went on to forge a Hall of Fame career. He would retire with more than 3,000 hits and break two cherished records. In 1974, at the age of thirty-five, he stole 118 bases to break Maury Wills's single season record of 104, and he retired with 938 career steals, topping Ty Cobb's lifetime mark of 892. Both records have since been shattered by Rickey Henderson, but Lou

Brock left no doubt he was one of the best ever. He also helped the Cards into another pair of World Series in 1967 and '68, starring in each when he hit .414 and .464. He had a combined 25 hits and 14 stolen bases, showing the baseball world all over again just what kind of player he was.

As for Ernie Broglio, well, it went just the other way. He pitched in 18 games for the Cubs to finish the 1964 season and went just 4-7. After that, he would pitch just two more years and win a total of three games. He had simply lost it and the Cubs received virtually nothing from the trade, in spite of their high hopes. So it now becomes obvious how the fortunes of two teams could have been affected if the trade was never made.

Without Lou Brock, the Cardinals still would have had a very competitive team. It's doubtful they would have overtaken the Phillies in 1964, since Brock provided the spark and was great down the stretch. In '67 they won the pennant by a full 10 games, so without Brock they still might have prevailed, but it would have been closer. A year later they won it by nine, led by the great Bob Gibson, who won 22 with a 1.12 ERA. So they might have won that one as well without Brock, but he sure made it a lot easier. Plus his stolen base exploits focused much attention on the Cards and put a lot of fans in the seats. His presence was a boon to attendance, as well.

The Cubs didn't get the arm they thought they were getting with Broglio, but think what they might have done if they held on to Brock. The team had a trio of sluggers in Banks, Santo, and Williams. Add the speed of Lou Brock to the top of the lineup and this team might well have thrived. When the fiery Leo Durocher took over the managerial reins in 1966, the Cubs began to climb. They were third in both 1967 and '68, and led much of the way in 1969 before the Mets caught and passed them in September. By then the team had solid pitching with ace Ferguson Jenkins, Bill

Hands, and Ken Holtzman. What they lacked was speed, and a catalyst at the top of the lineup. Had they kept Lou Brock they might well have held off the Mets in '69, which would have squashed one of baseball's great stories. The team finished second to Pittsburgh in the NL East in 1970, missing the division by five games. Would having the Cardinals' version of Lou Brock have made up those five games? There's a good chance it would have.

One final question. Would Lou Brock have been just as good if he had stayed with the Cubs? Probably, especially if he had a manager who saw his talents the way Johnny Keane did, and turned him loose on the bases. Durocher certainly would have. He was simply too great a talent to hold down.

WHAT IF THE WASHINGTON SENATORS HADN'T TRADED THEIR MANAGER TO THE NEW YORK METS?

Now this one sounds odd. It seems ridiculous to trade a manager, but that's exactly what happened in November 1967 when the Washington Senators dealt their manager, Gil Hodges, to the New York Mets in return for pitcher Bill Denehy and $100,000. Maybe they felt Hodges would have eventually left anyway so they tried to get something in return. What it accomplished initially was to return a hero to his roots. Gil Hodges had been a star for the Brooklyn Dodgers of the 1940s and '50s, one of the great Boys of Summer, part of a team that had gone to six World Series from 1947 to 1956 and played them all against the New York Yankees.

When the Dodgers moved to Los Angeles in 1958, Hodges went with them, though his best days as a player were behind him. He came back to New York in 1962 to join the expansion Mets and hit their first ever home run, but by 1963 he was clearly done. At the age of thirty-nine he played just 11 more games before the Washington Senators, also an expansion team, asked the Mets to release Hodges so he could become their manager. They did.

Hodges retired with 370 lifetime home runs and a reputation as the best-fielding first sacker of his generation.

Managing an expansion team without much talent, Hodges had them out of the basement the first year. Though the Senators remained under .500 for the next four years, by 1967 they had 76 victories and Hodges was quickly earning a reputation as one of the finest young managers in the game, a decisive presence on the bench and a real leader. He was firm, but fair, and his physical demeanor demanded respect. All the while, the people in New York were watching.

The Mets, it seemed, continued to be the worst expansion team ever. They lost a record 120 games their first season of 1962 and didn't get out of the National League basement until 1966, when Wes Westrum had taken over from Casey Stengel. That year they finished ninth,

The next year, however, they were back in a familiar place, last, losing 101 times despite the presence of a talented rookie pitcher, Tom Seaver, who would win 16 games. After the season, the Mets made their move. They wanted Hodges and soon learned the only way to get him was to make a trade.

The deal was finally made that December. Bill Denehy was a marginal pitcher who would be out of baseball in just a few years. Maybe the Senators just wanted the money. Whatever the reason, they pulled the trigger and Gil Hodges became the manager of the Mets for the 1968 season.

In a sense, what happened next is almost like a Shakespearean tragedy, and none of it would have occurred if the Senators hadn't agreed to trade their manager to the Mets. The New Yorkers had a mixture of youngsters and veterans in 1968, including a second good young pitcher in lefty Jerry Koosman. With Koosman compiling a surprising 19-12 mark and Seaver finishing at 16-12, the Mets were ninth and out of the basement at 73-89. But even that didn't prepare the baseball world for what would happen the next year. Veteran third sacker Ed Charles gave a hint when he talked about what Gil Hodges immediately brought to the team.

"Hodges changed the losing mindset," Charles said. "He was an upfront type of manager, very knowledgeable about the game, very firm in what he expected from the players. . . . A few guys were prima donnas when he took over and there were some early confrontations. But he established the fact immediately that he was the boss and that things wouldn't be like they were in the past. . . . Once he established that he was the boss the guys took notice in a hurry. I remember him getting mad once and telling us he would bring up the whole Tidewater [triple-A] ball club if he had to. We believed him."

By 1969, Hodges had tweaked the team. He picked up a few players he knew from the American League the year before (Tommie Agee, Al Weis), had a strong catcher in Jerry Grote, and was willing to platoon at several positions. He added another rookie pitcher, Gary Gentry, to go with Seaver, Koosman, and veteran Don Cardwell, and had a strong bullpen with Nolan Ryan, Tug McGraw, and Ron Taylor. A June 15 trade with the Montreal Expos brought slugging first baseman Donn Clendenon, who would platoon with Ed Kranepool, and his acquisition completed the team.

The Mets started slowly in 1969, but after 36 games they were surprisingly at .500 with an 18-18 record. A five-game losing streak caused optimism to wane, but these weren't the old Mets. The team subsequently embarked on an 11-game winning streak and suddenly they were at 29-23 and no longer the laughingstock of the league. Hodges continued to run a tight ship and, slowly, the Mets began showing everyone they were for real. The 1969 season was the first year of divisional play and soon it became apparent that the National League East was coming down to two teams, the Mets and Leo Durocher's front-running Chicago Cubs.

Under Hodges' guidance, the Mets continued to get stronger. Seaver was putting together a Cy Young year and Koosman, after some early-season arm problems, was right behind. On September 10, the Mets forged into first place for the first time in their history and they never looked back. They would win 101 games, take the division, then sweep the Atlanta Braves in the first ever divisional series before upsetting the powerful Baltimore Orioles in the World Series in just five games. The Series featured clutch hits, great catches, and top pitching performances by a team that seemed to have destiny on its side, and the Mets credited their manager for all that had happened.

"I always felt that Gil was the smartest manager in the league," said Jerry Koosman. "The more time you spent around him the more you realized he was always one or two steps ahead of the opposing manager. [With us] there was never any hollering or screaming. He might shake your hand or give you a pat on the butt. But mostly he sat quietly and ran the club on an even keel. He wouldn't let us get too high or two low. But by late in the season he did expect us to win."

The team would forever be know as the Miracle Mets, going from ninth to first, then winning the World Series against a Frank and Brooks Robinson–led Orioles team that had won 109 games during the regular season. And it only happened because the Mets had decided to take the unusual step of trading for a manager, and the Washington Senators accepted. Had they refused, the Mets would have had to look elsewhere and the miracle probably would not have occurred.

How can anyone be so sure? Well, it was one of those magical seasons when everything went right, every decision Gil Hodges made was the correct one, and the trade for Clendenon paid dividends. When a great pitching performance was needed, they got it, and when a great catch had to save a game, it happened, right through to the end of the World Series. With a different manager—any manager—the decisions would have been different; the personnel would have been somewhat different, and the team might have responded differently. Without Gil Hodges and the trade that brought him back to New York, a real piece of baseball history would have been lost.

Why, then, call it a Shakespearean tragedy? On September 24, 1968, toward the end of his first season with the team, Gil Hodges suffered a mild heart attack. Coach Rube Walker managed the team over the final week or so of the season. By the start of the next campaign, Hodges had been given a clean bill of health and returned to work. After the miraculous '69 season, he managed the team the next two years. Both times they finished third with identical 83-79 records. Koosman had a recurrence of arm trouble and some of the young players, as well as the veterans, just couldn't duplicate the event of 1969.

Near the end of spring training in 1972, the players went on strike in one of baseball's periodic work stoppages. On April 2, Gil Hodges had just finished a round of golf with some of his coaches when he had a second and massive heart attack. He died two days before his forty-eighth birthday. The short but sweet Gil Hodges era was over, but as long as baseball is played in New York, the 1969 season will be remembered as a real miracle, orchestrated by a manager who had been acquired via a trade.

WHAT IF JOHN SMOLTZ HADN'T BEEN TRADED BY DETROIT TO THE ATLANTA BRAVES?

This is an interesting trade because one team was looking for the quick fix while the other was taking a chance on the long haul. In that sense, it was similar to the Lew Burdette–Johnny Sain deal, and while it looked at first as if the quick fix team got the better of the deal, it definitely turned out the other way when all was said and done. The trade occurred on August 12, 1987, when the Atlanta Braves shipped thirty-seven-year-old veteran right-hander Doyle Alexander to the Detroit Tigers in return for a twenty-year-old righty named John Smoltz. At the time of the trade, the Tigers were in a battle for the American League East title with the Toronto Blue Jays, while the Braves were headed for a 69-92 finish, a step out of the National League East basement. Guess which team wanted the quick fix?

Alexander was a journeyman whose career had begun in 1971. When he moved to the Tigers in '87 it would be his ninth and final big league stop, including two stints with both the Yankees and the Braves. He was an up-and-down player, good one year, not so good the next. You never quite knew what you would get from Doyle Alexander. He won 17 games with Texas in 1977, and had a pair of 17-win seasons for the Blue Jays in 1984 and '85. Yet he was 9-10 and 5-7 for the Rangers following his 17-win season, then bounced back to go 14-11 for the Braves in 1980. Two years later, he was just 1-7 on a very good New York Yankees team. That's the way it was.

When he went to the Tigers, Alexander exceeded everyone's expectations. He started 11 times down the stretch and finished the regular season with a perfect 9-0 record and 1.53 earned run average. Suddenly, Doyle Alexander looked like Grover Cleveland Alexander. The Tigers also won in the two starts when he didn't figure in the decision, making the team 11-0 when he took the mound. They would win the division by just two games over the Blue Jays. Guess who received a great deal of credit for bringing them a division title? Doyle Alexander, of course, and rightly so. Had the trade not been made, the Tigers would not have been division champs. Team brass deserved a pat on the back for that one. Mission accomplished.

On the other end of the trade was John Smoltz. Smoltz was a minor leaguer in 1987, having been drafted in the twenty-second round by the Tigers in 1985, but he was considered a prospect. A year later he got a taste of the majors, 12 starts and a 2-7 record with a 5.48 earned run average. Did the Braves make a mistake? The next two years, however, Smoltz began to get his legs. Installed in the rotation, he was 12-11 and then 14-11 on teams that lost 97 games each year. But in '91 the Braves came to life, going from last to first in the National League East as Smoltz compiled a 14-13 record. That would start a run of fourteen consecutive division titles for Atlanta with John Smoltz playing a huge part in a rotation that also featured Tom Glavine and later Greg Maddux.

In 1996, Smoltz went 24-8 with 276 strikeouts and a 2.94 ERA to win the National League Cy Young Award. That wasn't all. When he began having some recurring arm problems, he volunteered to become a closer, feeling a relief role wouldn't put much strain on his arm. He quickly became one of the best, saving 55 games in 2002 and winning the Rolaids Fireman of the Year Award. He saved 45 and 44 games over the next two seasons. Then, in 2005 at the age of 38, he returned to the rotation and over the next three years compiled records of 14-7, 16-9, and 14-8. At the age of forty he remained one of the better pitchers in the National League.

That still isn't all. During the Braves fourteen-year playoff run, which included one World Series triumph and four trips to the Fall Classic, John Smoltz became one of the best big game pitchers of his generation. His overall postseason record is an amazing 15-4 with a 2.65 ERA. In the World Series he's just 2-2, but his 2.47 earned run average says how well he's pitched. In the divisional series he's 7-0, and in nine championship series 6-2. With 207 career victories and 154 career saves as a closer, there's little doubt where John Smoltz will wind up. In Cooperstown.

Now how does the trade look? Doyle Alexander helped the Tigers into the playoffs, but it was a last hurrah. He did have a 14-11 season in 1988, but in '89 he was an abysmal 6-18 and promptly retired. That same year, John Smoltz was still getting started. It's pretty safe to say that had the Braves not made the deal for John Smoltz, they would not have set a record by winning fourteen straight divisional titles. They certainly would have had a very good team and would have won more than their share, but Smoltz was a steady and sometimes spectacular performer who helped them get there every year, and without him closing for those three seasons (2002–04), the team might not have gotten the job done then, either.

So do you trade for the quick fix or long haul? Both. When pulling the trigger on a deal for a quick fix, however, you have to gauge what you're giving up. "Win now" might be the immediate mantra, but every team has a long haul and you don't want to give up too much. Detroit did.

Shine On, Superstar

Great athletes don't come along every day. The truly special ones are only a select few considering the thousands upon thousands of athletes participating in sports. It's always a sad day when a truly great athlete retires—for the athlete, his teammates, his league, and his many fans. To know you'll never again see Willie Mays chasing a long fly ball, or Bill Russell blocking a shot, or Muhammad Ali dancing around the ring, or John Unitas throwing a touchdown pass is a bit of a traumatic experience for the true sports fan who appreciates greatness. Unfortunately, some of these athletes stay too long, to the point where they can't perform the way they used to. But what's even sadder is the athlete who has to leave too soon. Maybe it's an injury or illness that forces him out, or maybe he just decides he's lost the passion and wants to do something else. At any rate, when an athlete goes too soon there's always the question of what he would have done had he played the length of a normal career. Then you always have to wonder what could have been.

But what if these superstars didn't have to leave too soon?

★　★　★　★　★

If you're a real sports fan, you appreciate the really great athlete, the superstar who dominates his sport and makes what we all find very difficult look easy. These special few combine great talent with a work ethic and competitive drive that takes them to the top, and they work to stay there, game to game, month to month, and year to year. Some sports, of course, lend themselves to longer careers than others, but most of the great athletes find a way to keep going. They love what they do, love being around their team-mates, and love the cheers of the crowd. Years ago, they did it even though they didn't make much money. Today, they can make millions while still getting the same primal satisfactions.

Sadly, there are also those who manage to rise to greatness only to leave it behind before they're really ready to go. Some can't continue because of an injury, or can only continue at a lower level of performance. Others have the misfortune to become ill and are forced to retire, and a few simply decide they've had it, that they want to leave while on top and do something else. In each case we're left to wonder just how great they would have been had they continued for the normal length of a career, and what their final place would be within their sport if they had. It's an intriguing question, and here are a group of those athletes about which it can be asked.

ADDIE JOSS

Baseball was a very different game a hundred years ago, and it may be tough to envision a Hall of Fame player as having had an incomplete career. But that's what happened to a right-handed pitcher named Adrian "Addie" Joss, who pitched for the Cleveland Indians from 1902 through 1910. Nine years do not normally make for a Hall of Fame career, but Addie Joss's nine glorious years did. His career did-n't end because of an arm injury or because he drank too much. It ended in a very tragic way. On April 14, 1911, two days after what would have been the start of his tenth season in the big leagues, Addie Joss died of tubercular meningitis. Both a career and a life were over.

But what a career he had. Joss, who was born in Woodland, Wisconsin, was uncommonly tall for his day, standing a gangly 6'3" and he weighed 185 pounds. He threw with what has been de-scribed as "an exaggerated pinwheel motion" that resulted in the nickname "the Human Hairpin." Joss was essentially a fastball, curveball pitcher but his trump card was pinpoint control. He av-eraged just 1.43 walks per game, the third best in big league history. Addie Joss joined the Indians in 1902 and pitched a one-hit shutout in his debut, showing his great talent from day one. He would win 17 games that year and lead the league with five shutouts.

From there, his career simply took off. He won 18 his second year and had his first 20-win season in 1905. That was the first of four-straight 20-win seasons, topped by his 27-11 mark in 1907. The year after that he won 24 and had an earned run average of 1.16. On October 2, 1908, Joss faced the White Sox's Big Ed Walsh in a pivotal, late-season game. Walsh would win 40 games that sea-son, and on that day, he allowed the Indians just four hits, but a sin-gle in the third allowed an unearned run to score. That was more than enough for Addie Joss. That afternoon he retired twenty-seven White Sox hitters in succession—a perfect game!

Joss also had his share of illness and injury. He missed the final month of the 1903 season with a high fever and then con-tracted malaria in 1904. Back problems slowed him in 1905. But he persevered. Joss threw a second no-hitter in April 1910 as he started the season with four straight wins. But soon after that he developed a sore arm, and after his record dropped even at 5-5, he was sent home to rest. The following spring he looked strong again, throwing six good innings in an exhibition game, but his teammates noticed he looked very thin. After fainting on the bench at Chattanooga, he was sent home and died soon afterward.

Addie Joss finished his career with a record of 160-97. He had a career earned run average of 1.89, which continues to be the second best of all time. The great Ty Cobb, who had an incredible .367 lifetime batting average, hit just .071 against Addie Joss. Joss also allowed fewer baserunners per nine innings (8.73) than any other pitcher in big league history.

But what if he had a career of, say, sixteen years? That would have added another seven seasons to his resume. Not counting the 1910 season when Joss had the sore arm, he averaged 19.3 wins for his first eight years in the bigs. Had he avoided more arm problems, he could have had, say, as many as 16 wins per season for those seven years. That would be another 112 victories, giving him 272 for his career.

It might not put him in the same category as Cy Young or Walter Johnson, but it would have made for a great career, and any pitcher with great control who stays healthy can keep winning. He had already thrown a perfect game and another no-hitter, and he certainly could have added a third or even a fourth no-no before he was through. Joss completed 234 of his 260 starts, another amazing statistic, and his earned run averages in years he didn't win big are yet another tribute to his talent. He led the league with a 1.59 ERA in 1904, when he was just 14-10, and had a 1.71 ERA in 1909, when he was just 14-13.

For years, Addie Joss was a largely forgotten figure in baseball annals. He didn't qualify for the Hall of Fame because there was a rule saying a player had to be in the majors for ten years. Finally, in 1978, the Veterans Committee did the right thing. They waived the ten-year rule and voted Addie Joss into the Hall, preserving the memory of a great pitcher forever.

Unlike many of his contemporaries, Joss wasn't a rough-and-tumble, hard-drinking, uneducated ballplayer. In the off-season, he was a sportswriter for the *Toledo News-Bee*. Another town paper, the *Blade*, wrote an editorial about Joss that said, in part, "Baseball was a profession, as severe as that of any other. . . . In taking his vocation seriously [Joss] was, in return, taken seriously by the people, who recognized in him a man of more than usual intelligence and one who would have adorned any profession in which he had elected to engage."

ROSS YOUNGS

Like Addie Joss before him, Ross Youngs was an early star now largely forgotten because his career was cut short by illness and early death. Youngs was an outfielder for John McGraw's New York Giants from 1917 to 1926. In June of 1926, he was leading the club in batting when he was hospitalized with a severe urinary tract infection, which was the result of another infection that had passed from his throat to his kidneys. Though he returned to the team in mid-August, he had to finish the season under the constant care of a nurse. That was the last time he played. Youngs was bedridden for all of 1927 until he died on October 22 from kidney disease.

It ended a bright life and career. Youngs was originally from Shiner, Texas, born April 10, 1897, and was a star halfback on the football team at West Texas Military Academy. He had played baseball in various leagues in Texas from 1914 through 1916 when a scout recommended him to John McGraw. By 1917, he saw his first big league action and became a regular the next year.

Youngs wasn't a power hitter, but he made great contact, had great speed, and in the outfield had an extremely powerful throwing arm. He was a McGraw ballplayer all the way, hitting over .300 in seven of his eight full seasons, with a high of .356 in 1924. He played in four World Series with the Giants from 1921 to 1924 and stole home 10 times during his career. His career batting average was .322, but his .264 mark in 1925 might have been the result of the beginnings of his illness.

Youngs was a compact 5'8", 162-pounder who might well have had a twenty-year career if his health hadn't failed. The 1930s were approaching, a time when hitting picked up tremendously in the National League. Having averaged 171 hits a year during his eight full seasons, if you give him that average for another nine years—and being the type of hitter he was, he might well have done that—you would have to add another 1,539 hits to his ledger. Put that together with the 1,491 he had and you have 3,020. Every player with 3,000 or more hits is remembered today as a great player.

His manager, John McGraw, was not one to pass out compliments easily. He was as tough and critical as they come, yet of Ross Youngs, McGraw said, "He was the greatest outfielder I ever saw. He could do everything that a baseball player should do and do it better than most players. As an outfielder, he had no superiors. And he was the easiest man I ever had to handle. . . . On top of that, a gamer player than Youngs never played ball."

It's said that John McGraw always kept two pictures above the desk in his office. One was the legendary Christy Mathewson. The other was Ross Youngs. The Veterans Committee must have agreed with McGraw. They voted Youngs into the Hall of Fame in 1972.

DIZZY DEAN

His name was Jay Hanna Dean, or maybe Jerome Herman Dean, depending on what he felt like saying that day. To make things easy, everyone called him "Dizzy," and he generally referred to himself as "Ol' Diz," though he was still in his twenties. He had his own way of speaking, his own vocabulary. When he struck out a hitter, he'd say he "fogged" one past him. When someone asked him why he told reporters different stories, he replied, "I was helpin' those writers out. Them ain't lies; them's scoops."

It's no secret that Dizzy Dean is a legend, the National League's last 30-game winner, a member of the famed St. Louis Cardinals Gas House Gang team of the mid-1930s, and a Hall of Famer who became an iconoclastic broadcaster once his playing days ended. What people sometimes tend to forget is that Dizzy Dean won just 150 games and really had only five and a half peak seasons before a freak injury curtailed his effectiveness. Because those five and a half peak seasons came at the beginning of his career, Dizzy Dean presents one of the great "What-Ifs" in baseball history.

Diz was born in Lucas, Arkansas, on January 16, 1911, the son of a sharecropper. He had a poverty-filled childhood, dropped out of school in the fourth grade and enlisted in the army at sixteen. He was already pitching by then and used to sharpen his control by throwing potatoes whenever he had KP. Signed by the Cardinals in May of 1929, he was sent to the St. Paul Saints of the Class A Western League. He had a 17-8 record when he was promoted to the Houston Buffaloes in the Texas League. The fast track continued. He was 8-2 with Houston and got a late-season call-up by the Cards. His major league debut was a complete game, three-hit victory in which he gave up just a single run. The kid could pitch.

A year later, at the age of twenty-one, he began his five-year run. His record over the next five seasons was phenomenal: 18-15, 20-18, 30-7, 28-12, and 24-13. He led the league in strikeouts the first four years and fanned between 190 and 199 hitters in each of the five seasons. Like a lot of stars back then, Diz started and relieved when needed, and led the National League in complete games four times. And then, of course, there were all the zany antics.

255

In 1934, Diz predicted the Cards would win the pennant. His younger brother Paul was now on the team. He was dubbed "Daffy," and Diz boldly predicted that Paul would win 18 to 20 games while he would win 20 to 25. Diz ended up winning 30 and Paul came in with 19. On September 21 of that year, the Deans pitched a doubleheader against the Dodgers at Ebbets Field. Diz took a no-hitter into the eighth inning of the opener and won it, 13-0, finishing with a three-hitter. Then, in the nightcap, his brother Paul pitched a no-hitter, allowing just a first-inning walk.

"If I'd known what Paul was gonna do, I would have pitched one, too," Diz said. And a lot of people believed him.

"If there is such a thing as getting a kick out of losing, I got it today," said Dodgers catcher Al Lopez after the double-header loss. "I think we were all up there with our mouths open in admiration of the stuff those two were throwing."

In the World Series that year, Diz predicted he and Paul would win two games each and that's just what happened. The Deans and the Cards beat the Detroit Tigers in seven games. Diz pitched a six-hit shutout in the final game while going on just one day's rest. That's the kind of pitcher Dizzy Dean was. At the end of the 1936 season he was just twenty-five years old and had already won 121 games. There was no telling what his final numbers might be.

Of course, things rarely turn out perfectly. Paul Dean won 19 games again in 1935, but the next year he held out for more money, and when he finally came to camp he tried to throw too hard too soon. He hurt his arm and was never the same. In fact, he never won more than five games in a season again, hanging on until 1943. Diz, however, seemed as good as ever. In 1937 he seemed on his way to another big season. Though he preferred going fishing during the All-Star break, his wife persuaded him to pitch in the game. In the third inning, the Indians' Earl Averill slammed a hard line drive that struck the little toe on Diz's left foot.

When told it was fractured, Diz replied, "Fractured, hell! The damn thing's broken!"

The problem was that you couldn't keep Diz down. He was back on the mound in two weeks, wearing an oversized shoe. To compensate for the pain he said was stabbing up to his hip he changed his pitching motion. He described what happened next. "As the ball left my hand, there was a loud crack in my shoulder, and my arm went numb down to my fingers."

Because of the injured arm, Diz was just 13-10 in 1937, and when his arm didn't come around, Cards president Branch Rickey traded him to the Cubs for three journeyman players and $185,000. Apparently, the Cubs were willing to take a chance that he'd regain his form. Diz pitched sparingly in 1938, but managed to compile a 7-1 record with a 1.81 earned run average in just 13 games, but by the next year it was clear he wouldn't get the magic back. He hung on until 1941, only winning nine more games. One of baseball's most talented pitchers and colorful characters was done at the youthful age of thirty.

But what if Dizzy Dean had not been hurt in that All-Star Game? He was just twenty-six years old when it happened and well on his way to a fifth straight 20-win season. Though he was a fast-ball pitcher, there's a good chance he could have lasted another twelve years. Assuming that he would have had several more 20-plus-win seasons, it's pretty safe to say he could have averaged 18 wins a year. That would have added another 216 victories to the 121 he had before the start of the 1937 season, giving him 337 wins and putting him in a class with the game's elite. Even a more modest 15 wins a year would have squeezed him past the 300-win mark.

That isn't all. Diz was averaging 194 strikeouts a season during his peak years. Drop that to 180 Ks over a final projected twelve seasons and Diz would have fanned another 2,160 hitters to go with the 975 he had through 1936. That would give him 3,135 Ks for his career and would have made him the second pitcher after Walter Johnson to record 3,000 strikeouts. Diz also fancied himself a hitter and actually slammed eight home runs during his peak seasons. A healthy Diz making 30 to 35 or more starts a year could have wound up among the top-slugging pitchers of all time.

Despite only having 150 career wins, there was no denying Diz's talent. No one objected when he was voted into the Hall of Fame in 1953. But had it not been for the bad luck of one line drive, what a pitcher he could have been.

SANDY KOUFAX

In a way, you can compare Sandy Koufax with Dizzy Dean. The Dodger left-hander of the 1950s and 1960s won 166 games and retired at the age of thirty-one because of an injury to his pitching elbow. Both were outstanding pitchers who could have had much greater careers, but there was a difference, besides the fact that one was right-handed and the other a southpaw. Dean's best years were early in his career, right out of the gate. After his injury, he hung around another few years probably hoping to find the magic again.

Sandy Koufax was just the opposite. Possessor of a rising, electric fastball, Koufax had trouble controlling it in his early years with the Dodgers. It wasn't until he got some advice from catcher Norm Sherry and a part-time scout who helped change his motion to give him better vision—as well as telling him to relax and not try to overpower every hitter—that Koufax became nearly untouchable. In Sandy's case, it was the first six years of his career that were mediocre. In the last six, he was as good as any pitcher who ever lived. For example, in his final season of 1966 he compiled a record of 27-9 with a 1.73 earned run average, 27 complete games, five shutouts, and 317 strikeouts. That kind of season matches up with most other great pitchers' best.

Why, then, did he call it quits if he was still so good? Two years earlier, in 1964, Koufax was in the midst of another great season. On August 16, he had a 19-5 record with seven shutouts when he banged his left elbow on the ground diving back into second base. He didn't pitch again that season and the injury caused an arthritic condition to develop in the elbow. His last two seasons he rarely threw between starts, stopped using a slider and a sidearm delivery to lefties, yet still kept setting records. His elbow only felt good when he pitched, but he feared if he continued, the arm would be permanently crippled. So he packed it in. Interestingly, some say that modern day arthroscopic surgery could have alleviated the condition and allowed him to continue.

Sandy Koufax in his prime was absolutely overpowering. From 1962 to 1966 his record was 111-34. He had the lowest earned run average in the league each year and threw four no-hitters (then a record, pre-Nolan Ryan), including a perfect game. He set a record of 382 strikeouts in the 1965 season (also broken by Ryan with 383) and shut out the Minnesota Twins in the seventh game of the 1965 World Series pitching on just two days rest.

One of his Dodger teammates, fellow pitcher Claude Osteen, once said, "You know how a guy fouls a ball straight back and you gasp, because he just missed it and is going to get the next one? With Koufax, they never got that next one."

Sandy was born on December 30, 1935, in Brooklyn. His original name was Sanford Braun, but he took the name of his mother's second husband, whom she married before Sandy's third birthday. He began playing on the schoolyards in Brooklyn, eventually going to the University of Cincinnati on a basketball scholarship. In 1954, the Dodgers signed the hometown kid to a bonus of $14,000. Under the rules of the day he would have to stay in the majors for two years. Catcher Rube Walker saw Sandy work out one day and said to Dodger management, "Whatever he wants, give it to him. I wouldn't let him get out of the clubhouse."

At 6'2", 210 pounds, Koufax was extremely strong. He had large hands and long fingers, which made his curve break off the table and his fastball move. One spring, Manager Walt Alston thought he noticed a little flab on Sandy's side just above the beltline. He thought maybe his lefty had gained weight over the winter and playfully grabbed the area to tease Koufax. As soon as he grabbed it he let go and jumped back, astonished. It wasn't flab, but a rock-hard ridge of pure muscle. That's how strong Sandy was.

Sandy began finding himself in 1961, when he reversed an 8-13 record from the year before (and almost decided to quit) to go 18-13 with a league-best 269 strikeouts. The next year he was sailing along at 14-7 when a circulatory problem in one of his pitching fingers ended his season. Over the next four years (1963 to 1966) he was 25-5, 19-5, 26-8, and 27-9. Those four seasons stack up against any season by any other pitcher ever, and the 19-5 year was shortened by the elbow injury.

It's hard to believe that Sandy's career began in 1955, the only year the Dodgers won a World Series while in Brooklyn, but he was just 2-2 that year, then 2-4 and 5-4 in the next two before the team moved to Los Angeles. Brooklyn fans never saw their native son at his best. The first three years in L.A. weren't much better. He was still inconsistent, going 11-11, 8-6, and 8-13. Mostly starting by then, he also pitched some out of the bullpen and continued to have control problems. When he was 11-11 in 1959, he had 131 strikeouts in 158.2 innings, and he also walked 105 batters. That wouldn't do, but by the time he set the record with 382 strikeouts in just 335.2 innings in 1965, he walked just 71. That's how it came together for him.

He was also a ferocious competitor who always knew he'd have to pitch well to compensate for the Dodgers' lack of hitting, and if you watch slow motion film of his delivery, you can see how much he put into every single pitch. The mystery of Sandy Koufax was why it took him so long to find himself. The talent was obviously always there. There's an old adage in baseball that says left-handers tend to develop slowly, especially hard-throwing lefties. Maybe with the right coaching, or if he received earlier the advice that he got in 1961, he would have matured more quickly. Either way, Koufax's career is a big What-If.

As it stands, there are people today who still feel Sandy Koufax is the greatest left-hander ever, maybe the greatest ever. Certainly for the final five years of his career you can make a strong case. His final record was 166-87. He threw 137 complete games, 40 shutouts, and struck out 2,396 hitters in 2324.1 innings. That's more than a strike-out per inning. Let's look at his career in two ways.

What if he had pitched for another five years at the same level of his final five? He would have been barely thirty-six years old then, so it was certainly possible. Sandy always kept himself in tip-top condition and without the arthritic elbow should have been fine. Just averaging 20 wins a season would give him another 100 victories, bringing him to 266. And if he averaged just 250 strike-outs a season, not the 307 that he averaged his last four years, he would have had another 1,250 Ks, giving him 3,646 for his career. These are all great numbers, and who's to say that a healthy Koufax couldn't have pitched another few years. Three more years of just 12 victories would have put him over 300 and 150 strikeouts in those years would have bumped him past the 4,000 mark.

There is still another side to the Koufax What-If. Suppose he had found the magic three or four years earlier, maybe in 1958. Tack on another 50 victories and maybe 600 strikeouts and then do the math. With a long career, Sandy Koufax would not only be considered one of the best, but would have also put up numbers that could have shown he was the best. As it was, despite his shortened career and *only* 166 victories, he was elected to the Hall of Fame in 1972, the first year he was eligible.

DON MATTINGLY

There was a time when New York Yankees first baseman Don Mattingly was considered the best player in baseball. Period. In fact, when the *New York Times* conducted a poll of major league players in 1986, asking them to choose the best player in the game, Mattingly was the overwhelming choice. Just how good was the man dubbed "Donnie Baseball" in New York? Let's put it this way. While not a pure slugger, he had become one of the best all-around hitters in the game, capable of the timely homer, the line-drive double, singles all over the place, and a batting average often well above .300. He also drove in a lot of runs, and on top of that, he was clearly the best fielding first baseman in the league and one of the best of his era.

From 1984 through 1989, Mattingly played the game the way the greats played it, with ease, joy, intensity, and tremendous talent. He worked at it, too, honing his swing, taking endless hours of batting practice and ground balls at first. He also became the Yankees' leader in an era when the team wasn't dominant. Here are a few things that Don Mattingly accomplished during that six-year period.

In his first full season, in 1984, the twenty-three-year-old Mattingly won the American League batting title with a .343 average. He added 23 homers and 110 RBIs. A year later, he smacked 35 homers, drove in a league-best 145 runs, collected 211 hits with 86 for extra bases, batted a solid .324, and was named the American League's Most Valuable Player. But he still wasn't through. The next year he was a .352 hitter with 238 hits, 53 doubles, 31 homers, and 113 runs batted in. His hits and doubles were both Yankees team records.

And that still wasn't the end of it. In 1987, Mattingly tied a longstanding record when he homered in eight consecutive games, and when he slammed a grand slam homer off Boston's Bruce Hurst on September 29, he set a major league mark by hitting six grand slams in a single season. His batting average was .327 that year and he hit 30 homers while driving in 115 runs, all despite missing 21 games to injury. The next two years he slacked off, but just slightly, hitting .311 and .303. In 1988, he had just 18 homers and 88 RBIs, but missed another 18 games, and in 1989 he rebounded to 23 homers and 113 runs batted in.

In those six years Don Mattingly had 1,219 hits, 257 doubles, 160 home runs, 684 RBIs, and a .327 batting average. Per season that becomes an average of 203 hits, 43 doubles, 27 homers, 114 RBIs, and a .327 average. Throw in a Gold Glove for his stellar defense each year and the picture you get is that of a first-ballot Hall of Famer. In addition, his Yankee legacy was already such that he was being mentioned in the same breath as icons such as Babe Ruth, Lou Gehrig, Joe DiMaggio, and Mickey Mantle. He was already part of the New York lineage of all-time greats.

Then something happened. In reality, it began in 1987 when Mattingly wound up on the disabled list for the first time with an injured back. There were rumors of horseplay in the locker room causing it, but Mattingly said it happened while he was fielding ground balls. It involved two disks in his back, and Donnie Baseball himself referred to it as a "serious injury." He returned after his DL stint and continued to have an outstanding season, but when his back flared up again, it was something else.

He struggled with the bat early in the 1990 season and eventually went on the DL in July, not returning until late in the season, but this time he didn't hit like the old Donnie. In 102 games he batted just .256, with 5 homers and 42 runs batted in. The following year he was healthy enough to play in 152 games and then another 157 in 1992, but something was missing. He batted .288 each year, not bad, but definitely not Mattingly. The big difference was in his power numbers. He hit 9 and 14 homers and drove in just 68 and 86 runs. Even the fans began to realize that this wasn't the same guy they were so used to seeing.

Mattingly would play three more years (including the strike-shortened year of 1994), never appearing in more than 134 games in a season. While his batting average was still respectable (.291, .304, and .288), his power production continued to drop—the homers from 17 to 6 and then 7, and the RBIs from 86 to 51 and 49. Then, at the end of the 1995 season, he called it quits at the age of thirty-four. Ironically, the Yankees made the playoffs that year for the first time in Mattingly's career, and in a five-game series against Seattle he was outstanding. He had 10 hits, 5 for extra bases, 6 RBIs, and a .417 batting average. Still, the Yanks lost and Mattingly retired without a World Series ring.

Because he was a mere mortal during the final six years of his career it now appears that Don Mattingly will never make it to the Hall of Fame. Some say that he should. They compare his numbers with those of the late Kirby Puckett, who had to retire early after his lost vision to glaucoma, but Puckett was still at the top of his game when he had to quit. Mattingly wasn't. Yet when you play "What If" with Don Mattingly's numbers, you get some incredible results.

Remember, you not only have to prorate his final six years, but probably add at least four more. As hard as he worked, and because he always kept himself in top condition, it's not a stretch to think that Mattingly could have played at least to the age of thirty-eight. Let's, then, take a look at his numbers, allowing a natural decline for age using that same ten-year window.

In his six peak years Mattingly averaged 203 hits a year. So let's say he averaged just 180 over his final ten seasons. Those 1,800 more hits added to his six-year total, and the few hits he got his first two part-time seasons would make him the first Yankee ever to top 3,000 hits. His total would be 3,190. He averaged 43 doubles a year at his peak. Make it 35 for the next ten and you have a total of 622 doubles, way above all-time Yankee leader Gehrig, who had 534. Not a huge slugger, Mattingly averaged 27 homers a season during his run. Make it 22 for the remainder of his prorated career and his total would read 384, ahead of Joe DiMaggio (361) and good enough for fourth place on the all-time Yankee list. If he averaged just 95 RBIs a year for the balance of his career, he'd have wound up with 1,655 and that would put him behind Gehrig and Ruth, in third place on the all-time Yankee list, ahead of Joe D., the Mick, and Yogi. And assuming his .327 batting average would come down a bit, to maybe .320, he'd still be the fifth-best Yankee all-time hitter.

Accept the math and he also would have been a definite first-ballot Hall of Famer. There were even those who felt Mattingly should have continued longer with the Yanks, especially given the way he hit in the 1995 playoffs. If he had been healthy and played the extra four years, he would have been part of the Joe Torre era and the team that would win three World Series in four years, and he might have stayed for the fourth one in 2000, giving him a nineteen-year career.

"I did make some adjustments the final half of my last year," Mattingly said. "I was watching Straw [Darryl Strawberry] with the leg kick. I started messing with it and got the hang of it. I felt I could do some things I wish I had done early. I think I could have got it back to the 20-home run range. So I felt I could have kept playing because my leg kick was giving me power again. My biggest problem wasn't baseball, but it was being on the road, being away from family. My kids were getting bigger and I felt I was giving up too much."

So Donnie Baseball retired and baseball was the loser. In his prime, he was a joy to watch, both at the bat and in the field. And those who saw him and knew what happened to him have at one time or another all said the same thing. Oh, what could have been!

JIM BROWN

Whenever there is a who's-the-best sports debate, the word *arguably* usually comes up. He's arguably the best hitter, or arguably the best point guard, but there's one area of one sport where the word is never used. Whenever someone asks about the greatest running back in NFL history, the answer is simple. Jim Brown. No ifs, ands, buts, or arguablys. Despite a parade of outstanding running backs down through the years—and many of them were great—one name continues to stand head and shoulders over the rest, even more than forty years after his unexpected and early retirement.

Jim Brown never changed from his first NFL carry in 1957 to his final one in 1965. He was simply electric, the perfect combination of speed and power, a runner who could beat you several ways and who fought for every single yard. At 6'2", 232 pounds, he was a rock-solid performer who never missed a single game during his nine-year career with the Cleveland Browns. Playing in the days of the 12- and 14-game schedule, he was over the 1,000-yard mark seven times, topped 1,500 yards twice, and had a career best of 1,863 yards in the 14-game season of 1963. That year, he carried the ball 291 times and averaged an incredible 6.4 yards a carry while gaining 133 yards a game.

Brown was born on St. Simons Island in coastal Georgia on February 17, 1936, and then moved to Long Island in New York, where he grew up. He was an outstanding athlete from the start, earning thirteen letters at Manhasset High School in football, basketball, baseball, lacrosse, and track. From there he went to Syracuse University where he became an All-American in both football and lacrosse, gaining 986 yards his senior year of 1956 in just eight games. That's an average of 6.2 yards a carry, which was typical Brown. When the Cleveland Browns made him their top pick in the 1957 draft, they got more than they expected. They got a ready-made star.

Brown gained 942 yards on 202 carries as a rookie in 1957, averaging 4.7 yards a tote. Though he was named NFL Rookie of the Year, the best was still yet to come. The very next season, he ran for 1,527 yards in just 12 games, carrying 257 times for a 5.9 average, and he did it not so much by running wide, which he certainly could do, but by pounding the ball off tackle. It was a case of give him an inch and he'd take a lot more. Once he was past the line he was as good in the open field as any runner, and if he got behind the defensive backs they couldn't catch him. Today he remains the personification of speed and power. No one has ever been quite like him.

Jim Brown had more going for him than just his football ability. He was intelligent, articulate, and very handsome—with enough notoriety that Hollywood came calling. He had a small part in the movie *Rio Conchos* in 1964, and then when the 1965 season ended he was offered a leading role in what was expected to be a blockbuster film, *The Dirty Dozen*. Already looking for life after football, Brown accepted.

He had just completed his ninth season in the NFL and was twenty-nine years old. No one could say he was slipping because he had put together a year in which he ran for 1,544 yards on 289 carries, an average of 5.3 yards a pop, and once again led the league in rushing. When it was time to report to training camp for the 1966 season, however, he was still filming. Finally, the Browns gave him an ultimatum, report or else. Never one to be threatened, Jim Brown simply announced his retirement, and he meant it. He would go on to a very successful movie career with several major starring roles, but being a lead actor wouldn't obscure what he did on the gridiron.

When he retired, Jim was the NFL's all-time leading rusher with 12,312 yards on 2,359 carries. He was a three-time Most Valuable Player and appeared in nine straight Pro Bowls. His career average of 5.2 yards a carry continues to be the best ever, a further testament to his talent in an era when NFL defenses were very tough and geared to stop the run.

Today, while Jim Brown is still universally acclaimed as the greatest ever at his position, he is only the eighth-best rusher in NFL history. That begs the question of just how far he could have gone if he continued his career. It's an interesting question because Jim Brown was a complete natural. He was always in top shape, yet rarely lifted weights. He had great strength and leg drive, and, of course, all his instinctive moves. A firm believer in hard-nosed football, he never intentionally ran out of bounds unless it was to stop the clock. He's always put his head down and drove for those extra few yards.

Comparing Brown's stats with the two leading rushers in history is interesting. On top is Emmitt Smith, who ran for 18,355 yards on 4,409 carries, an average of 4.2 yards a carry, and behind him is the great Walter Payton, who gained 16,726 yards on 3,838 carries, an average of 4.4 yards a pop. Both Smith and Payton were extremely durable and played for fifteen and thirteen seasons respectively. Neither, however, had Brown's speed or his power. Smith carried the ball 2,050 times more than Brown; Payton 1,479 more times.

Multiply those carries by Brown's career average and the numbers become astounding. Give Jim Brown 2,050 carries at 5.2 yards a pop and he would have had another 10,660 yards or 22,972 yards. Give him Payton's carries and he would have added 7,690 yards to his total, gaining 20,002 yards.

If that sounds unrealistic, there's another way to do it. Suppose Jim Brown had played just five more years, until he was thirty-four. Because of his conditioning and his history, chances are he wouldn't have slowed down much. For his nine-year career he averaged 262 carries and 1,368 yards. Suppose for those final five years he averaged 250 carries and a per-rush average of 4.9 yards a carry. That would be another 1,250 carries for 6,125 yards. If he did that, Jim Brown would have finished his career with 18,437 yards, just slightly ahead of Smith's all-time mark. With 3,609 carries, he would have averaged 5.1 for his career, still the best.

There's a feeling, even today, that Jim Brown could have pretty much done whatever he wanted on a football field. He was that good. If he wanted to play another five years, or maybe even eight years, he probably could have done it. And had he done that, he would undoubtedly still own every single rushing record in the books. As it was, he was simply the best, bar none. And not *arguably*.

GALE SAYERS

Gale Sayers wasn't Jim Brown. He was a completely different type of runner, a guy who may have had no equal in the open field. He was quick, fast, electric, an instinctive runner who once said he didn't think about the moves he made, they just happened. Unlike Brown, who never missed a single game to injury but retired prematurely, Sayers' career was badly truncated by knee injuries. His career with the Chicago Bears was the equivalent of just over four and a half seasons, and when it came time for the Hall of Fame voting some felt he wouldn't qualify because of his relatively short career. Yet the committee's vote to elect him was unanimous, and when they announced it they said, simply, "There never was another to compare with him. What else is there to say?"

That's really what is so intriguing about Gale Sayers. It has been more than forty years since he erupted onto the NFL scene, a lightning bolt out of Kansas where he was also considered by many the greatest open-field runner in college football history. He then joined the Bears and put together one of the greatest rookie seasons ever. So it is natural to wonder just what kind of career Sayers would have had if he had stayed healthy. A great What-If.

The Kansas Comet was born on May 30, 1943, in Wichita, Kansas, and after graduating from Omaha Central High became a two-time all-American at Kansas, where he gained 3,917 all-purpose yards. The Bears picked him the same year they chose linebacker Dick Butkus, which could make the pair the best two first-round choices ever. Butkus became an immediate starter and Sayers an immediate superstar. Listen to what Sayers did as an NFL rookie.

In his first start against Green Bay he scored both Bears touchdowns in a 23-14 loss. A week later against the Rams he took a screen pass and ran 80 yards for a touchdown and threw a touchdown pass off the option in a 31-6 Chicago victory. Veteran Rams tackle Rosey Grier would never forget Sayers' long touchdown jaunt.

"I hit him so hard I thought my shoulder must have busted him in two," Grier said. "I heard a roar from the crowd and figured he fumbled. Then there he was, 15 yards away and going for the score."

And it continued. A week later, he scored four touchdowns as the Bears beat the Vikings, 45-6, with one of his TDs coming on a 96-yard kickoff return. Finally, on December 12, on the next-to-last week of the season, he put on a show on a muddy field in San Francisco that is remembered to this day. He scored a record-tying six touchdowns that afternoon as the Bears won, 61-20. He scored on runs of 21, 7, 50, and 1 yard/s. He also had an 85-yard punt return and scored on an 80-yard pass reception. While everyone else was slipping and sliding on the muddy field, Sayers simply glided.

"It was the greatest performance I have ever seen on the football field," said longtime Bears coach George Halas, who had been watching NFL football since the beginning.

When the year ended, the NFL Rookie of the Year had scored a then record 22 touchdowns. He ran for 867 yards on 166 carries, an average of 5.2 yards a carry; caught 29 passes for another 507 yards, an average of 17.5 yards a catch; and ran back 16 punts for 238 yards and 21 kickoffs for 660 yards, a league-leading 31.4 yards a return. When he led the league in rushing with 1,231 yards in 1966, his future seemed limitless. Even though the Bears were just 5-7-2, Sayers had set an NFL record with 2,440 all-purpose yards.

In 1967 he gained just 880 yards from scrimmage, but still had three kickoff returns for scores. His yardage might have been down a bit because the Bears alternated him with halfback Brian Piccolo to save wear and tear, and the two became close friends. Then in 1968, Sayers was leading the league with 856 rushing yards after eight games and averaging a career best 6.2 yards per carry when he suffered his first knee injury, tearing the ligaments in his right knee. He had surgery, and with Brian Piccolo's help, worked extremely hard to rehab for the following season.

He came back in 1969 to again lead the league with 1,032 yards, but the knee injury had robbed him of some speed and mobility. It didn't help that the Bears finished a franchise-worst 1-13. There was more bad news when it was learned that Piccolo had been diagnosed with cancer. Then things got worse. In 1970, Sayers sustained an injury to his left knee and once again needed surgery. Later that year, Brian Piccolo died. Though Sayers didn't know it immediately, he was already at the end of the line. He carried the ball just 23 times in 1970, tried it again the next year and could carry only 13 times. An aborted comeback in 1972 never got off the ground. That's when he knew he had to retire.

In his abbreviated career, Gale Sayers carried the football 991 times and gained 4,956 yards, an average of 5.0 yards per carry. He was just twenty-six years old in his final full season of 1969, and only twenty-nine when he officially retired. As a testament to his greatness, he was the youngest player ever elected to the Hall of

Fame (thirty-four) and had the shortest effective playing time of anyone enshrined at Canton. Had Gale Sayers remained healthy, just what heights might he have scaled?

Running backs normally don't have exceptionally long careers, and health is always a concern. Jim Brown was never hurt and probably could have played well into his thirties. Sayers' effectiveness may have been determined by the way the Bears used him, whether they continued to have him run back punts and kick-offs, and how much he ran the ball from scrimmage. If he remained healthy for just ten years, through the 1974 season, he probably would have gained between 10 and 12,000 yards, assuming the Bears used him mostly at running back. His per catch average of 17.5 as a rookie was like that of a wide receiver. But after that the Bears didn't throw to him nearly as often.

The biggest difference if Sayers had had a long career would be the incredible highlight film that his best runs would have created. It's still an absolute treat to watch films of his moves in the open field. He would seemingly cut on a dime, moving laterally with a quick burst and then turning back upfield past the defender, his long strides taking him away from pursuers with each step. There's little doubt that had he played for ten effective years he might well have had no peer in the open field. None. The Kansas Comet was simply that good, one of the few players who was a threat to go all the way every time he touched the football.

BILL WALTON

They called him the big redhead, all 6'11" of him, and he came to the NBA out of UCLA, where he divided his time between protesting against the Vietnam War as a late-1960s radical and being the best collegiate basketball player in the land. Bill Walton led coach John Wooden's Bruins to a pair of national titles, including a 1973 victory over Memphis State in which he hit on 21 of 22 field goal tries and scored 44 points in a truly memorable performance. In addition, he was also the fulcrum for a pair of 30-0 seasons and part of a record 88-game winning streak. The redhead followed Lew Alcindor (Kareem Abdul-Jabbar) as the Bruins' center, and there were some who felt that Walton was the better all-around player.

When the Portland Trail Blazers made him their top pick in the 1974 draft, they knew there was something of a risk. On the one hand, they could be getting a center who might eventually rank among the best in NBA history and around whom a championship team could be built. But on the other, they could find themselves with an extremely talented player with a history of injuries who might find it very difficult to stay healthy through the rigors of the NBA season. As it turned out, they got both.

"Bill Russell was a great shotblocker. Wilt Chamberlain was a great offensive player," said Dr. Jack Ramsay, Walton's coach at Portland. "But Walton can do it all."

Born on November 5, 1952, in La Mesa, California, Bill Walton was already a star when he reached Helix High School in La Mesa, and he had already begun suffering from the injuries that would derail his career. In high school, he broke an ankle as well as a leg and several bones in his feet. He also underwent a knee operation, all of which could have made him damaged goods. Despite all this, he remained relatively healthy at UCLA, though he had bouts of tendinitis in his knees and some back problems.

After the draft, he hit the NBA running. In his first seven games with Portland, he averaged 16 points, 19 rebounds, 4.4 assists, and 4.0 blocks a game. The numbers were incredible, especially for a rookie who had to adjust to the bigger, faster game. Not only could he score and rebound, but he passed as well or better than any center in the game.

"I was with the Celtics when Russell came into the league," said Lakers coach Bill Sharman. "Walton is the same type of player. Extremely intelligent, and he had great basketball instincts."

Unfortunately, his rookie year was cut short by—what else—injuries. This time it was foot problems, and he wound up playing just 35 games as a rookie and averaged 12.8 points and 12.6 rebounds. The next year he played in just 51 games, though when he was in there he was dominant. His dossier of injuries already included more foot problems, a sprained ankle, a broken left wrist (twice), a pair of dislocated toes, and two dislocated fingers. His medical chart was getting longer than his game stats.

Walton and the Trailblazers reached their zenith in the 1976–77 season. This time the big redhead played in 65 games and managed to be in there when it counted . . . in the playoffs. The Blazers finished second in the regular season as Walton averaged 18.6 points and led the league with 14.4 rebounds. He also led in blocked shots with 3.25 a game. Aided by the strong play of guard Lionel Hollins and power forward Maurice Lucas, the Blazers roared through the playoffs, beating the Denver Nuggets, then the Los Angeles Lakers, and finally the Philadelphia 76ers in the Finals. The Sixers had Julius Erving and George McGinnis that year, but the Finals MVP was Bill Walton.

By this time, the entire league knew how good Bill Walton was. He truly could do it all on the basketball court, and when the Blazers got off to a 55-10 start the next season Walton was not only proving dominant, but a consummate winner. In February, however, an injured left foot forced him to the sidelines once again. He tried to come back in the playoffs against the SuperSonics, but after the second game, the foot was again hurting. X-rays showed the navicular bone below his left ankle was broken. Though no one knew it at the time, the death knell for Walton's dominance and for a long NBA career had just sounded.

Before the injury he had been averaging 18.9 points, 13.2 rebounds, 5.0 assists, and 2.52 blocked shots a game. So good was he was that he was still named the NBA's Most Valuable Player, but after that his career became an injury-filled odyssey. He sat out the entire 1978–79 season and then was shipped to San Diego, where he played in just 14 games in 1979–80. He had re-fractured the same bone in his left foot. After that he sat out the next two more seasons before trying it again. He underwent radical surgery in 1981 to restructure his left foot. He had an abnormally high arch which doctors felt was causing stress on the bones when he landed. So the arch was lowered.

He returned in 1982–83, but was permitted to play just one game a week, which he managed without pain. The foot seemed to be getting better. He played in 33 games that year, but increased to 55 the next and 67 the year after that. Still, the Clippers weren't winning and he wasn't the same dynamic force he had been with the Trail Blazers. In the 1984–85 season, he averaged just 10 points and 9 rebounds, and only 2.3 assists. Not Walton-like. The team was also losing. He must have known he didn't have a lot of time. He wanted to win, and he let that be known. That's when Red Auerbach and the Boston Celtics traded for him.

The 1985–86 season turned into a dream for Walton. The Celts had a great team led by Larry Bird, Kevin McHale, and Robert Parish, and the redhead served as a backup for the two big guys, McHale and Parish. He played in 80 games, averaging just 7.6 points and 6.8 rebounds, but his presence was invaluable, and the Celts swept to the NBA title. Finally, Bill Walton was on another winner, and for his efforts he received the NBA's Sixth Man Award. By that time he was thirty-three years old, but his play led to Kevin McHale saying, "You watch an old guy like that with the most hammered body in sports, acting like a high school kid—it's both funny and inspiring at the same time. Every game was a challenge, and he didn't let any of us forget that."

Unfortunately, it was a last hurrah. After playing just 10 games the following season, the injuries returned and Walton promptly retired at the age of thirty-four. It had been thirteen years since he first hit the floor running for Portland, and he had missed three complete seasons and parts of the rest. In fact, the 80 games he played for the Celtics in 1985–86 were the most of his career. But what if he had played those thirteen years in a relatively good state of health? What then?

In one sense, it's difficult to imagine what Bill Walton could have been, but if you take the first two-thirds of the 1977–78 season you'll get a good idea. That's when the Trail Blazers went 55-10 before Walton's foot injury. Take away the center and Portland did not have a great team. It was Walton's presence that year made them nearly unbeatable. He was scoring close to 20 points a game, rebounding as well as anyone, blocking shots, and passing out of his center position better than any big man in the NBA. He always played with a joy and an intensity that were difficult to match. He knew the game extremely well and knew how it should be played. So how would Bill Walton rank with the other great centers of an era filled with great centers had he remained healthy? It's not a stretch to say he would have been very close to the top.

Bill Russell is still considered the best center by many who believe that his play made his entire team better. He may have rebounded and blocked shots a bit better than Walton, but he didn't score and didn't pass as well. Wilt Chamberlain was the game's best scorer and rebounder, and once even led the league in assists when he decided he needed to prove something. Wilt certainly had an enormous talent, but with it an enormous ego, which sometimes got in the way. Walton didn't have that. It was always team first, and do anything you have to do in order to win. So Walton was probably the better team player.

Kareem Abdul-Jabbar is the NBA's all-time leading points scorer and had a long and very successful career, especially after he went to the Lakers and was teamed with the likes of Magic Johnson and James Worthy, just to name two. The Lakers were a great team. Bill Walton was never surrounded by a great team except that one year in Boston when he was a bench player. He didn't score as well as Kareem, but you can make a case that he did everything else better—rebound, pass, run the floor, block shots. With that same great Laker team around him he would have won just as much, and maybe more than Kareem. His one title with the Trail Blazers came with a less than stellar supporting cast and had a healthy Walton remained in Portland, it's a safe bet that the team would have contended for several more championships.

The second-tier top centers just don't compare. Nate Thurmond, Willis Reed, Wes Unseld, Bob Lanier, Jerry Lucas—none of them offered as much as a healthy Bill Walton. They all had talent and were winners, and all made positive contributions to their teams, but none had the all-around talent of Walton, or the ability to do so many things on a basketball court. So the answer to this What-If is pretty simple.

Had he stayed healthy, Bill Walton would be in the company of the three best centers ever to play the game and would be mentioned in the same breath as Bill Russell and Wilt Chamberlain, the two who are usually acknowledged as the benchmarks by which all others are judged. Walton himself has said that Kareem was the best player he ever played against, so that has to mean something, too, and he has also said that Bill Russell "was my favorite player of all time."

But the man he gives the most credit to is his UCLA coach, John Wooden. He once said that "growing up, my parents were very, very strict. And then I went to UCLA with John Wooden, who was just off the charts." Walton also said that "Wooden didn't teach basketball, he taught life." But Bill Walton learned basketball somewhere, and when healthy played it as well as anyone.

If only.

About the Author

BILL GUTMAN is a longtime freelance writer who has written about all the major sports for more than three decades. Over the years he has published numerous sports histories, as well as biographies of "Pistol" Pete Maravich, Magic Johnson, Lance Armstrong, and Bill Parcells. Some of his recent books include *Won for All: The Inside Story of the New England Patriots' Impossible Run to the Super Bowl* (with Pepper Johnson), *Twice Around the Bases: A Thinking Fan's Inside Look at Baseball* (with Kevin Kennedy), and *Heroes of Football: The Story of America's Game* (with John Madden). Mr. Gutman lives in upstate New York with his wife, Cathy.

Index